LITERATURE OF
Greece AND Rome

TRADITIONS IN WORLD LITERATURE

National Textbook Company
a division of NTC/CONTEMPORARY PUBLISHING GROUP
Lincolnwood, Illinois USA

Cover Illustration: Head of Apollo Sculpture / Relief
Christie's / SuperStock
ISBN (student edition): 0-8442-1191-5 (hardbound); 1192-3 (softbound)
ISBN (teacher's edition): 0-8442-1287-3 (softbound)

Acknowledgments begin on page 299, which is to be considered an extension of this
copyright page.

Published by National Textbook Company,
a division of NTC/Contemporary Publishing Group, Inc.
4255 West Touhy Avenue,
Lincolnwood (Chicago), Illinois 60646-1975 U.S.A.

Library of Congress Cataloging-in-Publication Data

Literature from Greek and Roman antiquity
     Literature of Greece and Rome.
          p. 320 cm. 23 (Traditions in World Literature)
     Includes index.
     Summary: Presents selections from the writings of such well-known classical authors
as Aesop, Homer, Sappho, Horace, Ovid, and Pliny with biographical material, discussion questions, and writing prompts.
     ISBN 0-8442-1191-5 (hard), — ISBN 0-8442-1192-3 (soft). — ISBN 0-8442-
1287-3 (teacher's guide)
     1. Classical literature—Translations into English. 2. Greece—Literary collections. 3.
Rome—Literary collections.
     [1. Classical literature—Translations into English. 2. Classical literature—
Collections.] I Title. II Series.
     PA3621.L48   1998
     880—dc21   98-31286
                                                                        CIP
                                                                        AC

890 QB 0987654321

Contents

LITERATURE OF ROME

INTRODUCTION

CLASSICAL LITERATURE AND THE WORLD OF TODAY

John Lewin

Looking at today's world, we become aware of what seems a desperate flight from the past. "It was good enough for Grandfather," (or even Father) is no longer an adequate reason for the maintenance of any value. New developments in science change our picture of reality from day to day; historical events flip everything upside down. (Since the Vietnam War, how many perspectives have changed?) In art, in "popular culture," the cry is "Are you with it?" whatever "it" happens to be at the moment.

Under such circumstances, the past and anything *of* the past begin to seem unreal, irrelevant. In many respects this is healthy: a neurotic, after all, is a person who is compulsively bound to past reaction-patterns, most of which are not only irrelevant and unrealistic but stultifying and wildly destructive. But a neurotic is not only not free to escape from the past; he is also not free to use its positive elements creatively in the present.

In the context of the present essay, this obviously leads to the question: what is the value, what is the relevance, of classical literature in our own time and situation? We know the textbook answer: a "classical" work is "classical" because of its universality, because what it says and how it says it speak to people of all times and places. There are other arguments, but most of them can be reduced to the dubious proposition, "It's good for you"—dubious because we have come to distrust the prescriptions handed out so arbitrarily by various authority-figures: parental, educational, religious, military, political, artistic, and scientific. Our judgment on a writer is pragmatic: a writer establishes a rapport or doesn't—speaks to me or talks at me. Edward Albee, we may say, is speaking to us: what he says and how he says it come out of an involvement with our own time and situation. We'll grant that Aeschylus (again for instance) was doing the same for his own time; still three facts remain. First, most of us—the present writer included—will be able to read a vast number of "classical" writers only in translation; and a writer's use of his or her own language (or in a few cases an adopted one, for example, Nabokov and Conrad) is an indispensable element of the writer's artistry. Second, no good writer starts out with the conscious idea of "producing a classic"; he or she writes for human beings in a specific time and situation, and much that was of concern *then* is not of concern *now,* or has been superseded by other concerns. Whole areas of commonly shared response might be touched off by the stimulus of a single name, a symbol or phrase: "Hiroshima," "Kennedy," or even "Pentagon" can evoke a reaction in us that will not be experienced (or not to the same degree) by audiences of a millennium from now. Third, the form of expression used by a writer of another time and culture—how the writer says what he or she says—is likely to be full of artistic conventions which now seem unbearably artificial and obscure.

These are formidable barriers to approaching a classical author. Why, then, bother?

The world of Greek and Roman civilization from which "classical" literature arose was full of currents which run through our own age: in Greece there was the agonizing conflict between old and new value-systems, between "the light of the mind and the voices of the blood." In Rome there was the strange sense of inner decay that we see arising in a nation which has attained to a position of supreme world power. In both there was a vivid sense of the reality of the body, of the inscrutability of fate, and of the *immediacy* of life, into which we have found ourselves shaken today after centuries of smug belief in the "spirit" and in "Universal Order."

The world from which classical literature sprang was called the "pagan world." Today we are said to be moving into a "new paganism." But one of the outstanding features of the Renaissance, the "rebirth" of the individual and the development of new social forms to replace the repressive and superstitious patterns of medievalism, was a renewal of interest in the literature of the classical, or pagan, world. Perhaps something similar is occurring today. Certainly a "rebirth" of some kind is in order. The only alternative, as our contemporary writers have not ceased to assure us, is death.

In the seventh century the city of Alexandria was conquered by the Moslems. Alexandria had the finest library in the ancient world. What should be done with it? the Caliph Omar was asked, and he wrote: "The contents of those books are in conformity with the Koran or they are not. If they are, the Koran is sufficient without them; if they are not, they are pernicious. Let them, therefore, be destroyed." And so they were, and humanity was a little poorer.

Today, of course, we need not burn books: we can ignore them. The point is that, whatever fundamentalists claim, the Koran is the product of a mind and a heart (or several of them) as is the Bible, as is the *Iliad,* as is the *Oedipus* or the *Metamorphoses* or Edward Albee's *The American Dream* or Saul Bellow's *Herzog.* And no individual vision of reality can replace another: Homer and Sophocles and Ovid can give us excitement and insights that Albee and Bellow cannot, and vice versa. And getting used to the formal conventions of "classical" writers does not really require much more effort than coming to terms with the seemingly "formless" conventions of contemporary authors.

We come, then, to the question of translation. The wrong translator of a work in a foreign language, like the wrong teacher or actor of Shakespeare, let us say, can turn wine into water with appalling thoroughness. Here pragmatic judgments are very much in order. Whether or not a translator has a Ph.D. in classical literature is largely irrelevant. It is not enough to turn Greek or Latin words into their nearest English equivalents. The translator, like the teacher, like the actor, should have an intuitive, empathetic understanding of the wordless thought—and feeling—processes that must have gone on in the mind of the original author *in order* for them to be articulated in the words and images the author chose to use. The translator, having re-created these in his or her own mind, must then express them in new language. He or she must, therefore, be able to write *English* prose, poetry, or dramatic speech exceedingly well: clearly, beautifully, excitingly. A translator must, occasionally, make changes in emphasis, by condensation or even (more dangerously) by expansion, according to his or her own judgment of what is "relevant" (or universal) and what has ceased to be so. He or she must love, appreciate, understand, but not slavishly worship.

It will be seen that a large element of subjectivity enters into this, and an equally large element of presumption. Here we tread the fuzzy boundaries between "a translation of X," "an adaptation of X," and "an original work based on X." One of the best discussions of this issue is by D. S. Carne-Ross, in an article called "Translation and Transposition." After quoting from Christopher Logue's version of Book XXI of Homer's *Iliad*—one of the most brilliant, gutsy, excitingly alive renderings ever made of a piece of classical literature—Carne-Ross says:

> If you say that this isn't translation at all, but paraphrase, a new poem suggested by Homer, I can only repeat the sentence from Dudley Fitts which I quoted just now—"I have simply tried to restate in my own idiom what the Greek verses have meant to me"—and ask what the translation of poetry can be if it is not the re-creation in a new language, by whatever means are open to the translator, of an equivalent beauty, an equivalent power, an equivalent truth.

The melancholy fact remains that a huge amount of classical literature in translation appears to have been done by machine, or by scholars whose veneration for their subject has caused them to repress any relish they might have taken in it, or in their own mother tongue. The result is like nothing so much as painting by the numbers, and the apathy it provokes is understandable.

There is, on the other hand, the occasional temptation for the translator or adapter, in making the "changes of emphasis" mentioned above, to simply expurgate something in the content of the original which goes against his or her temperament and convictions. If only, one thinks, Aeschylus had not delivered himself of the rather shabby advice that aggressive impulses should be taken out on strangers rather than fellow citizens! But there it is, and it is a matter for the translator or adapter's own conscience to wrestle with. Perhaps the high pedestal of "classicism" itself prevents us from regarding even the greatest writers as human beings with whom we are free to disagree. It may be that, exciting though we may find Edward Albee, we feel free to differ with him intellectually or artistically without burning or ignoring his books because Albee is not (or not yet) an author of "classical" status.

An essay of this nature may seem to be making the point, "Everyone *should* read and like classical literature." This is nonsense. Not everyone is going to read and like *contemporary* literature, because if it is of any artistic quality it will, even if enticingly violent and sexy, make certain demands on us, require us to meet it halfway. Anything done purely for commercial purposes will make no demands; it will be simple and safe; it will operate by a formula designed to please everybody; it will not be the voice of a complex individual speaking from his heart. We must put up with a great deal of obscurity and apparent formlessness from contemporary authors in order to come to their vision of the life of men. Similarly, we must recognize that classical authors did not value compression as highly as we do in an age of capsule news, digests, and obsession with rapid change. A work of art was a great tree that sank its roots among mud and stones and dung and rotting corpses and grew into branches, leaves, and flowers, not a missile on a launching-pad. A translator practiced in contemporary literary techniques can sometimes give us the best of both worlds—richness and directness.

READING TRANSLATIONS

Since every language is a unique and complex structure of sounds and meanings, translation cannot be a simple matter of substituting a word from one language for a word in another. When a work of literature is being translated, the challenge is even greater. In that case, the translator must attempt to create something that is both faithful to the work in the original language but also reads well in the language into which the work is being translated.

At the top of page xi is a passage from Book 22 of Homer's *Odyssey* in the original Greek. Three English translations follow. The first was done in the early 1700s by the English poet Alexander Pope, who created translations of Homer that remained standards throughout his century. The other two translations were done in the recent past by Americans, Robert Fitzgerald and Robert Fagles.

This passage from the *Odyssey* describes how the goddess Athene ("Pallas") assists the hero Odysseus in killing his enemies ("the suitors") by waving the *aegis,* a snake-fringed shield that causes those who see it to run mad with terror.

δὴ τότ’ Ἀθηναίη φθισίμβροτον αἰγίδ’ ἀνέσχεν
ὑψόθεν ἐξ ὀροφῆς· τῶν δὲ φρένες ἐπτοίηθεν.
οἱ δ’ ἐφέβοντο κατὰ μέγαρον βόες ὣς ἀγελαῖαι·
τὰς μέν τ’ αἰόλος οἶστρος ἐφορμηθεὶς ἐδόνησεν
ὥρῃ ἐν εἰαρινῇ, ὅτε τ’ ἤματα μακρὰ πέλονται.
οἱ δ’ ὥς τ’ αἰγυπιοὶ γαμψώνυχες ἀγκυλοχεῖλαι,
ἐξ ὀρέων ἐλθόντες ἐπ’ ὀρνίθεσσι θόρωσι·
ταὶ μέν τ’ ἐν πεδίῳ νέφεα πτώσσουσαι ἵενται,
οἱ δέ τε τὰς ὀλέκουσιν ἐπάλμενοι, οὐδέ τις ἀλκὴ
γίγνεται οὐδὲ φυγή· χαίρουσι δέ τ’ ἀνέρες ἄγρῃ·
ὣς ἄρα τοὶ μνηστῆρας ἐπεσσύμενοι κατὰ δῶμα
τύπτον ἐπιστροφάδην· τῶν δὲ στόνος ὤρνυτ’ ἀεικὴς
κράτων τυπτομένων, δάπεδον δ’ ἅπαν αἵματι θῦε.

ALEXANDER POPE (1726)

Now *Pallas* shines confess'd; aloft she spreads
The arm of vengeance o'er their guilty heads;
The dreadful *Aegis* blazes in their eye;
Amaz'd they see, they tremble, and they fly:
5   Confus'd distracted, thro' the rooms they fling,
Like oxen madden'd by the breeze's sting,
When sultry days, and long, succeed the gentle spring.
Not half so keen, fierce vulturs of the chace
Stoop from the mountains on the feather'd race,
10 When the wide field extended snares beset,
With conscious dread they shun the quiv'ring net:
No help, no flight; but wounded ev'ry way,
Headlong they drop: the fowlers seize the prey.
On all sides thus they double wound on wound,
15 In prostrate heaps the wretches beat the ground,
Unmanly shrieks precede each dying groan,
And a red deluge floats the reeking stone.

ROBERT FITZGERALD (1961)

At this moment that unmanning thunder cloud,
the aegis, Athena's shield,
took form in the great hall.
                    And the suitors mad with fear
5   at her great sign stampeded like stung cattle by a river
when the dread shimmering gadfly strikes in summer,
in the flowering season, in the long-drawn days.
After them the attackers wheeled, as terrible as falcons
from eyries in the mountains veering over and diving down
10 with talons wide unsheathed on flights of birds,
who cower down the sky in chutes and bursts along the valley—
but the pouncing falcons grip their prey, no frantic wing avails,
and farmers love to watch those beakèd hunters.
So these now fell upon the suitors in that hall,
15 turning, turning to strike and strike again,
while torn men moaned at death, and blood ran smoking over the
    whole floor.

ROBERT FAGLES (1996)

And now Athena, looming out of the rafters high above them,
brandished her man-destroying shield of thunder, terrifying
the suitors out of their minds, and down the hall they panicked—
wild, like herds stampeding, driven mad as the darting gadfly
5   strikes in the late spring when the long days come round.
The attackers struck like eagles, crook-clawed, hook-beaked,
swooping down from a mountain ridge to harry smaller birds
that skim across the flatland, cringing under the clouds
but the eagles plunge in fury, rip their lives out—hopeless,
10 never a chance of flight or rescue—and people love the sport—
so the attackers routed suitors headlong down the hall,
wheeling to the slaughter, slashing left and right
and grisly screams broke from skulls cracked open—
the whole floor awash with blood.

ǝ

THE DELPHIC ORACLE

Delphi, the most celebrated sanctuary in ancient Greece, was located on the lower slopes of Mount Parnassus. The Greeks believed the spot to be the center of the earth, saying that Zeus had released two eagles, one from the east and one from the west, and flying toward each other they had met there. The site was originally sacred to the earth-goddess Gaea (jē′ ə).

The Greeks told the story of a monstrous serpent, Python, who guarded the spot. The god Apollo came to Delphi, slew Python, and established his oracle there. An *oracle* is a shrine where prophecies, believed to be of divine origin, were delivered. There were a number of oracular shrines in the Greek world. Apollo was called *Pythian* in memory of his deed. The priestess of Apollo who gave the oracle was called the *Pythia* or the *Pythoness.* The Delphic oracle was consulted on a variety of questions, both private and public.

Those who wished to consult the oracle first performed the rite of purification and sacrificed to Apollo. Precedence among pilgrims was generally determined by lot, although occasionally granted as a privilege. A male priest, the sole attendant of the Pythia, related the questions and interpreted the answer. The priestess, seated on the sacred tripod, gave the oracle while in a frenzied state. How this condition was induced is not completely clear. Excavation at Delphi has shown as improbable the theory that the priestess inhaled vapors issuing from a hole in the earth. Such practices as chewing laurel leaves and drinking the water from the Castalian spring that flowed near the sanctuary, may have helped induce a prophetic state, but the major cause was probably the priestess' own complete faith in the power of the god to speak through her. The influence of Delphi, felt throughout the entire Mediterranean world for several centuries, began to decline from the fourth century B.C. onward. The sanctuary was finally closed by the Christian emperor Theodosius in A.D. 390.

Literature of Greece

AESCHYLUS

(525–456 B.C.)

Generally regarded as the "father of tragedy," Aeschylus was probably the first dramatist to grapple with the painful and unanswerable questions of human life and to create characters who were grand in their suffering. He also transformed Greek stage productions from simple choruses with a leader to genuine dramas involving character interaction, dialogue, scenery, costumes, and heroic action. Aeschylus wrote about 90 plays, of which only 7 survive. His most famous work is probably the *Oresteia*, a trilogy (series of three literary works) consisting of the *Agamemnon*, *The Libation Bearers*, and *The Furies*. This trilogy appears here in an adapted form under the title *The House of Atreus*.

One of the most enduring myths of all time, the story of the downfall of the House of Atreus has been the subject of dramas and stories for over 25 centuries. Agamemnon, who led the Greeks against Troy, belonged to this famous family, as did his brother Menelaus, the husband of Helen. A curse seemed to hang over the family for several generations, a curse that started with an atrocious act committed by Agamemnon's great-grandfather Tantalus. When Tantalus was invited to dine with the gods, he killed and cooked his only son, Pelops, and served him for dinner. Realizing that the dish contained human flesh, the gods restored Pelops to life and devised a hideous punishment for his father. Tantalus was placed in Hades with a pool of water at his feet and luscious fruit trees over his head. Whenever he bent down to drink, the water drained away, and whenever he reached for fruit, the wind blew it just beyond his grasp. Thus he stood forever, thirsty and hungry in the midst of plenty.

Pelops had two sons, Atreus and Thyestes, who also brought disgrace to the family. Thyestes fell in love with Atreus' wife, and Atreus retaliated by killing Thyestes' two small children and serving them to their father to eat. Thyestes was powerless to take revenge, since Atreus was king. However, Atreus' children were doomed to suffer for this crime.

The curse created by the murders and cannibalism of previous generations descended full force on Atreus' son Agamemnon, who is the subject of the first play in this trilogy. As commander of the Greek army, Agamemnon had sought advice from a seer named Calchas about a problem that arose as his fleet of ships was sailing to Troy. A strong north wind had stranded the ships near the coastal town of Aulis. The seer Calchas told Agamemnon that he must sacrifice his daughter Iphigenia to the goddess Artemis in order to get the ships moving again. Agamemnon finally agreed to kill his daughter, an act that enraged his wife Clytemnestra and turned her thoughts toward revenge. After the sacrifice of Iphigenia, Agamemnon set off for Troy, where he fought valiantly for 10 years, at last returning home as a conquering hero.

As the play *Agamemnon* opens, the Greek army is returning from Troy, and Agamemnon is awaited by a crowd of townspeople who are eager to honor him. Clytemnestra has brooded for 10 years planning her revenge on her husband with her new lover, Aegisthus (the son of Thyestes). The events that follow are viewed differently by different writers throughout the ages. Some writers depict Clytemnestra as a vengeful monster, while others see her deeds as the justified acts of a grieving mother. ■

THE HOUSE OF ATREUS

An adaptation of the Oresteia *by John Lewin*

ACT ONE. AGAMEMNON

CHARACTERS

WATCHMAN

CLYTEMNESTRA, *wife of Agamemnon*

HERALD

AGAMEMNON, *king of Argos*

CASSANDRA, *daughter of Priam, King of Troy; Agamemnon's prisoner*

AEGISTHUS, *Clytemnestra's lover*

Scene: *Argos, a city in the Peleponnesus. The palace of* AGAMEMNON. *In the foreground, an altar.*

(It is just before dawn. There is a watchman on the roof.)

WATCHMAN. O gods, give me an end to this chilly watch.
    It drags on with the dying year while I
    Crouch like a dog above the house of Atreus
    Watching the marching armies of the stars,
5   The summer battalions and winter companies;
    But of that other host, no news.
    A flash of fire and I will know the job is done,
    Troy town is taken, my king makes for home,
    And I can come down from this hard and dew-wet bed,
10   Where that man-hearted woman who rules the palace has
        placed me,
    And sleep, perhaps, with sweet dreams.
    But not now. No. Fear is up here with me
    And no man sleeps that shares a bed with her.
    I sing in the dark, but it sounds like weeping
15   When I think of this great house, what once it was
    And how it is managed now.

(singing)

Bring good luck, immortal gods,
Throw the dice, but grant us odds—

(He sees a light in the distance.)

They've lit the beacon! It's done!
20   Queen! Town! Wake up!
Light the fires! Break out the wine! They're coming home!
Troy is down! Look! I'll start the dancing myself!

(*lights and movement in and beyond the palace*)

O gods, let it all turn out well.
Let me see my master again; put his hand back on the reins.
25   The other things—let me not think of them.
I cannot speak; an ox stands huge on my tongue.
If the stones of that palace could talk, you would hear a tale.
Until then—if you can, fill in my thoughts.
If not, forget even these few words I have said.

He exits. Enter the CHORUS.[1]

30   CHORUS. Ten years since Agamemnon and Menelaus,
The twin bronze fists of the house of Atreus,
Led forth a thousand ships to the doom of Troy.
The cry of war that rose from the throats of the Greeks
Was like the eagles' scream when their nest is found
35   Empty, their young taken away.
And as Apollo, Pan, or Zeus,
Hearing that song of blood high in the air,
Rolls the rock of Justice down on the transgressor,
So the house of Atreus rolled on to crush the house of Priam.[2]
40   For one woman[3] and her loose love
The long line of man's flesh stood among the hacking swords,
Straining muscle to muscle and knowing rest
Only when eyes darkened and knees struck the dust.
Greek and Trojan are caught on the Great Wheel,
45   And it will not be stopped by flame of altar or water of eyes
Until the anger of the high gods is satisfied.
Meanwhile we wait, the empty of honor, the stay-at-homes,
Half-existing, as a dream remembered by day;
Babies that crawl on four feet, we that totter on three,

CLYTEMNESTRA *enters.*

---

1. Chorus: The chorus is an essential element of Greek drama, though its function varies widely in the hands of different dramatists. In Aeschylus' plays, the chorus provides eloquent commentary on the actions of the characters. Much of the tragedy's power comes from the imagery and poetic rhythms of the chorus. LEADER (see line 105) refers to the leader of the chorus.

2. Priam: King of Troy. He and his entire family were either killed or taken hostage during the Trojan War.

3. one woman: Helen, for whose sake the Trojan War was fought.

50	While the men that stand on two are gone
	To kill and die in the fields at high-walled Troy.
	But you, Clytemnestra,
	Lady of Argos, wife of Agamemnon our lord,
	Surely you have news. Has a change come?
55	You have commanded the altars to burn with constant fire
	All over our city, consuming holy oil
	From the deep vaults of the royal treasury.
	The high gods snuff up the pleasant smoke.
	Surely this augurs well. If you have something to tell us, speak.

(Without answering, she re-enters the palace.)

60	I sing that day of gold and thunder when the youth of the world
	Shook the mane of his bronze helmet into the sun
	And laughed like a horse at the patient and narrow grave;
	When the roadstead blackened with lean and shark-nosed ships
	Scenting the distant blood of Troy.
65	Then to the captains and kings an omen appeared:
	On the right hand, the hard hand that holds the scepter and spear,
	Two eagles fell from the sky, one black as iron, one blazed with silver,
	And struck at a running hare. In a spray of blood
	They tore the wet blind young from her swollen belly.
70	Sorrow is great: may good come out of it all.
	Calchas the prophet-priest knew the eagles to be
	Agamemnon and Menelaus, sharers of one fierce heart,
	And thus he made clear the sign: From coping-stone to corner-stone the belly of Troy
	Will be ripped by the savage ram, and the Argive[4] host
75	Will feed upon blood and gold, on flesh and wine.
	But Artemis, the huntress of wild beasts,
	Is their protector, and her holy heart
	Shall swell with pity for the helpless prey,
	And the winged hounds of her father, their pinions sticky with blood,
80	Must fear her wrath and the high clear song of her bow.
	Sorrow is great; may good come out of it all.
	For she is tender and kind
	To the young things of wood and meadow, the harmless hare
	And the mighty lion;
85	But Artemis, protector of wild beasts,

---

4. **Argive:** Greek

Is their fierce huntress, and the omen must be fulfilled.
A young and helpless thing
Must fall to the iron talons, and the sweet earth
Must be watered with blood to cause fair winds to blow.

90   Thus the dark words of Calchas. Apollo our trust,
You see how men may be caught in a double snare,
Damned if we tug to the right, and damned if we pull to the left,
Drowning in blood whichever way we turn.
Apollo, break the circle and show us a way:

95   Sorrow is great: may good come out of it all.
Almighty Zeus, whatever your secret name,
God omnipotent, do not turn away.
My own brain's light cannot pierce the darkness,
And I must turn to you if ever I am to know.

100   You have ordained that knowledge is bought with sorrow,
But ignorance of this hanging, voiceless threat
Is sorrow also.
O Zeus, if there is joy, then show her face to us;
If there is doom, do not let us meet him in the dark.

105   LEADER. I see the shores of Aulis, long ago:
The Greek ships rock in the roaring of the tide
And a wind blows out of the north to hold them back from Troy.
I see great Agamemnon sway and groan like a giant tree in a
      storm;
Tears fall from his eyes; he strikes the earth with his staff.

110   He is given his choice: the ships rot and the men starve
Or Iphigenia, his daughter, dies on the altar-stone
To charm the wind towards Troy.
He is woven into a net, and the cords are the curse of murdered
      children.
He has chosen. They lift her above the altar.

115   She cries his name, as once, at feasts, she sang in his honor.
They gag her mouth. The knife gleams in the dull light through
      the clouds.
The prophet Calchas sings of the will of the gods.

CLYTEMNESTRA *enters.*

CHORUS. Say no more; we shall see what is to come when it
      comes; until then, let us not ask for misery.
Knowledge will come whether we want it or not;

120   We must speak only of good, as she who protects our land
      would desire,
Our lady here, Clytemnestra.

LEADER. Great Queen, I beg again, if you know that which we do
      not know, let us hear it.

We can only ask you humbly, and if you wish not to speak, so be it.

CLYTEMNESTRA. You shall have it all.
125   This was a night blessed above all other nights,
      For on it Troy fell, and there is a great king who has seen his last dawn.

CHORUS. You said—can I believe—no!—Say that again!

CLYTEMNESTRA. Our armies hold Troy. Is that plain enough for you?

CHORUS. But—there have been so many rumors—what proof—

130   CLYTEMNESTRA. Do you accuse a god of lying?

CHORUS MEMBER. This is a dream. It can be no other.

CLYTEMNESTRA. You think of me, perhaps, as some greensick girl?

CHORUS. But what kind of messenger can come with so great speed!

CLYTEMNESTRA. A god I said, and a god it was.
135   The god of fire leaped the night-shrouded valleys
      From peak to peak,[5] and beacons cold these long years
      Burned under the hands of joyful men
      On Ida, Lemnos, Athos, and over the great sea;
      And on Macistus, men whose eyes had strained long years
140   Until they saw false fires saw the true one
      Leaping toward them, and lit their beacons in turn,
      So that a current of flame streaked across the waters of Euripus
      And the laughing watchmen on Messapius' hills
      Heaped high the heather, and a crackle of orange fire
145   Made the god laugh too, in joyful strength
      Increased, and he soared and swung like a scytheman
      Across a frosty harvest of stars, and touched with light
      The cold valleys of Asopus, and shone on Kithaeron
      Like the autumn moon. The great marsh of Gorgopis felt his power
150   As the god raced on to Aegyplanctus' peak.
      A hot spark struck amongst the high-stacked pine
      And the god laughed again, and shook his beard of flame,
      And leaped headlong across the Saronic Gulf,
      Until last on Arachnus the great torch burst into bloom
155   And the flames fell on the house of Atreus, bringing news of joy.
      There is my proof.
      What have you to say now?

---

5. **peak to peak:** Clytemnestra's bonfire-relay runs from Ida, a mountain near Troy, across the northern Aegean Sea, and down the east coast of Greece, ending at Arachnus, a mountain near Argos.

CHORUS. Nothing but thanks to the gods for this great day,
         And wonder.
160   Feed my heart with more such news, if more you know.

CLYTEMNESTRA. I know only what must be, now:
         The look of things in Troy.
         Women lie crying on the hacked corpses
         Of those that lay with them in love;
165   Children shake the stiff bodies
         Of those that bore them, crying old sweet names
         From throats that soon will be collared with the slave's iron.
         But the Argives, drugged already with blood
         And weary from the last great fight on the citadel wall,
170   Have ground out the spark of strength
         On the bodies of once-proud women, and filled their throats
         With a wine of which no more will ever be drunk,
         And now sleep like children
         In soft beds without owners,
175   No more standing the nightly guard
         Or lying open-mouthed to the icy stars.
         But let them be satisfied.
         The people and the city
         Are crushed by the wheel. Let them go no further
180   And lay violent hands on the property of gods
         Leave the shrines standing, soldiers of Argos,
         Or the gods may reach out as you go over the sea.
         But yet there is blood in the earth that will cry for blood;
         There is wrong done with the knife, and though the gods smile,
185   There are those of the dead who will not let old wrongs sleep.
         —You see me, elders of Argos, a timorous woman,
         But one whose dearest wish is that right prevail.

LEADER. And no man could speak more wisely.

CLYTEMNESTRA *exits.*

         Now let us praise the gods for this,
190   For the joy was worth the pain.

CHORUS. O Father Zeus,
         Your net of darkness
         Is cast on Priam
         And Priam's son:[6]
195   A dreadful beauty
         That gives me wonder:
         Your bow is bent
         And justice done.

---

6. **Priam's son:** Paris, who stole Helen from Menelaus, prompting the Greek expedition to Troy.

For those whose feet
200 Tread down the holy,
In no great house
Is any room
Whose doors ring not
To the knock of Justice,
205 No gold yet minted
To buy off doom.

That arrogant boy
The son of Priam
That spat on kindness
210 And shamed his host—
For him high Troy
Was damned with beauty
And Hellas armed
For a lovely ghost.

215 Tonight in Hellas
Will hear great weeping.
All over Troy
The corpse-fires burn:
Those who were tall
220 In youth and valor
Are homeward borne
In a little urn.

The people mutter
Against great leaders;
225 Blood will have blood;
The high may fall;
The ghosts of those
Who died for nothing
Will walk and wail
230 By a ruined wall.

CHORUS MEMBER. So, it seems, we cannot keep the shadows back.

LEADER. Only because we doubt the light.

CHORUS MEMBER. Why depend on false hopes?
If they are disappointed, it would not be the first time.

235 LEADER. We have the queen's word.

CHORUS MEMBER. Did she not say she is only a timorous woman?
Women believe what they want to believe, and are we such
fools as to call hope and fear arbiters of truth?

ANOTHER CHORUS MEMBER. Look there! A herald coming from the
shore!

LEADER. Now we shall know the reality for what it is,
240   And whether to laugh with joy or—

CHORUS. No! No!

LEADER. No, I would not have said it.
    Things are too delicately balanced
    To disturb them with evil words.

245   CHORUS. Oh, let all be well.

LEADER. Yes, let all be well.
    He who would wish other for our city,
    Give him what he richly deserves.

Enter the HERALD.

HERALD. O God, this good soil of Argos!
250   I thought this strange filth that covers me
    Would cover my bones also.
    Now I am home.
    Even the sunlight is better here than in other lands.
    A man can lose everything in ten years:
255   Health, friends, every illusion gone,
    But kind are the gods who have given me my one wish:
    To come home.
    Apollo, I hope everything is all right between us.
    By Scamander Water[7] you were not good to us.
260   Our old quarrel is groundless now: there is no more Troy.
    Great Agamemnon, who even now beaches on the shore,
    His black ship whirled here by the storm-wind,
    Has exacted full justice.
    That golden city now looks
265   Like a dumping place for cinders and burnt bones.
    The land is sterile, her seed dead,
    The altars of her gods smashed to dust,

(*The* CHORUS *reacts. He does not notice and goes on.*)

    The dust plowed into the ground.
    Now let playboy Paris say
270   That the joy was worth the pain.

CHORUS. May you continue happy, O herald.

HERALD. I *am* happy now. Now I could die and count myself blessed.

---

7. **Scamander Water:** a river that flowed near Troy.

(*a slight murmur from the* CHORUS)

LEADER. This because you missed home so much.

HERALD. When you gave me that welcome, I could hardly hold my tears.

275 LEADER. Homesickness is a pleasant pain.

HERALD. I don't understand.

LEADER. Because you know that those whom you miss also miss you.

HERALD. Yes, that is good. Then you remembered us, eh?

LEADER. Remembered you? Black fear was on our hearts while you were away.

280 HERALD. Fear? Of what?

LEADER. Of that which, as you said, made us think that death might be a blessing.

(CHORUS MEMBER *shakes his head in warning.*)

But of that no more. Better to keep silent now.

HERALD. Well, it's come to a happy end.
There were times when we doubted that anything would come out right again,
285 But up-and-down is the law, except for the gods.
You back home can't have any idea.
If it was rotten, dirty, miserable, we got it.
Imagine the stink of a ship packed to the gunwales with men,
Under a blistering sky—
290 And when we got ashore, we wished we were back being seasick:
The fool officers always picked our campsite
Just within range of a good Trojan bow;
And after a day of fighting or standing around
We'd fall down to sleep in the sopping grass
295 Until our clothes smelled like bad cheese and the harness rotted.
And if you find a few Trojan lice in your clothes tonight
You can thank me for them.
Oh, and the winter: you think it's cold in Greece?
This was unbelievable.
300 Every time a wind would blow off Mount Ida
Birds would fall from the air as if they'd been struck by a slingstone.
But why go on? It's all over now—
All over for the dead; they're out of harm's way;

And we won't worry about them: sometimes we even called
them lucky.

CLYTEMNESTRA enters quietly.

305 But now we're all of us lucky: lucky as Agamemnon,
And he rides higher in fortune than any man ever rode.
And soon we'll stand in bright morning in the temple square
And watch them nail the spoils to the temple walls,
And write on the walls: "This to the gods, in payment,
310 From the men of Argos who broke the spear of Troy."

CHORUS MEMBER. Now I know it was true, and not a dream.
I am not too old to change with newborn knowledge.

LEADER. Then let us tell the queen
This news that has made us young again.

315 CLYTEMNESTRA. Why tell me? My dancing time is done.
Some hours ago the fire-god hurled the news at my heart.
Since then, this square has been in shadow
While toothless old mumblers pronounced on the lightness of
my mind.
Others, who were faithful to me, kept the fires I commanded
320 Fed with ox-fat and sweet-scented herbs,
But here, I see, this is not done.

(*The* LEADER *attempts to speak.*)

There is nothing I wish to hear from you.
I say my dance is danced:
No. It will not begin
325 Until my lord is safely inside that house.
Herald, go swiftly to the shore:
Say to the Captain-General his city awaits him;
Say that a watchdog waits him in his house—

(*The* HERALD *registers incomprehension.*)

And that is his wife, who will love him as he has never been
loved.
330 Say my heart has forgotten nothing
Since he took sail, and left his seal on me;
And as for taking pleasure with another man—
I could as easily dye metal scarlet.

She exits.

HERALD. She speaks like a lady, there's no doubting it.

335 LEADER. We are glad you understand.

But tell us one thing, herald, before you take your message:
How is it with Menelaus?

HERALD. I would like to tell you a happy lie.

CHORUS. There are no happy lies. We know when we are prepared
or when we are not prepared, one or the other.

340 HERALD. His ship is missing.

CHORUS. Ah—

LEADER. You spoke of a storm-wind. Was it that—

HERALD. Enough; your first arrow hit the mark.

CHORUS. Does no man know of his fate?

345 HERALD. Only the sun on the waves.

CHORUS. It seems the gods were angered.

HERALD. I came here to tell of victory.
Why do you make me end with all this woe?
Yes, it *would* seem the gods were angered,
350 For fire and sea conspired against us,
And many men whose eyes were bent on home
Are eyeless now in the cavern of fishes
And their ships broken; driftwood on nameless shores.
Our own ship rode the storm, but Menelaus'
355 Is gone out of sight.
But let me end with good words. If he is alive
He may be grieving for *us,* as we for him,
And he will soon come home in the happy sunlight,
To the smiling god—
360 Let me speak good—there may be hope—

His words choke him. He runs out.

CHORUS. A child's name
May carry a shadow,
A hint in sound
If named too well:
365 What god stood by
At the birth of Helen
To name that beauty
The bride of Hell?

She smiled while borne
370 From her great lord's chamber,
A smile uncaring

For all men's tears;
And over the sea
There followed after
375 A thousand ships
And a forest of spears.

She walked great Troy;
Her smile was changeless;
They lit bright torches
380 And cried her name,
Till the bridal song
Was turned to screaming;
The laughing dancers
Were bathed in flame.

385 So with the man
Who stole from a lion
And bore to his house
Its small soft young:
It rolled in play
390 Like a harmless kitten
And licked the hand
With its tiny tongue.

But the beast waxed strong
And its name was Lion,
395 With blood its hunger
And death its will.
It walked the house
Like a thing of terror,
Too cunning to capture,
400 Too great to kill.

Was Helen sent
To bring down Fortune
And spill the blood
Made hot with Pride?

The sound of the approaching host begins to be heard.

405 Have we not seen
The end of evil?
Will many die
As many died?

The host begins to enter. With AGAMEMNON *in his chariot, drawn
by four Trojans of noble rank, is* CASSANDRA.

CHORUS. Eternal glory
410 By Zeus all-seeing
Now to our king
Be freely given;

And may swift Justice
Steer to fulfillment
415   All things moving
In earth and heaven.

Great Agamemnon!

LEADER. O my dear lord, I would wish no better thing
Than for you to believe my joy at seeing you
420   My own like the voice of breath or beat of blood.
I will not give you false, twisted smiles
And lick the floor with praises of your mighty deeds,
But speak fairly and frankly.
My thoughts were against you in the beginning,
425   When your glorious words lashed so many of our young men
To rush unthinking to the hungry grave
For the honor of one wild young girl.
But the outcome is good, as your messenger said,
And thereby approves the means.
430   You have succeeded, and we love you.
Ask about the city; you shall find
We have been true, though others have not.

AGAMEMNON. First I hail Argos and her gods,
Who know the right cause from the wrong
435   And brought us safe to shelter, while their wrath
Sent Justice, through our arms, to break great Troy.
Through them I have triumphed, and let them now see
That I do not forget a debt.
We were executors of no human judgment;
440   The gods themselves withdrew mercy
From the proud dog Priam and his lax race.
They are no more.
We were right, and therefore ruthless.
We fell like a lion on their towered city:
445   The smoke of her burning still goes up,
Carrying perfumed lust and painted glory
In a storm of ashes.
Now the gods are thanked, and I turn to you.
For what you said—remember those last phrases.
450   I know how false a friend can be—
A shadow in a glass, a whispering specter—
When envy of another's fortune strikes the heart.
Only one man was not a backstabber,
A malcontent, a frustrator of my plans,
455   And that was Ulysses, who at the beginning
Was least eager of all those mouthing warhawks
To follow my spear to Troy. This to his credit, wherever he
     may be.

I am of a great mind now to call the Council
And begin the reordering of the state, which it doubtless needs.
460   I can see from the joy that greeted me that cancers have grown
That need the gentle knife and white-hot iron.
I go now to my home, my true seat, the palace of my fathers,
And for this victory, may our name live forever.

Enter CLYTEMNESTRA.

CLYTEMNESTRA. You will all forgive me, I know, if I seem
immodest
465   In looking such love at the man who owns my heart,
But it has been a long time, and I am not good at pretending.
What can a woman do? The world of men
Is more important to them than her love.
But I am not thinking of "men" and "women";
470   I am thinking of what went on in my own heart
While this man was away.
I am thinking of all the tears I shed,
Of nights black with fear and days gray with terror.
Did you know how many times, when messengers came saying
475   That your bones lay in the ground by the walls of Troy,
I hanged myself, and was cut down by frightened slaves, and
    went on living,
Till I ran out of tears and my heart dried up.
Do you know what it is like, in a city without a king?
Prowling cutthroats, desperate men,
480   Troublemakers, subverters of the state,
Come out like bone-crunching hyenas at night;
And only one lonely woman to stave them off.
It is for that reason that your son
Does not stand by me to welcome his father.
485   I have put Orestes in safe hands;
An old comrade of yours, Strophius, has taken him far away,
Clear of this anarchic nightmare, Argos.
But now! Why, now all is changed: the king is back;
Sun shines once more; the earth drinks in your majesty like rain;
490   The very pillars of our house, this aged tower,
Stand tall for confidence.
Come, dear my love,
Enter and claim the reward you so richly deserve.
Yet stay!
495   It is not meet that one whose foot
Was sanctified by God to crush high Troy
Should walk on this foul courtyard.
Maidens! Slaves!
Let a path of crimson spring up into the house

500   That our high king may walk where Justice leads him,
    To a welcome that he never thought to see.

        CLYTEMNESTRA'S *handmaidens spread a carpet of purple stuffs*
                from the chariot to the palace door.

AGAMEMNON. This farce has gone far enough.
    I am thoroughly persuaded that you missed me—
    You said so in a speech almost as long as my absence—
505   But to treat me as some damned Persian
    Who sucks up flattery and sits limp-wristed on a godlike throne
    Is something I will not bear.
    I am a soldier, and if you give me a general's honors, I will take
        them;
    I am a king, and it is my place to command and to be
        obeyed;
510   But I am a man, and I can walk on the ground as other men do.
    To soil these beautiful things with my boots,
    To grind them into the dirt, to waste them, for my own
        glory—
    Why, that is as if I sacrificed to *myself,*
    My own god and my own priest,
515   And that is arrogant, blasphemous madness, that is spitting in
        the face of true gods, that is mocking the divine order and
            daring it to revenge itself;
    And, make no mistake, *it will.*

CLYTEMNESTRA. Does all this mean you are afraid?

AGAMEMNON. I meant exactly what I said.

CLYTEMNESTRA. If *Priam* had won, would *he* have acted as if he
    were ashamed of his greatness?

520 AGAMEMNON. Priam? He would have trod on the purple without a
    thought.
    Perhaps that is why he did not win.

CLYTEMNESTRA. Of course, if what people will say is troubling
    you—

AGAMEMNON. Do they need to say it? Look at their faces.

CLYTEMNESTRA. Envy! Great men are measured by small men's envy.

525 AGAMEMNON. Is this the woman I remember?
    Can this be a woman still?

CLYTEMNESTRA. I *had* thought that if you loved me you would
    desire to please me;
    But no one makes up Agamemnon's mind but Agamemnon
    himself.

(*pause*)

AGAMEMNON. Take off my boots.

(*The boots are removed. He still hesitates.*)

530   And how do we know who is watching from the sky
     As I crush these fair things into the courtyard's filth?

CLYTEMNESTRA. This is not a pauper's house, O King.
     There is Tyrian purple[8] in the royal stores
     Enough to carpet Argos with these footcloths.
535   I would have walked this path a thousand times
     If such had been the price of your return.

(*pause*)

AGAMEMNON. The girl Cassandra should be looked after kindly.
     It is not her fault that she has been made a slave.

He enters the palace.

CLYTEMNESTRA. God, God, you who bring all things to pass,
540   You know my prayers. Now let them be fulfilled.

She follows him. The rest of the host exits.

CHORUS. Why should I fear? The city lies
     Under my master's hand;
     The keel that plowed the waves to Troy
     Lies beached in Argos' sand;

545   But one has yet to reach the shore,
     And fangs of rock still wait
     That ship which sails uncharted waves:
     Great Agamemnon's fate.

     No siren's song, no sybil's speech,
550   Not all of wit and worth
     Can charm back home the innocent blood
     That soaks the innocent earth.

     One chamber of the human heart
     Holds pride and strength within,
555   The next, a mad, sick animal,
     And the wall between is thin.

     Yet still I track some slippery hope
     Among my icy fears.
     Angling for a phantom fish
560   In a lake of tears.

CLYTEMNESTRA *re-enters.*

---

8. Tyrian purple: A purple dye produced in the city of Tyre in ancient Phoenicia. Cloth colored
with this purple dye was much prized by the Greeks and Romans.

CLYTEMNESTRA. You, girl—Cassandra or whatever your name is:
We have work for you within.
You may bear a warm bowl of scented water.
Did you hear me, you proud slut?

565   Thank the gods you were sent to a house old in power and
      wealth,
And not to some new-rich upstart who would thrash you as
      someone once thrashed him.

LEADER. Perhaps she speaks a language strange as the crying of
      swallows
And cannot understand.

CLYTEMNESTRA. She had better understand.

570   LEADER. Cassandra, if you know what is being said to you, we beg
      of you, obey.
You will only be forced to, later.

CLYTEMNESTRA. Oh, she knows what I am saying, well enough.
I fancy she spoke excellent Greek in Agamemnon's tent.
Very well, then, stay. If you like that chariot so much

575   We will have you chained in it until you rot.
I waste no more time. There are greater things to be seen to.

She goes back into the palace.

LEADER. Come, Cassandra. We do not hate you.
Yield now to Necessity. Better bow than break.

CASSANDRA. God! God! God! Apollo! Apollo! Apollo!

580   LEADER. She is mad, or the handmaiden of the god.

CHORUS MEMBER. Or we are mad, or all the world is mad.

CASSANDRA *comes down from the chariot.*

CASSANDRA. Apollo, my trust, have you brought me to ruin?
What is this house? Who is the king here?

LEADER. This is the house of Atreus.

585   CHORUS MEMBER. The home of Agamemnon, your master.

CASSANDRA. This is the house of Hell.
This is the winepress of death. Are you not all drowning in blood?

(*She points at the altar.*)

The flesh of the children is roasted, that their father will be fed.
Do you hear their cry?

590   CHORUS MEMBER. We have had enough of evil speech in this
      courtyard.

(*pointing toward the seashore*)

If you must prophesy, prophesy to the waves.

LEADER. Wait. What does she see?

CASSANDRA. I see that doom is certain,
　　For gray and stinking, from their caves beneath the earth,
595　The Furies[9] have come, and huddle like bats about this god-
　　　　hated house,
　　Eating into the brain with their high unbearable song.

LEADER. What this is I do not understand,
　　But it is black horror.

CASSANDRA. Red, red!
600　She has lain with him in love, and now that hand,
　　That hand caressing, feels for the cold hilt—no, no!
　　Draw the water, cast the net;
　　You are fishing for doom. Gather here, dark ones;
　　Your prey is walking within;
605　The great beast is going to the water
　　And the sting of death.

CHORUS MEMBER. O gods, what do you call down upon this
　　　house?

(*The* LEADER *restrains him.*)

CASSANDRA. Now I will sing my own doom,
　　Not for the ears of men but for Apollo who loved me,[10]
610　Whose body touched mine by Scamander Water,
　　And whose breath mixed with mine.
　　You have set me upon a hard path, Apollo.
　　Now no more will I drink at the stream of my fathers,
　　Or walk the white city in the morning light;
615　For he whose foot ground out the flame of Troy
　　Will soon go down to darkness, and his strength,
　　My last help, shall be gone,
　　And I will be the bride of cold iron
　　And queen forever in a land of soundless night.

---

9. **The Furies:** goddesses who punished those guilty of certain crimes, principally crimes against
　parents or guests, afflicting them with madness. They were conceived of as hideous women with
　snakes curling about their faces.

10. **for Apollo who loved me:** Cassandra was once loved by the god Apollo, who gave her the
　power to see the past and foretell the future. When she refused his love, he took revenge by
　making sure that no one ever believed her. A god's gift, once given, cannot be taken away, but
　Apollo turned the gift into something worthless.

620 LEADER. This is great sorrow. This deadly second sight is the curse
of a god?

CASSANDRA. The curse? No, no; the *gift;*
It was the bride-price of great Apollo;
To possess my body he touched my eyes with light.

LEADER. And you . . . ?

625 CASSANDRA. I swore to yield myself;
But I was of no mind to enter such a dreadful dynasty
By bearing a god's child. When the time came I refused.

LEADER. But the gift of prophecy was given,
And a god cannot withdraw his word.

630 CASSANDRA. Oh, this was seen to. When I told the truth, I never
was believed.

LEADER. We believe you. Though from a far country
You know of the Feast of Thyestes, a thing
That is spoken of in whispers even here.

(*The spell seizes her again.*)

The holy evil is upon her.
635 May some god pity her agony.

CHORUS MEMBER. What monstrous thing will we be made to see now?

CASSANDRA. The children! The children!
I hear their cry! I see them!
The generations go down in blood;
640 Doom walks in fire, Time is a falling mountain;
The innocent begets the cold-eyed jackal;
The all-destroying lion falls;
His mate becomes the jackal's bitch,
And both together lap the lion's blood.
645 That great golden beast, stiff and fly-blown on a marble floor,
How could he know? She is no woman, nor any animal,
But a monster, a spawn of hell, chaos, not nature.
Her eyes turn toward me!
I see my doom now like a moving flame!
650 Agamemnon! Dead!

LEADER. You have said enough.

CASSANDRA. I have not said anything, if you have not understood.

LEADER. We pray that such a thing may never happen.

CASSANDRA. Yes, pray. Pray while *they* act.

(*She removes her crown of fillets and casts it and her staff to earth.*)

655 There, Apollo, take them back;
 Make some other woman miserable with your kindness.
 We two are done. You have turned everyone I loved against me,
 But that does not matter because they are all dead now
 Under the broken walls of Troy.
660 Having starved and lived in ditches,
 I am no longer as beautiful as when you sought me
 By Scamander Water, but it is all the same.
 I have seen an altar-stone swilled with my father's blood.
 And mine will soon be shed.
665 I only pray the stroke will be quick
 And the pain not too great.

(*She looks at the* CHORUS.)

 I need friends.

CHORUS MEMBER. Is there no way you can escape?

CASSANDRA. Not when the day is here.
670 Now indeed I can cry my prophecies to the waves;
 But of darker waters than the ones you meant.

LEADER. You are a brave woman. You will be remembered.

CASSANDRA. I remember those who were brave: my father and
 brothers.
 I must be brave for them.

(*She moves toward the palace, but turns at the door.*)

675 I am going in now.
 Do not weep. I die in royal company,
 And I shall be avenged.
 Sun, I see you for the last time:
 Guide with your light that wandering man;[11]
680 For when at last he comes again to Argos
 And passes through these doors, his bright sword drawn,
 That day shall Agamemnon's mighty ghost
 And the small shade of one forgotten girl
 Lie down to rest forever.
685 Poor Humankind. Your happiness ends with the fall of a
 shadow
 But your misery only with eternal night.
 And to know this—that is the worst of all.

She enters the palace.

---

11. **wandering man:** Orestes, Agamemnon's son.

CHORUS. No man is wise who cannot say to Fortune,
    "Enough from your golden hands,"
690   For he sees himself the master of all around him
    And famous in many lands;

    He strides like a walking tower in the sun of glory
    And all bow down before;
    And then one day, enthroned in pride and greatness,
695   He hears a closing door.

    He is all alone, in his mouth the taste of ashes
    That he knows for the sum of his life;
    And the only light, as he sits in the hollow darkness,
    Is the gleaming edge of a knife.

(AGAMEMNON *screams within.*)

700 LEADER. It is done.
    What shall we do?

CHORUS. Raise a hue and cry. Get the townspeople to back us.
    Then we can act.
    No. Burst in on them now. Take them with their butcher-work
    still red on their hands.
    I think that may be the best thing. This is a situation that calls
      for immediate action.
705   He's right. No time to waste—It's clear they mean to set up a
      tyranny.
    We must act now. We can't let them trample down our rights.
    Better death than submission.
    But first we must be sure we're doing the right thing.
    That's true. Mere good intentions won't bring back the dead.
710   Besides, how do we know the king *is* dead?
    Hearing a scream proves nothing.

CHORUS MEMBER. Let us get the facts straight.
    Then our rage can burst forth.

    Enter CLYTEMNESTRA, *her hands and dress stained with blood.*

CLYTEMNESTRA. I spoke so many empty words,
715   Words of love, and my heart a cinder of hate.
    Now I throw them all to the ground
    And think no shame on it.
    My smooth words wove a snare that caught and held;
    My lies built a circle of sharp stakes
720   That even that great beast could not leap over.
    The gods know how long this was in coming—
    How many times he earned his due
    Helpless and naked in his bath, I cast the rich robes about him,
    Netted him, held him fast,
725   And pushed a blade of iron through the silk.
    Twice I drove it home, and he screamed like a beast

And that great purple sack pitched and buckled to the floor.
They say the third time is the charm, so I brought down the
    edge
And the air squelched from him, and a fountain of bright blood
730   Shot up and fell on me like the sweet rain on the young shoots
    in spring.
Now you know, and may it make you happy.
For me, I glory. This man filled our cup
With pain unspeakable;
Now he is home, and has drunk it to the dregs.

735   LEADER. You glory in it—and this man was your own lord.

CLYTEMNESTRA. Yes, that man was my husband . . . Agamemnon.
Now he is dead, and this hand, this good workman, did it.
That is all that makes any difference.
What you think of it means nothing to me.

740   CHORUS. Whether you did this coldly
Or whether some poisonous herb worked your brain to madness,
In those three strokes you cut yourself away
From humankind, from love, from rest on this earth.

CLYTEMNESTRA. You judge me? You threaten me with exile?
745   You should have said those words to this dead dog
When his yellow-toothed priests tore the throat from the lamb
    of my womb
To charm the winds of Thrace.
You should have hunted *him* from this land
With stones and curses, as you would use me now.
750   Very well, then. If you can make good your threats, so be it,
But if the power falls to me, be assured
You shall learn wisdom, late
Though it is for you to learn.

CHORUS. You will remember this some day:
755   Some day, when there is no appeal.

CLYTEMNESTRA. For that, I swear to you
By the crying of my child's blood, that now is stilled,
And by the dark goddess of Hell, to whom I now consign
    Agamemnon's ghost,
I shall fear nothing while the presence of Aegisthus
760   Warms this house like a fire, and stands between me and
danger like a rock.
As for this other, he lies as was his custom,
Bedded with a gilded whore of Troy,
Though this a prophetess, her legs spread on the marble
As on the rough planks of her late lord's ship,
765   Her swan song dead upon her lying lips.

There let them lie. Their memory will give
A sharper pleasure to my bed's delight.

LEADER. You mock our grief, in your hatred and pride,
But the gods who give us sorrow give us tongues to mourn.

770   CHORUS. So it has come to undying fame:
The flower of blood that is Helen's name.
Great cold, great sleep
Cover our town.
The strong tower is fallen,
775   The great shield is down.

CLYTEMNESTRA. A double waste of old men's breath:
To curse Helen, and pray for death.

CHORUS. Who will weep for you now, O King?
And who to the grave your bones will bring?
780   Great cold, great sleep
Cover our town.
The strong tower is fallen,
The great shield is down.

CLYTEMNESTRA. Let the daughter he murdered greet him with
tears,
785   For I have had none, these many years.

CHORUS. The spider-queen has stung your life,
But the curse of Atreus drove the knife.
Great cold, great sleep
Cover our town.
790   The strong tower is fallen,
The great shield is down.

CLYTEMNESTRA. Then never the hand of queen or wife,
But the hand of Justice, drove the knife.

CHORUS.
    (*to* CLYTEMNESTRA)

That blood on your breast will be fresh one day,
795   And death for death will another repay.
Great cold, great sleep
Cover our town.
The strong tower is fallen,
The great shield is down.

800   CLYTEMNESTRA. Listen to me. I ask no more than this:
The knowledge that I have set the balance straight,
Wiped clean the print of blood, and laid to rest
The doom that has walked this house so many years.

CHORUS. Who can decide this thing? And who
805   Can wash off blood with blood?
          I only know, as one does,
          To him shall it be done,
          And so following,
          World without end.

Enter AEGISTHUS *with his bodyguard.*

810 AEGISTHUS. So: the bright day of Justice, and at last
          I can begin to feel there is a God,
          Watching this dead beast tangled in the purple
          Paying in full for the tricks his father contrived.
          Do you know that story, Argives? It is time
815   The tale of the Feast of Thyestes was cried to the clouds.
          Atreus, this man's father, drove his own brother from the
              land—
          My father, Thyestes—in a dispute about the throne.
          Then, when Thyestes came in misery after long years
          A suppliant to his hearth, Agamemnon's father
820   Smiled his dog's smile, and invited him
          To a feast of reconciliation, roast meat and wine.
          But the meat that was served that day
          Was Thyestes' own children, and when that royal jester
          Showed Thyestes the heads of the game he had eaten
825   He leaped up, and vomited the meat from his mouth,
          And kicking over the laden table, cried,
          "May the gods do this to the whole house of Atreus."
          Then was he driven into banishment again
          To share with me, his third-born,
830   Those years of voiceless, impotent sorrow.
          But now I have found a voice, and an arm,
          And now I have come home.
          I planned this deed, and if I die, I die.
          The slate is clean.

835 CHORUS. Nothing is clean, Aegisthus. The slate is sticky with
              blood.
          You have added blood-guilt to blood-guilt, and piled it on your
              own head.

     AEGISTHUS. I am going to tell you something, old men:
          Don't meddle in royal matters.
          It serves little for the galley-slaves to spit
840   At the ship's master on the deck above.
          Not while there are whips, and chains, and hunger's iron tooth.
          Is my meaning clear?

     CHORUS. So you have found an arm, you coward:
          Yes, a *woman's* arm.

845 AEGISTHUS. Why, naturally. Should I have come to Argos
   With "I am here to kill Agamemnon" written above my heart?
   My motives for hatred were too well known.
   No, the deception was the woman's part,
   And well has she done her work.

850 CHORUS. O god of the sun, make Orestes tall and strong
   And light his way home to vengeance on these two.

   AEGISTHUS. You have howled enough. Disperse now,
   Before I have my men whip you to your kennels.

   CHORUS. Men of Agamemnon! Soldiers of Argos! Help us!

855 AEGISTHUS. The soldiers of Argos will follow the man who pays
       them,
   And pay them I shall, with Agamemnon's gold.

   LEADER. Let every man take up stock and stone.

   AEGISTHUS. Guards! They threaten us. Let your swords do their
       work.

   CHORUS. To the death, then, usurper! The gods judge between us!

       (CLYTEMNESTRA *comes between them.*)

860 CLYTEMNESTRA. No more, my dearest. We have seen a bitter
       harvest-time,
   A letting of foul blood from ancient sins.
   Now let the grass grow over the torn earth,
   The scarred flesh heal.
   Let us all learn to say "Enough."
865 Old men of Argos, you have sustained your honor;
   Go to your homes before you meet with harm.
   What was done, we had to do,
   And what is done, is done.

   CHORUS. You think this tale of blood is finished?
870   It has not yet begun.

   AEGISTHUS. Listen to that. Treasonous old fools,
   I am your king,
   And I will not forget this day.

   CHORUS. If you do forget, you will be reminded when Orestes
       comes home.

875 AEGISTHUS. Exiles are eaters of wind and empty dreams.
   I was one long enough. I know.

   CHORUS. You have turned a royal palace to a slaughterhouse and
       an honored kingdom to a dunghill.

Now crow over it, like a cock with his hen.

CLYTEMNESTRA. Dogs bark loudest that cannot bite.
880   Forget them, dearest. We hold the power,
        And you and I shall order all things well.

They go into the palace.

DISCUSSION QUESTIONS

1. If you were retelling the story of Agamemnon and Clytemnestra
based on the general outline of the myth, what details would you
emphasize if you wanted your readers to sympathize with
Agamemnon? What details would you emphasize if you wanted to
direct your readers' sympathies toward Clytemnestra?

2. Where do Aeschylus' sympathies seem to lie, with Agamemnon or
Clytemnestra? How does he persuade the audience to share his view?
Notice which details he provides to defame the other character.

3. *Agamemnon* is famous as a play that creates an atmosphere of
impending doom. How does Aeschylus create this atmosphere?

4. Clytemnestra claims that her motive for killing her husband is
retribution against the man who "tore the throat from the lamb of
my womb." Her motivation, however, is more complex than simple
sorrow over the death of Iphigenia. What other motives does
Clytemnestra have for wanting her husband dead?

5. Clytemnestra's meeting with Agamemnon quickly develops into a
contest of wills as they argue about walking on the purple carpet.
What tactics does Clytemnestra use to try to persuade her husband?
How does he respond? What impression do we get of these two
characters from this discussion?

6. After Clytemnestra and Agamemnon enter the palace, the chorus
chants:

> One chamber of the human heart
> Holds pride and strength within,
> The next, a mad, sick animal,
> And the wall between is thin. (lines 553–556)

How do these lines apply to Clytemnestra? Can they also be applied
to other individuals in the long history of the House of Atreus? Do
you think they apply to human nature in general?

ACT TWO. THE BRINGERS OF OFFERINGS

CHARACTERS

ORESTES, *the son of Agamemnon*

PYLADES, *Orestes' friend*

ELECTRA, *Orestes' sister*

SERVANT

CLYTEMNESTRA

CILISSA, *Orestes' old nurse*

AEGISTHUS

CHORUS OF MAIDSERVANTS

Scene: *Argos. The tomb of* AGAMEMNON; *the palace. Some years have passed.*

> *The tomb of* AGAMEMNON. *Enter* ORESTES *and* PYLADES

ORESTES. Hermes, lord of the dead,[1]
　　Be with me now. I stand by the grave of my father,
　　On the soil I called home.

(He lays a lock of hair on the tomb)

　　Hear me, Father. I leave this lock of hair,
5　　An offering of manhood and of grief
　　I was not here when they struck you down,
　　Not here to stretch out my hand as they carried your corpse to
　　　　this tomb.

> *A procession of women approaches.*

　　What does this mean? Has death come again to our house?
　　Or does someone still remember my father!
10　　O God, that girl—it must be—
　　Pylades, look—my sister—Electra.
　　Come, out of the way.

> *They conceal themselves.*

CHORUS. I come from a house of blood
　　　　With blood upon my breast,
15　　　　For as my nails have torn my flesh
　　　　Foul dreams have torn my rest.

　　　　Last night one cried in the dark
　　　　The scream of a horrible birth:

---

1. **lord of the dead:** the god Hermes conducted the souls of the dead to the Underworld.

She had borne a dream of the restless dead
20   And the fires beneath the earth.

I am sent to bribe the dead
From that palace that all men shun
By the godless woman who rules the house
That never sees the sun.

25   The glory of old is gone
With the loveliness of light;
High Fortune capers and dances there
On the terrible edge of night.

There Murder walks with Lust,
30   And where their fingers stray
Not all the waters of all the earth
Can wash the blood away.

Meanwhile, I serve them both
And close a silent gate
35   On bitter tongue and raging heart,
Sorrow, and secret hate.

ELECTRA. You women, maidservants of the house of Atreus,
    Tell me what to say.
    Give me the words to pour out with these libations
40   On my father's grave.
    Should I say "I pour out the love and tears of a faithful wife"—
    And mean my mother?
    Or is this better: "Reward the givers of these sweet offerings
    For their gift of—a filthy crime?"
45   Or should I just spill them out, dumb and dishonored, the way
        my father died,
    With my face turned away as if I were emptying slops?
    Tell me, please. I truly don't know.
    Don't be afraid. Remember we're sisters in hatred.
    Remember the hour strikes for the free man
50   As well as for the slave.

CHORUS. Because I respect your father's grave as I respect the holy
        places,
    I will tell you my thoughts.

ELECTRA. Speak them.

CHORUS. As you pour, pronounce blessings on those of good will.

55   ELECTRA. Who do I have to call friend?

CHORUS. Yourself first; then all of those who hate Aegisthus.

ELECTRA. Shall I include you then?

CHORUS. The naming of names is for you to decide.

ELECTRA. Who stands with us in this?

60 CHORUS. Though he's far away, remember Orestes.

ELECTRA. Thank you. I shall not forget.

CHORUS. Then the murderers. Pray against them—

ELECTRA. Yes. Tell me. Give me the words.

CHORUS. That there may come a man, or more than man . . .

65 ELECTRA. To judge, or to punish?

CHORUS. To take blood for blood. Say only that.

ELECTRA. Is this a seemly prayer in the eyes of the gods?

CHORUS. You have been struck. Is it impious to wish to strike back?

ELECTRA. Hermes, lord of the dead,
70   Be with me now. I stand by the grave of my father.
  Father, hear me. I say this prayer for myself and for your son
      Orestes.
  Our mother made us slaves and homeless wanderers;
  She traded us for Aegisthus, the man who planned your murder.
  O Father, let Orestes come back home.
75   Let me see him again.
  And let me never be like my mother.
  For our enemies, let them be killed as they killed you.
  This is my prayer.

CHORUS. Between good and evil,
80   Stand beside this mound:
    Here, where the tear falls
    And breaks on the ground
    As our king was broken,
    Make a solemn sound.

85   Hear us from your darkness;
    Hear and befriend.
    Strong bow, sharp sword
    Let the just gods send
    To this house of terror:
90   Come, and make an end.

ELECTRA. Women, look here.

CHORUS. What is it?

ELECTRA. Here, by the tomb—a lock of hair.

CHORUS. What man's? Or is it a girl's?

95 ELECTRA. No one would have done this but myself.

CHORUS. Yes, the ones who *should* do these things are eaten up
    with hate.

ELECTRA. It isn't mine—and yet it's so very *like* mine . . .

CHORUS. Orestes?

ELECTRA. I don't know—what else to think.

100 CHORUS. Then he—

ELECTRA. No. He might have cut it and sent it by some stranger.

CHORUS. Perhaps. And all the sadder if it's true. It means he'll
    never set foot upon this land again.

ELECTRA. To think of that is like a sword in my heart.
    Is *this* the answer to my prayer?
105 No—if I start to cry I'll never stop.
    What common man who lives in this kingdom of terror
    Would put his hand in the fire with such an act of devotion?
    My mother? No. Expect a sweet act of grief from one who no
        longer even belongs to nature?
    And yet—how can I be sure it comes from that most loved of
        men?
110 If only it could speak, could whisper a word
    To stop this tearing and twisting of my heart, to tell me
    Whether to throw it away like a hated thing
    Or to water it with a fellow-mourner's tears
    And replace it proudly on our father's grave.

115 CHORUS. We call upon the gods, who know
    How the winged seed of hope is tossed by the storm;
    And yet, if it chance to fall on fertile ground,
    How mighty a tree may rise up from that place.

ORESTES *appears from his hiding place.*

ORESTES. Thank the gods. They have answered half your prayer.
120   Now pray for the rest.

ELECTRA. What do I have, that I should thank the gods for it?

ORESTES. What you sought.

ELECTRA. How do you know what was in my heart?

ORESTES. I know that Orestes was there.

125 ELECTRA. Then how is half my prayer answered?

ORESTES. You prayed to see him. Look before you.

ELECTRA. Is this a trap?

ORESTES. If it is, I am the one who's caught in it.

ELECTRA. You overheard me. You're making fun of me.

130 ORESTES. Look in my eyes, if you think I'm laughing.

ELECTRA. But—how can I be sure—

ORESTES. You saw only a lock of hair,
          And it was as if I stood before you.
          Now here I am, and you won't believe it.
135   Look. Here is the place the lock was cut from.
          Is it still the gift of a stranger?
          Look at this sash.
          Your hands were smaller when you wove the cloth
          With its design of running beasts.

          (*She starts to cry out.*)

140   No, no, dearest,
          We are too close to those who hate us
          To lose our heads for joy.

ELECTRA. O my own, my four-times beloved,
          Because you have come to stand in our father's place,
145   And because the love that I would have borne our mother goes
                to you,
          And my love for our sister, sacrificed at Aulis,
          And because you of all men have come to stand up for me
          And bring us to our own.
          Trust now to your strength, and let Might and Right
150   And Zeus, the great third, stand beside you.

ORESTES. Zeus. Zeus. Hear these grave words, and guide what we
                must do.
          You see here the children of the eagle
          Stricken down by the deadly snake.
          The nest is deserted, and the young ones perish.
155   Save them, O Zeus. It is myself I mean,
          And my sister Electra,
          Homeless the one and helpless the other,
          Sustain us, O Zeus. If you leave us naked to the winds,
          The children of a father who honored you so greatly,
160   What will become of the faith of men?
          The stump of this royal tree can still serve as your altar,
          But not if you let it be blasted to the ground.
          Cherish it, and a shoot may still spring to immortal glory,
          Though now it seem dry and low.

165 CHORUS. Children, children, saviors of your father's house and honor,
          No more of that. Idle ears may hear,
          And busy tongues carry your thoughts to those who hold the
                power,
          Those whom I long to see
          Stiff on the pitch-pine pyre,
170   Black in the heart of the flame.

ORESTES. Apollo holds the power, and he will not forsake me.
    His oracle told me to stake all on this chance:
    "Give them a taste of their own," he said,
    "Come down upon them like a blood-crazed bull."
175   If I did not, he promised nothing but horror.
    The undone deed would come out upon me
    In cancer, in rotting sores: my flesh would die alive;
    Or the dark ones would haunt me, the Furies that eat the brain.
    He spoke of the sudden terror in the dead hour,
180   The monstrous shadow approaching the bed;
    Told how a man may be driven from city to city, from road to
        road,
    Sharing no cup of friendship in a welcoming house,
    Turned back from holy altars by a father's curse,
    Until at last in some ditch, gnawed by cold and wretchedness,
185   He finds his only friend, Death.
    Should I believe such an oracle? What difference does it make,
    When even if I do not, the thing must still be done?
    I have motives enough to drive me on:
    The will of the gods, the giant grief of my father,
190   Myself driven from my estates, and the people of Argos,
    My people, that wrestled down the might of Troy,
    Slaves to a brace of women: for Aegisthus is woman-hearted,
    Or, if he is not, he can prove it soon in my face.

CHORUS. Great Zeus, we pray that your thunder-stone
195   Be dashed in the teeth of those grinning mouths
    Dripping with venom of hate;
    That the great wheel be turned again,
    Blood-greased, groaning with the voice of living men,
    That tells the cycles of fate.

200 ORESTES. Father, how can I reach down through the darkness?
    What word, what act can throw a gleam
    Into your stone-sealed night?
    From my eyes should fall fire, not sickly tears,
    Remembering the greatness of your days,
205   The roaring blood, the light.

CHORUS. Child, the red teeth of the flame
    Eat only the body of the dead;
    His will is a stubborn stone,
    White-hot; but touch it with a tear,
210   The stone will break, the ghost will rise,
    Dreadful, to claim his own.

ELECTRA. Father, Father, hear us! Hear our cry!
    We have only your low grave to shelter us
    Against the black wind,

215   Against the iron night.
    Before the monstrous darkness fall,
    Tall-plumed, terrible in arms,
    Rise! Rise into the light!

ORESTES. If you had died in the storming of burning Troy,
220   Your great heart split by a bronze-tipped spear
    Or under a falling tower,
    You would lie today in a cairn like a mighty mountain,
    Your dead face covered by a mask of gold
    With a smile of immortal power.

225 CHORUS. And Agamemnon's giant ghost,
    Among the great companions, the Argive heroes,
    Would move to his place of pride
    As a great star walks in fire among lesser stars
    Through the country of night, to a royal throne
230   By death-lord Hermes' side.

ELECTRA. No! No! I wish he had never died!
    Not by the side of blood-churned Scamander
    With the broken yield of the spear;
    But that those who wished him evil were dead
235   By some nightmare means, in distant lands
    Whispered in silent fear.

CHORUS. Child, you are spending the gold of dreams.
    The north wind blows vain wishes away
    And scatters them far and wide.
240   But the lash that shall punish those of bloody hand
    Screams over their heads in the darkened air:
    The gods have taken your side.

ORESTES. Ah, this agony pierces me like a sword!
    So let my cry speed like a singing arrow
245   To sting these powers awake!
    Zeus, Zeus, let some Vengeance rise up from the ground
    To crush those two into dust.

CHORUS. I claim the right to sing my savage joy
    About the pyre where their corpses burn.
250   I have bitten my lips too long
    Against the indignation of my heart,
    Whipped by anger as the prow by the howling salt-blast.

ELECTRA. Aie! Zeus, smash their skulls with your fist!
    Hear me, Earth! Hear me, you gods of darkness!

255 CHORUS. Blood cries for blood. The seed of the second death
    Is sown in the stroke of the first.
    See it done, you Furies. Give us a sign.

ORESTES. You Curses that wander the land beneath the earth,
Powers of the kingdom of death, give us a sign.
260   We are the last of the house of Atreus
And we have nothing. O God, where shall we turn?

ELECTRA. We have one thing: our mother's inheritance—
The gift of the wolf, a savage implacable heart—
She who without a tear shoveled our father into the ground.

265 CHORUS. Ah, that day I clawed at my streaming cheeks; I battered
       my head and breast and wailed the high deathsong to the skies.

ORESTES. I ask this of the gods:
Let me live long enough to kill my mother.

CHORUS. Listen: to cripple the strong hand of your father's ghost
270   They chopped the corpse's hands from its body.

ELECTRA. Ah! And while they were butchering you, Father,
They flung me into a room and locked the door
As if I were a mad dog, and left me to drown in my tears.
Hear this, Father. Listen to these words.

275 CHORUS. Let these words burn deep.
Let them eat into the quiet soul.
Only so will the rage of blood awaken.
Pray for that time so long delayed,
And let your will, when you have prayed,
280   Have the simplicity of fire or stone.

ORESTES. O Zeus, give me my kingdom.

ELECTRA. O Persephone,[2] let me see Aegisthus die.

ORESTES. O Earth, when I face those two
Let my father come forth to see!

285 CHORUS. My flesh crawls to hear their prayer.
Let it come, let it come, this dreadful thing they ask,
For the blood thickens with cold; the heart of this house
Is numb with ingrown pain,
The agony not to be borne, the worm that eats all away.

290 ELECTRA. Father! Father, be with your children!

ORESTES. Remember the shame of your death!

ELECTRA. They netted you like a beast!

ORESTES. Helpless, naked, they struck you down!

ELECTRA. Does that not rouse you from your darkness, Father?

---

2. **Persephone:** queen of the Underworld.

295   ORESTES. Will you not rear upright that beloved head?

ELECTRA. Do not let your house perish, Father.
    A man's children are the voices of his blood
    When he is gone from earth,
    Like floats that hold the net from sinking in the deep.
300   Hear us, Father. Our grief and shame are yours,
    And our prayers for ourselves are also prayers for you.

CHORUS. Children, you have spoken well.
    Now the rest must be action.

ORESTES. It will be. But tell me first why my mother sends you
    with libations.
305   Some hypocritical remorse?
    Tell me what you know about it.

CHORUS. I know all about it, for I was there.
    It was a dream she had.
    That godless woman was shaken
310   By drifting terrors in the night.
    Because of it, she sent these offerings out.

ORESTES. Can you tell me exactly what it was?

CHORUS. Yes; she told me. She dreamed she gave birth to a serpent.

ORESTES. Was there more to the dream?

315   CHORUS. She dressed it as if it were a baby
    And when it was hungry, she gave her breast to it.

ORESTES. So that it tore her nipple with its fangs.

CHORUS. Yes, and drew in blood along with the milk.

ORESTES. This is no empty dream. This is the vision of a man.

320   CHORUS. She woke up screaming in the blind dark.
    They had to light lamps all over the palace.
    At any rate, this is why she sends these offerings to be poured:
    To free her of—whatever it was.

ORESTES. By the earth and my father's grave
325   I pray that this omen is meant for me.
    Yes, it must be; the parts all fit.
    If this snake came out of the place from which I came,
    Fastened its jaws on the breast from which I drew milk
    And pierced the flesh with its fangs, drawing forth blood and
      savage pain,
330   It must mean that my mother will be murdered by the creature
      she bore.
    I am the snake; I am the one who will kill her.

CHORUS. You have interpreted well.
    May it all happen as you have said.
    Now tell your friends what they must do—
335   Or not do, as need be.

ORESTES. This is how it will be:
    Electra will go inside,
    And at all costs keep secret what has happened.
    Let me make this emphatic: it must be this way
340   If those two are to be tricked to their doom
    As they tricked a noble and open-hearted man to his.
    And that is how it will happen; Apollo has said so,
    And Apollo's word has never been false.
    Now. My friend Pylades and myself, disguised as travelers
345   And talking like outlanders, go to the outer gate
    And ask to see Aegisthus.
    Then, once I am over that doorstone, and through those gates,
    And find that man sitting on my father's throne,
    The minute he rises, and looks me in the eye,
350   And says "Who are you?" I'll give him an answer
    Swift, and sharp, and cold, through the middle of his body.
    Electra, go in now, and keep your eyes open and your lips closed.
    You other women,
    If you can say something that will help our plot, say it;
355   If not, keep quiet.
    Pylades, you will second me: you and the god Apollo,
    Whom I call on now to guide the work of my sword.

                   Exit ELECTRA, ORESTES, *and* PYLADES.

CHORUS. The earth crawls
    With unnumbered terrors;
360   Monstrous forms
    In the sea-depths lie;
    The storm-wind howls,
    And far in the darkness
    Things like torches
365   Fall through the sky.

    But none can measure
    The heights of daring
    Man's pride may scale
    Till it falls to doom,
370   Or fathom the blind
    Down-dragging darkness,
    The animal power
    Of the woman's womb.

    Althea lit
375   The torch that measured
    By length of burning

Her own son's life;[3]
And Scylla, all
For a golden necklace,
380   Her father's charmed hair
Shore off with a knife.[4]

But why should I tell
Of ancient treason
When near at hand
385   Is the bitter tale
Of the brazen-hearted
And scheming woman
Who slew the hero
In war-lord's mail?

390   The sword is forged
Upon Right's hard anvil
That shall lay the guilty
Low to earth,
And the son brought home
395   By unswerving Justice
Stands even now
At the door of his birth.

Before the palace. Enter ORESTES *and* PYLADES.

ORESTES (*knocking at the gate*).
    You there! Inside the palace!
    Is there no one at home?
400   Can't you hear me—or has Aegisthus no respect for the laws of
      hospitality?

SERVANT. All right, all right.

(*opening*)

Who are you, stranger, and where from?

ORESTES. Just tell the masters of this house
    That I have news for them.
405   Be quick about it, will you?
    The darkness is coming on, and it's time for travelers to find
      shelter.

---

3. Althea . . . life: Althea was the mother of the hero Meleager. At his birth it was prophesied that
his life would last until a piece of wood then burning on the fire was consumed. Althea snatched
the wood from the fire, put it out, and hid it away. Years later, Meleager killed her brothers in a
quarrel. Enraged, Althea retrieved the partly burned piece of wood and threw it into the fire,
causing Meleager's death. Afterwards, full of remorse, she hanged herself.

4. Scylla . . . knife: Scylla was the daughter of Nisus, king of Megara. When King Minos of Crete
besieged Megara, Scylla, out of love for Minos, clipped a magical lock of her father's hair, on
which the safety of the city depended. She gave the lock to Minos, who then succeeded in
conquering Megara. Minos, repelled by Scylla's treacherous act, had her drowned.

Send the lady of the house to the door—
Or wait; better yet the lord.
Then we can talk as man to man
410   Without having to stand on the usual ceremony.

Enter CLYTEMNESTRA.

CLYTEMNESTRA. Friends, if you want lodging for the night you have
           only to say so.
       There are all the comforts you could wish for in this house—
       The beds are soft, and we'll draw a bath if you'd like one—
       I can take care of that.
415   If you have important business to discuss, of course,
       That's for the man of the house to see to, and I'll call him.

       ORESTES. I'm from Phocis,⁵ Madam. While I was on the road to
           Argos
       I met a man, a stranger to me, and we fell into talk.
       He told me his name was Strophius, and he said
420   "As long as you're going to Argos anyway, my friend,
       I'd appreciate it if you'd give Orestes' parents
       A message from me: tell them that he is dead.
       Please don't forget. I'm sure they'll want to know.
       Then they can tell you whether they want his remains sent
           home
425   And you can bring the message back to me
       On your return. Tell them, anyway,
       That we've put his ashes in a nice bronze urn
       And there are many people who are sorry he is dead."
       That's all. I don't know if this concerns *you,* Madam,
430   But I think his father ought to know about it.

       CLYTEMNESTRA. Stranger, you can't know the terrible news you've
           given.
       It's like the final curse upon this house,
       Like a storm stripping an old tree bare.
       I tried so hard to keep him away from this swamp of death;
435   I hoped that some day he could come home safe,
       And be happy here, and make us happy,
       And now—it's all over.

       ORESTES. I wish I could have brought better news
       To someone as kind and hospitable as you.
440   But I thought it would have broken a sacred trust
       Not to keep the promise I made.

       CLYTEMNESTRA. And our hospitality will not be the poorer for it,
           believe me.

---

5. **Phocis:** a city in central Greece.

If *you* hadn't brought the news, someone else would have, eventually.

(*to* SERVANT)

Take these gentlemen to a guest room
445 And see to it that their treatment is worthy of this house
In the meantime I'll tell this tragic news to the master
And discuss with our many friends what we shall do.

Exit CLYTEMNESTRA, ORESTES, PYLADES, *and* SERVANT.

CHORUS. What words from our lips can help Orestes?
Great Earth, O you who cover the high king's grave,
450 The prince of the black ships of war,
Let subtle Persuasion pass through your gates of darkness
To win the aid of death-lord Hermes
To guide that unpitying sword.

Enter CILISSA.

But see, our wandering man is at work already
455 Sowing his crop of anguish, for here is Cilissa,
The old nurse of Orestes, and in tears.
Where do you go, Cilissa, and why does Misery walk with you?

CILISSA. It's that awful woman; she wants Aegisthus brought here
To meet the strangers and hear the news from *them.*
460 You should have seen her in front of the servants, trying to pull
a long face,
While all the time she could hardly keep from grinning
At how nicely everything's worked out for *her,*
Even if it is the last blow to this house, this terrible news;
And I'm sure it'll make *Aegisthus* happy when he hears it.
465 Oh, I'm so miserable!
It's been one thing after another, but never anything like *this.*
I tried to bear up under all the other things,
But to think of poor little Orestes—
You know, I worked my hands to the bone for that child;
470 I cared for him right after he came out of his mother,
And at night I'd have to walk the floor with him,
While he'd scream fit to wake the dead . . .
A baby hasn't got any sense; it's just like a little animal:
Poor little thing, *it* can't tell you when it's hungry or thirsty or
has to wet;
475 Its little insides just make up their own rules
And you have to keep guessing, and sometimes I wouldn't guess
right,
And then I'd have to wash out his little clothes—
I was nurse and laundrywoman too, and I did a good job—

I remember how I'd take him from his father's arms;
480 And now I have to go tell that awful man he's dead
And watch his face light up . . .
Oh, I'm so miserable!

CHORUS. Cilissa, did she say he should come alone?

CILISSA. What? How do you mean, alone?

485 CHORUS. I mean, did she say he should bring his bodyguard?

CILISSA. Why, as a matter of fact she did.
And she said they should all bring their weapons.

CHORUS. Cilissa, don't do it. He mustn't be alarmed.
Just tell him to come himself.
490 This is a case where the messenger has to correct the message a
little.

CILISSA. You sound almost happy about all this.

CHORUS. You can never tell. Zeus has ways of suddenly changing
an evil wind to a good.

CILISSA. What "good"? Orestes, the hope of this house, is dead.

CHORUS. Only a very bad prophet would be too sure of that.

495 CILISSA. Wait a minute. Do you know something you're not telling
me?

CHORUS. Don't try to outguess the gods, Cilissa.
Just do as we ask, and leave the rest to them.

CILISSA. Well, I don't understand, but I'll do it.
I only hope it all turns out for the best.

She exits.

500 CHORUS. Zeus, Zeus, father of the gods,
Stand up for Orestes.
You see the colt of that famous sire
Once beloved of you
Now hitched to a heavy load of sorrows.
505 Cut loose the traces, Zeus,
Give him his head,
And the thoroughbred's blood
Will attend to the rest.
And you, shining Apollo, lord of light,
510 Lord of the great and sacred shrine of Delphi:
When will the house of Atreus raise its head to the sun?
Great Hermes, sender of fair winds,
Send victory from your strong hand.
The future is darkness till you have made clear the sign,

515 And secrets under the night
Are secrets still in the day.

O, when may I sing for this house's unchaining
A song of hope—no longer the mourners' keening,
But of women who stand by the shore in a fair salt breeze
520 Singing the great ship home?

O my prince, it is nearly time, it is nearly time.
Strike home, and do not be afraid;
And if she cries "My child!" to you,
Cry back "My father!" to her.

Enter AEGISTHUS.

525 AEGISTHUS. I was asked to come here.
They say that Orestes is dead.
The news gives me no satisfaction.
This house stinks of death enough.
And how do I know that this is true?
530 A rumor started by a nervous woman
Flares up in the air and goes out again in smoke.
What do *you* people know about it?

CHORUS. We have heard the news, but of course we are women too.
Why not go in and hear it from the man who brought it?

535 AEGISTHUS. Yes, I'd better. I'll soon find out whether this man was
    there at the death
Or if he's just an irresponsible talebearer.
The eye of the mind can pierce the mask of deceit
And extract an answer that cuts to the heart of the matter.

Exit AEGISTHUS.

CHORUS. Zeus, Zeus, it is time now, it is time now.
540 The blade trembles, it edges near its target,
The quick-beating life of man.
He has gone in, our prince has gone in,
The doors are shut, there are two against him;
Apollo—

(*a scream from inside the palace*)

545 It is done.
One way or the other, it is decided.

SERVANT *comes running out of the main gate of the palace,*
toward the women's wing on the far side.

SERVANT. He's dead! My master is dead!
You there in the women's quarters! Open the door!
Someone tell Clytemnestra!

550 Aegisthus is dead!
Help! Someone!

Enter CLYTEMNESTRA.

CLYTEMNESTRA. What is this noise? What are you shouting about?

SERVANT. The dead man is killing the living!

CLYTEMNESTRA. I understand you—O God—too well.
555 Someone bring me a sword, or an ax, to kill!
I am at the end of my way; the curse has found us at last.
Bring me a sword, I say! Someone, bring me a sword!

Enter ORESTES—*with drawn sword*—*and* PYLADES.

ORESTES. You next; we've finished with the other one.

CLYTEMNESTRA. No, no! Aegisthus, my darling, my strong one,
have they killed you?

560 ORESTES. You love him? Very well, you can share a grave with him.

CLYTEMNESTRA. Wait, my son. I held you in my arms when you
were a tiny baby—
You'd go to sleep on my breast after you'd had your milk—

ORESTES. Pylades—can I let her go—do I have to kill her—

PYLADES. Orestes, let all men hate you, but not the gods.

ORESTES (*to* CLYTEMNESTRA).
565 Come here.
I'm going to kill you on his body.
His. In there.
The one you thought was a better man than my father.
You should have loved my father, but all you gave him was hate.
570 You have made your choice. You may sleep with this one forever.

CLYTEMNESTRA. I raised you from a baby. Will you let me grow old
in your company?

ORESTES. You killed my father, and now you want to come live
with me?

CLYTEMNESTRA. Fate had some part in that, my dear.

ORESTES. Then Fate says that this is the day you die.

575 CLYTEMNESTRA. If this meant a mother's curse on you, would that
make you stop and think?

ORESTES. What "mother"? You gave birth to me, and then threw
me away.

CLYTEMNESTRA. I put you in the house of a friend. I don't call that
throwing you away.

ORESTES. You sold me, if you prefer. That's what it amounts to.

CLYTEMNESTRA. I sold you. And what price did I get for you, then?

580 ORESTES. I could tell you, but it would be too filthy to say.

CLYTEMNESTRA. And what about some of the things your father
 did?
I don't suppose you'd care to talk about those?

ORESTES. Don't put the blame on him.
He was suffering hardships in a strange land while you were
 sitting here at home.

585 CLYTEMNESTRA. For a woman to be without her man for ten years
 is a hardship, child.

ORESTES. But you managed to bear it nobly, thanks to Aegisthus.

CLYTEMNESTRA. So you've condemned your own mother to death.

ORESTES. No, Mother. You have condemned yourself.

CLYTEMNESTRA. Do this thing, and my curses will follow you like
 hounds.

590 ORESTES. Let them. My father's would, if I failed to do this.

CLYTEMNESTRA. I might as well be crying to a tomb.

ORESTES. Yes. You might as well.

CLYTEMNESTRA. So you were the snake I bore and to whom I gave
 my breast.

ORESTES. Yes. Your nightmare was a good prophet.
595 Come. You did wrong, and now you pay for it.

   ORESTES *and* PYLADES *take* CLYTEMNESTRA *into the palace.*

CHORUS. Even this tears my heart, as I watch them pass into night.
But I cannot weep, for I see the hoped-for, the promised good:
That Orestes has not sunk down in the terrible ocean of blood,
And the eye of Agamemnon's house still opens to light.

600 As Justice came at the end to Priam and Priam's land,
So, after long years, to the halls of Atreus Justice returned:
Child of Zeus, the fury was hers in our prince's eyes that burned,
And the black wind of death that followed the sword in Orestes'
 hand.

Now to the cunning and might of Apollo we make our song,
605 Keeper of that great chasm in Parnassus' holy ground;
What is ordained on high by men upon earth is found:
The power that is of the gods will not serve evil for long.

Hail! To the light, to the gods, to the turning wheel of the Fates,

And to Time, that will cleanse the hearth of this palace of all
    that is vile,
610   Till its servants, once bowed with grief, can look up again, and
    smile
On the new generation of men that go in peace through its
    gates.

The doors of the palace open, revealing ORESTES *standing
over the bodies of* AEGISTHUS *and* CLYTEMNESTRA.
PYLADES *stands beside him, holding the purple robe in
which* AGAMEMNON *was entangled and slain.*

ORESTES. Look at them well.
    Here they lie, the double-headed dragon
    That killed my father and usurped my house.
615   Not long ago they sat on their thrones in full pride;
    Now they have only the love that binds them in death.
    They swore to kill my father; they swore to die together:
    They have fulfilled both vows.
    And now, you who would look upon evil,
620   Behold this. This was the web which caught my father,
    The robe in which she netted him for the bloody work.
    Spread it out. Come, gather in a circle
    And show it to that great father—not my own,
    But the golden eye of the all-seeing sun.
625   Let him see my mother's handiwork, and witness
    That I did right, when the day of reckoning comes.
    Aegisthus I do not count;
    He died the death adulterers die by law—
    But she, who plotted this foul thing against the man
630   Who gave her the children she carried in her womb—
    That once-sweet burden, now bearing the deathstroke's
        weight—
    What name will fit her? A deadly snake
    Whose very will, seething and envenomed,
    Rots a man's flesh even without a bite?
635   And this thing: when I look at it, words fail me.
    The sort of thing some crossroads-haunting thief,
    Some sneaking cutthroat, might devise
    To throw about his victims. Gods!
    Before such a woman should be called mine,
640   Let me be blasted, childless, from this earth.

LEADER. I have watched them pass into night, the guilty and
    guiltless,
    But no act of man have I seen that has stilled their crying
    Or given peace to those who are left to live on.

ORESTES. Did she do it or did she not? Here is the proof;

645   A great robe, three times pierced by Aegisthus' sword,
        Faded by time, darkened by blood . . .
        The last thing that touched my father when he lived . . .

(Burying his face in the robe, he weeps.)

        Our whole house . . . on and on . . .
        What filthy victory is this that I have won?

650   CHORUS. No man can pass to his life's end
        Untouched by suffering.
        One grief is here, and another is coming.

        ORESTES. Listen—you must know—tell me, when is this curse
            going to end?
        I'm afraid; I'm like a charioteer whose horses are running wild,
            off the course,
655   Plunging on into nothingness;
        Something I don't know has gotten into my heart and it's
            shrieking and dancing there.
        But my mind is clear . . . listen to me;
        I was right to kill my mother . . . the gods hated her . . .
        She was soaked with my father's blood . . .
660   And Apollo told me—his oracle told me—
        That if I did it no one could call me guilty,
        But if I didn't, well, no arrow from a bow
        Could shoot up to the heights of agony that would be mine.
        Look at me. I am going now to his shrine,
665   Home of the center-stone and the undying flame,[6]
        Out of this place of blood.
        There is nowhere else I can turn.
        Listen, you people of Argos: remember how these agonies came
            to be.
        For a moment I was home; now I go to be what I always was:
670   A wanderer and an exile, in life and in death;
        Leaving no legacy but the thing I did.

        CHORUS. No, Orestes, you must not speak this way.
        You did well; your act saved Argos;

(The FURIES *appear to* ORESTES.*)*
        You killed two serpents with a single—
675   ORESTES. No!
        Look at them!
        They're black—and there are snakes around them—they—

---

6. center-stone and the undying flame: A round stone in the sanctuary at Delphi, called the
omphalos ("navel"), was believed to mark the center of the earth. A flame was kept constantly
burning in the sanctuary.

CHORUS. Orestes, dearest son of your father,
What illusion is this?
680   Take hold of yourself. You have won the victory.
You have taken vengeance—

ORESTES. No—they are real. They stand there in the day.
I know what they are. They are the hounds of my mother.

CHORUS. They are visions, I tell you.
685   The blood that is still wet on your hands has shaken your brain.

ORESTES. Yes, the blood.
O God Apollo!
It's dripping out of their eyes!

CHORUS. Orestes, go to the shrine of Apollo as you had planned!
690   *His* touch will free you of this trouble.

ORESTES. You do not see them, but I do.
They drive me on—I can stay no longer—

Exit ORESTES, *pursued by the* FURIES.

CHORUS. Good fortune to you, and may the god be kind to you.
Now has the third storm broken on this house of kings.
695   First was the Feast of Thyestes, fed with his children's flesh,
Next the death of the war-king, cut down in his bath,
And now has the savior—or avenger—come and gone.
When will it all end?
When will this harvest of hate be done
700   And the fury lie down and sleep?

DISCUSSION QUESTIONS

1. A series of killings has occurred—Agamemnon sacrifices Iphigenia, Clytemnestra murders Agamemnon, and Orestes murders Clytemnestra. Which of these killings do you think is the worst, or do they all seem equally terrible?

2. What is the purpose of the opening scene at the tomb? (Why do you think Aeschylus began with this scene instead of having Orestes go directly to the palace?)

3. The women who accompany Electra to the tomb give Orestes a vivid description of Clytemnestra's dream the night before. Why does Aeschylus include this account of the dream? What is its symbolism?

4. What might be the purpose of including Orestes' old nurse Cilissa in the play?

5. This play contains several female characters from Clytemnestra's household who are not part of the main action but who, nevertheless, "take sides" in the conflict between Orestes and Clytemnestra. Whose side does each of the following characters take: Electra, the chorus of handmaidens, Cilissa?

6. How does Aeschylus prevent the reader from sympathizing entirely with Clytemnestra during the murder scene?

ACT THREE. THE FURIES

CHARACTERS

THE PYTHIA, *the Oracular Priestess of Apollo at Delphi*

APOLLO

HERMES

ORESTES

THE GHOST OF CLYTEMNESTRA

ATHENA

CHORUS OF FURIES

CITIZENS OF ATHENS

Scene: *Delphi: The shrine of Apollo. Athens: The shrine of Pallas Athena*

In the inner sanctuary of the shrine of Apollo is ORESTES, *surrounded by sleeping* FURIES. APOLLO *himself and* HERMES *stand by him. This area is in shadow. An unlit brazier stands near on a tripod. The area before the temple is dimly lit as by early dawn. Enter here the* PYTHIA, *the priestess of Apollo.*

> PYTHIA. I praise the dark Mother, the holy Earth,
>   First of all sybils, and that famous line[1]
>   By which this seat of prophecy was given
>   To great Apollo.
> 5   He came from Delos[2] to Parnassus' ground,
>   Sung on his way by the men of this land,
>   The masterful men who split the heart of the wilderness
>   With the straight spear of the road.
>   Here Zeus gave him the prophetic vision
> 10   And here, through me, he makes clear the cloudy will of his
>   father.
>   Here are the sacred precincts of gray-eyed Athena,
>   Here too the rock of Corycis,[3] the bird-loud hollow, walking
>   place of gods.
>   Great Dionysus haunts this spot,

---

1. **line:** Apollo's oracle was located on a spot said to be the center of the earth. Zeus had released two eagles, one from the east and one from the west, who flew toward each other in a straight line. The spot where they met, which was on the lower slope of Mount Parnassus, became the site of the oracle's sanctuary.

2. **Delos:** an island in the Aegean Sea, the birthplace of Apollo.

3. **Corycis:** a cave on Mount Parnassus.

He whose worshipers, the wild white women, tore King
     Pentheus[4]
15 As eagles do the trapped and shivering hare.
    I call upon the springs of Pleistus,[5] the power of Poseidon,
    And Zeus All-Father: inspire my mantic[6] heart.
    I go now to take my seat upon the sybil's throne,
    And may the children of Hellas come before me, to hear the
        will of the gods.

(*She lights the brazier, and the inner shrine springs into light.*)

20 Ahh, God, God, God, the shrine is made a nest of terror,
    And I broken from a holy priestess to a feeble old woman
    With the frightened heart of a child.
    Within is a man with the face of the god-hated,
    Sitting upon the center-stone,
25 In one hand a blood-smeared sword,
    In the other an olive-branch decked with fillets of wool so white
        they glow, and before him—
    Before him . . .
    I saw in a picture once things like harpies or gorgons[7]
    So frightful they blasted the eyes, but these . . . these . . .
30 Black, wingless, bloated, utterly abominable,
    The room full of the foul animal smell of their sleeping breath,
    Their eyes clotted with oozings of black blood . . .
    I do not know what hole in the earth could bear these things
    And not cry out in agony and sorrow.
35 I will not see more; a dreadful thing must run its course here,
    And the house of great Apollo must be cleansed by Apollo
        himself.

                                        Exit the PYTHIA.

APOLLO (*to* ORESTES)
    I hold the power, and I will not forsake you.
    Whether far or near, I stand your guardian to the end,
    And my hand shall not weaken against your enemies.
40 See now, I have cast sleep upon these filthy creatures,
    Handmaids of horror, wrinkled children of unreason,

---

4. **Great Dionysus . . . King Pentheus:** King Pentheus of Thebes refused to allow Dionysus, god
of wine, to introduce his rites among the Thebans. Dionysus retaliated by inspiring Pentheus
with madness. In this state he disguised himself as a woman and went to observe the revels held
by the female worshipers of Dionysus on Mount Kithaeron. In their frenzy these women, with
Pentheus' mother Agave among them, mistook him for a wild beast and tore him to pieces.

5. **Pleistus:** a river near Delphi.

6. **mantic:** pertaining to prophecy.

7. **harpies or gorgons:** female monsters.

Spawned by night and chaos, curled grublike in holes under the
   earth, vessels of poison and darkness,
Loathsome alike to gods, and beasts, and men.
You must flee on, and they will be at your back,
45   But hope will drive your feet across the long leagues of the
   earth,
And on the great water despair shall not be your shipmate.
You will come to sea-lapped cities, but only one will be your
   goal:
Athens, the home of Pallas.
There you will fall to earth, and embrace the knees of her
   ancient image,
50   And there you will find those who will render judgment
And speak powerful words, a spell of protection and peace.
This I swear: I who ordered you to strike down your mother.

ORESTES. Lord Apollo, you know what it means to do no wrong—
   Can you understand what it means to take responsibility?
55   If so, no man need mistrust your will.

APOLLO. Let no doubt weaken your heart.
   Hermes, my brother, they call you the god who guides;
   Be so indeed to this man.
   Have a care of him, for he is my suppliant, my—responsibility.

        Exit APOLLO, *then* ORESTES *led by* HERMES. *The* GHOST *of*
                CLYTEMNESTRA *appears.*

60   CLYTEMNESTRA. Have I found you asleep, while my blood screams
   from the earth?
I who walk dishonored among the other dead,
My disgrace does not sleep.
They call me manslayer and from their curses I find no rest.
No god takes *my* part, for all I suffered
65   From those I called my own.
There is a hole in my heart; think of where it came from.
Look at my scars with the inward eye
That sees in the darkness things unseen by day.
Remember that drink I poured for you by midnight,
70   That drink thicker and hotter than wine;
How you lapped it up at the hour unshared by gods—
All that is forgotten now, I see,
And your prey has skipped away like a young hare
From a pack of slow and stupid hounds.
75   Listen to me, you goddesses of the underworld;
I am pleading for my soul.
Listen to Clytemnestra crying in your dreams!

(*The* FURIES *moan in their sleep.*)

You may well whimper. He is on his way,
Guarded by friends who are no friends to me.

(*They moan again.*)

80 I suffer, the mother-killer flies,
And your brains are too thick with sleep to care.

(*They moan again.*)

Yes, you whine and then you fall back to sleep.
You've done nothing so far that wasn't wrong.

(*They moan again.*)

Sleep and fatigue have mixed their drugs together;
85 The serpent's eye dims, and its coils relax.

CHORUS. Get him, get him, get him, get him—
After him!

CLYTEMNESTRA. You chase a beast of dreams, belling like hounds
That can't stop hunting even in their sleep.
90 What do you think you're doing?
Up! Get up
And shake yourselves awake!
Think of how you have failed, and let it dig
Into your hearts like a goad.
95 After him! Suffocate him with your blood-reeking breath.
Chase him! Pursue him! Wear him down to the bone!

Exit CLYTEMNESTRA.

CHORUS. Wake, wake,
Up, up,
Out of the dark,
100 Come, come,
Ah, ah
Up, up,
Wake, wake.
Aaaeee!
105 I hurt, I am pain,
He is running, he is gone,
We have not got him,
We were asleep.
Aah!
110 Son of Zeus, Prince of lies,
You have ridden down the gray old powers,
Loved the mother-killer, helped him escape.
Was this right? Was this right?

An accusation struck in my dreams
115 Like a gouge from a goad in the herdsman's fist;

Hard in the ribs, a hole in the heart,
Burning and freezing, it bites like a lash.

This is the way the young gods deal,
Blind-drunk with power, on a blood-slippery throne,
120   Slimed with blood from the head to the heel,
Stains on the stone at the center of earth.

The all-high seer fouls his own nest,
Hales on the rebellion, the heart-pride of man,
And breaks the lines of order drawn by the gods of old.
125   He bedevils us now, but Orestes shall not escape;
Though he crawl in a hole in the earth, he will find us
breathing beside him;
With one curse cut off, another will push from his flesh.

APOLLO *re-enters from his sanctuary.*

APOLLO. Leave this holy place, and leave at once,
Before a dart of light strikes like a silver snake
130   From the string of my golden bow,
And you roll in agony, puking the black blood
You have sucked from the hearts of men.
This is no resting place for such as you;
Go where you belong, to a stinking shambles
135   Where condemned men are wrestled to the block and the heads
Leap from their shoulders in a spout of blood,
Where the sex of young boys is crushed or cut away,
And men spiked under the spine with a greased stake
Are hoisted high to howl away their lives.
140   These are the things you love, that turn the stomachs of gods.
What you look like shows what you are.
Some hole in the rocks full of rotten flesh-scraps and dung of
lions
Is where monsters like you belong,
Not mingling with worshipers in a holy shrine.
145   Get out, filth; go roam without guard or guide:
No self-respecting god would shepherd a flock like you.

CHORUS. My lord Apollo—if you have quite finished,
We too have a few things to say.
You are no mere accomplice in this crime—
150   If there is a crime—and there is—
The arch-criminal is you.

APOLLO. Explain that—and make it good.

CHORUS. It was by your oracle's command that this outlawed
wanderer killed his mother.

APOLLO. I ordered him to avenge his father—what of it?

155 CHORUS. You promised him protection, still dripping with blood.

APOLLO. It was by my will that he came here
    For purification and sanctuary, yes.

CHORUS. But we, who escorted him here, are abused and cursed.

APOLLO. No one asked for your presence in my house.

160 CHORUS. We are only doing our duty, my lord.

APOLLO. And what do you consider *that* to be?

CHORUS. Driving a matricide from place to place,
    Allowing him no rest.

APOLLO. And who does the same to a woman who kills her
    husband?

165 CHORUS. That does not count. It is not kindred blood,

APOLLO. So? Then you count as nothing
    The marriage of Zeus and Hera,
    The pattern of all consummations?
    You cast out of reckoning great Aphrodite,
170   From whom come the sweetest joys a man can know?
    I tell you that the love of a man and wife
    Transcends all oaths, and is watched over by Justice
    As it was sealed by Fate.
    If one of them can kill the other, and you wink your eye at it,
175   I say your pursuit of Orestes is not supported by right.
    You whip yourselves into a fine froth over the one,
    But to the other you are conveniently blind.
    Well, we shall see. The goddess Pallas will judge.

CHORUS. Nothing will make me leave that man alone.

180 APOLLO. Go on, then. Give yourselves enough rope.

CHORUS. Do not try to talk me out of my ancient privilege.

APOLLO. Privilege? I would not have such "privilege" as a gift.

CHORUS. No, of course not; not the lily-pure Apollo
    Who sits on the right hand of his father Zeus.
185   But a mother's blood drives *me,* and I shall have justice.
    I go to track him down.

They exit.

APOLLO. And I to protect him—for to betray a trust
    Is among gods and men a monstrous thing.

    He exits. The scene is now Athens. Some time has passed. Enter,
    to the shrine of Pallas Athena, ORESTES, *guided by* HERMES.

ORESTES. Pallas Athena, Lady, I have come here by Apollo's
    command.

190 The stain of blood has faded,
But there is a great weight upon me.
I have been blown by the winds of the sea
And worn down by many roads.
I am very tired. I pray you receive me.
195 I will wait here for my judgment.

CHORUS. He is here—we are close upon him. Follow the silent
guides
Clear as the beads of blood that lead the hunting-pack
After the stricken fawn, to the place where the quarry hides.
Orestes has gone to earth—follow upon his track!
200 By the welcome smell of blood I know he is near at hand . . .
Long with laboring lungs, blowing white spume from my lip,
At a man-killing pace have I ranged over endless oceans of land
And across the wide fields of water have followed his furrowing
ship.

There! See him,
205 Cringing at the feet of Pallas' ancient image,
Blubbering for absolution.
Not likely, that. It is not so simple
To bring a mother's blood that has soaked the earth
Back to her veins again.

210 Orestes, your turn has come; the wheel has turned again;
The sweet salt wine of your heart I will suck until, dry and white,
With nothing remaining of life but a mind that can still know
pain,
I shall carry you out of the sun to the country of absent light.

There will you meet them all, the sinners of violent hand
215 Against god or guest or parent, brought here when they come to
die;
For strictest of all accountants is the god of the underland,
And all old wrongs are tabled behind that watchful eye.

ORESTES. I have learned many things in the hard and bitter school
Of absolution. One is that there is a time to speak
220 And a time to keep silent.
This is a time to speak.
The stain of mother-murder is fading from my hand
And the blood sleeps.
I made sacrifice at the hearth of Apollo
225 While the blood was yet fresh and crying.
Since then, I have stood in the presence of countless men
And none of them has taken harm from me.
Time alters all things. It is from a pure mouth, I swear it,
That I call upon this country's guardian,
230 Holy Athena, to end this thing

Without more fall of blood.
Help me, great Goddess!
Wherever you may be, in the Libyan wilderness
Or by the waters of Triton,[8] where you were born,
235   Whether marching to battle
Or sitting to take counsel and aid your friends,
Or standing terrible in arms overlooking the Phlegraean plain,[9]
Hear me, gracious Lady, from far away:
Come, and deliver me from this thing that is upon me.

240   CHORUS. Never, never. No one will save.
Go down, go down, god-forsaken killer,
Bloodless shadow, gnawed by demons,
Hollow-hearted, go to the grave;
Go down, go down into the dark.

245   Come and join in the dance of hate,
Binding his soul with a terrible music:
Go down, go down, triple-damned Orestes,
Justice is pitiless, righteous, and straight;
Go down, go down into the dark.

250   Hold out your hands and if they are clean
You are safe from our anger and safe from our goad,
But if you have hidden them, knowing them stained,
You will find us in wait at the end of your road.

O Night my mother, O mother who bore me
255   To work out revenge on the blind and the seeing,
See how Apollo has scoffed at your laws
Ordained to endure to the end of all being,
Stolen to safety the shivering hare
Fattened for sacrifice under my claws.

260   Over the beast that is decked for the burning
Sing the song that eats at the brain,
Binding his soul with a terrible music;
The debt of outrage is paid with pain
Under the earth, and the worm is undying:
265   Go down, go down into the dark.

It is set down that none of the children of Heaven
Interfere in our dark and terrible office:
To pull down the pride and the guilt of great houses;
As we have no part in the rites of the gods,

---

8. Libyan wilderness . . . waters of Triton: Libya to the Greeks meant all of Africa. Lake Tritonis was once a large lake covering some 900 square miles in what is now Tunisia. It has shrunk considerably since classical times. Athena was sometimes said to have been born along its shores.

9. Phlegraean plain: a district in northeastern Greece, site of a battle between the gods and the giants.

270 In the robes blinding white in the sun, and the music.
For the work must be done that the children of Heaven,
The golden Immortals, will not soil their hands with:
To harrow the hearts of the killers of kinsmen,
Binding their souls with a terrible music.

275 All glories of men that rise high in the sunlight
Become as small dust as our shadow approaches
And our footbeats join in the dance of hate.
Hai! We come down like the fall of a mountain!
Let him run, let him run, for soon or late,
280 Though blinded with pride, the doer of evil
Shall feel us behind him, shall know we are with him
By a skin-rotting fog, by the closeness of darkness,
By a foulness about him, by the chill wind of fear, until
Hai! We come down like the fall of a mountain!

285 Let none who hear this dispute our will.
Despised by the gods, we yet play our parts:
Strength is ours, and wisdom, and skill,
Long memories, and implacable hearts.
Our way is set and ordained, and our right
290 Is old, as the darkness is older than light.

Enter ATHENA.

ATHENA. From far away I heard a cry for aid;
By Scamander Water I stood, where the lords of Hellas
Gave over to my hand the land of Troy,
War-won, to be my domain forever.
295 I have come swiftly, on untiring feet,
My great cloak catching the hard-buffeting wind
And drawn by it as if by chariot horses.
Here I see an assembly bizarre to say the least,
That makes me wonder, but not fear.
300 Who in the world are you? All of you—
This stranger huddled up beside my image,
And you—whoever—or whatever, if I may use the word,
May *you* be? I must say that even a god
Who knows the form of every living thing on earth
305 Would be hard put to find *your* category.
Pardon me—I have no intention of being unkind;
Here, of all places, one should speak without prejudice.

CHORUS. Daughter of Zeus, you shall be told all, and briefly.
We are the daughters of eternal Night.
310 We are called the Curses in the land below the earth.

ATHENA. Very well, now I know your names and your parentage.
What next?

CHORUS. You shall soon learn our privileges and powers.

ATHENA. Splendid. Tell me everything.

315 CHORUS. When a man has killed another, we hound him from his home.

ATHENA. Where to? Has the chase no end?

CHORUS. Only in that place where joy is never heard of.

ATHENA. And is this what you are doing to this man?

CHORUS. Yes. He deliberately chose to murder his mother.

320 ATHENA. Freely? Wantonly? Or was he forced to do so
By fear of some greater punishment?

CHORUS. What could force a man to make such a terrible choice?

ATHENA. An excellent question. And his to answer, I think.

CHORUS. It's no good asking *him*. He won't be bound by oath.

325 ATHENA. You seem to be more concerned with the forms of justice
than the reality.

CHORUS. And what does *that* mean, pray?
Explain it out of your immense subtlety of mind.

ATHENA. Legal technicalities can be used to make wrong seem
right.
That I will not allow.

330 CHORUS. Then examine him yourself, and give us an honest
decision.

ATHENA. You will really trust my integrity, and abide by my
judgment?

CHORUS. Why not? They say Nobility Obliges.
Perhaps Divinity will do the same.

ATHENA. Well, then. Stranger, it is your turn to speak.
335 Tell me your country and your parentage
And what trouble weighs on you, that you come a suppliant to
my hearth.
Remember that charges have been made against you which must
be answered.
I take it you have some faith in the soundness of your case and
the fairness of my judgment,
Or you would not be here at all.
340 Speak now, plainly and straightly.

ORESTES. Lady Athena, let me clear up one point.
I am not a suppliant, in the sense of some wretch craving
absolution from blood-guilt;
Your holy image took no pollution from the touch of my hand.

I know that by law the man of blood is not even permitted to
  speak in his own defense
345 Until he has been cleansed by ritual sacrifice.
This I have undergone. So much for that.
I am from Argos. For my parentage—
Thank you for asking, for I am proud to remember.
My father was Agamemnon, Captain-General and Lord of the
  Fleet,
350 Your comrade-in-arms when you made Troy
A land without a city. He came home
To a squalid, dishonorable death.
My mother in the darkness of her heart
Tangled him in a robe as he came from his bath
355 And butchered him. I was in exile then,
But I came home, after long years.
And killed the woman who bore me. I do not deny it.
I took revenge because I loved my father,
But I also did it because Apollo
360 Promised me an existence of lively horror
If I failed to take blood for blood.
That is all I have to say.
I have put myself in your hands, and I will accept your verdict
Whichever way it goes.

365 ATHENA. This is a matter of too far-reaching importance
For a mortal mind to decide.
I do not think that even I am qualified to judge
In a case where passionate anger was a motive.
Then too, you have declared yourself purified by holy ritual
370 And thrown yourself on my mercy,
And admittedly have done no harm to the city that is under my
  protection.
I respect your rights,
But these, too, have their work to do,
And if they are robbed of their victory
375 The poison of their resentment will soak the soil of this land
And plague it, world without end.
It is a dilemma: whether I send them away or give them their due
Someone will suffer for it.

Well, since it is my responsibility, and since a precedent is being
  created here,
380 I shall establish for all time a court of law
To judge cases such as this one.
Make ready your proofs; call your witnesses
To substantiate your causes under oath.
I shall select the best citizens, and they too shall be sworn
385 To judge this matter by nothing but the truth.

CHORUS. Unless we triumph
The old laws perish
And a Brave New Order
Shall reign instead,
390   Where parents' lives
Are spent in waiting
The day their children
Shall strike them dead.

Then we, who spy
395   On the guilt of mortals,
Will pour out wrath
On the heads of all:
Men shall seek false charms
From quacks and prophets
400   And see their doom
In their neighbors' fall.

Let no one cry
To *us* in anguish,
Broken by
405   Accidental woe;
Let none appeal
To the throne of Justice
When the house of Justice
Is fallen low.

410   There is need of fear
In the hearts of mortals;
It is well that knowledge
Is bought with sorrow:
No man today
415   Will stray from virtue
Who knows that Justice
May strike tomorrow.

Anarch and slave
Are both god-hated;
420   Safest of all
Is the middle way.
Daring and pride
Destroy that balance
That brings all good
425   For which men pray.

For him whose feet
Tread down the holy,
The shrine of Justice,
In hope of gain,

430	Who does dishonor
	To guest or parent,
	The gods make ready
	Unheard-of pain.

	Who sails with Justice
435	Without compulsion
	Fair winds, calm waters
	Will never fail,
	While the laughing pirate
	One day of darkness,
440	His mast storm-shattered,
	Must strike his sail.

	The blank sky deaf
	To his anguished crying,
	Who thought it clever
445	For such as he
	To trust blind luck
	And blinder Justice
	Goes down to death
	In the great blind sea.

Enter ATHENA, APOLLO, ORESTES, *and* CITIZENS.

450 ATHENA. Proclaim order, herald. Let the hard bright blast of the
Etruscan trumpet,[10]
Its brazen throat blown full with human breath,
Stab at the ear of this assembled host
And call them all to silence.

(*trumpet*)

It is best that attention be paid now,
455 For these new ordinances which I shall lay down
It is hoped will endure to the end of all being,
And this first case tried under them
Must be a model of fairness.

CHORUS. Lord Apollo, stick to your own bailiwick.
460 What right have you to meddle in this business?

APOLLO. I am here as a witness, because this man
Came to my hearth as a suppliant, and at my hands
Received absolution for the act of blood,
And also, in a sense, as co-defendant,
465 Because the ultimate responsibility for his mother's death is mine.

(*to* ATHENA)

You know the rules, having made them. Begin the trial.

---

10. Etruscan trumpet: The Etruscans were an ancient people noted for their metal work, which
was eagerly sought by the Greeks.

ATHENA. The prosecution has the right to open the case.
Let us know the truth of all that happened.

CHORUS. We are many, but our account will be concise.
470   Answer us point by point. Did you kill your mother?

ORESTES. Yes.

CHORUS. The first fall is ours.

ORESTES. But not the match.

CHORUS. Well. Then suppose you tell us *how* you slaughtered your
mother?

475 ORESTES. I took my sword and cut her throat.

CHORUS. And who prompted you to do this?

ORESTES. The oracle of Apollo. He will give testimony for me.

CHORUS. The prophet of a god ordered you to kill your own
mother?

ORESTES. Yes. And even now I do not regret it.

480 CHORUS. When sentence is pronounced upon you, you will sing a
different song.

ORESTES. I am not afraid. My father will aid me from beyond the
grave.

CHORUS. Cut down your mother, and then put your trust in a
corpse.
Straight thinking.

ORESTES. My mother was polluted twice over by her sin.

485 CHORUS. Perhaps you can explain that a little more clearly to the
court.

ORESTES. At one stroke she murdered her husband and my father.

CHORUS. If so, she has paid by her own death. Why should you
not do the same?

ORESTES. Why should *you* not have hounded *her* during her life of
guilt, as you have done with me?

CHORUS. Because the man she killed was not of her own blood.

490 ORESTES. Am I, then?

CHORUS. Murderer, she nourished you with her body! Do you
deny you were born of woman?

ORESTES. Lord Apollo, I call you now to give testimony.
Was there justice in my act, or was there none?

I do not ask you to deny that I did it, because I did.
495   I only ask: was I right to do it?

APOLLO. First let me assure you members of this court instituted
      by Athena
That what I say to you will be based on justice only.
As a divine augur, I am bound to use no deceit.
No word has been spoken from my throne of prophecy
500   Concerning man or woman or city
That has not come from the All-Father, Olympian Zeus.
Consider this carefully. It means that what I say reflects the will
      of the Father,
And no oath that may bind you is stronger than that.

CHORUS. And you maintain that your oracle
505   Was merely relaying the instructions of Zeus
In ordering Orestes to avenge his father
Regardless of dishonor to his mother?

APOLLO. Yes. How can you judge the two acts by the same rules?
    A great lord of many battles,
510   Endowed by heaven with the royal scepter,
Cut down by a woman, and not even
By the fierce dart of an Amazon in fair fight—
You shall hear the manner of it,
You who sit in solemn judgment here.
515   He came home from the war, having achieved, as most would
      agree,
A fair measure of success. She met him with a welcome
Fulsome in smooth graciousness,
And when he rose from his bath, naked and helpless,
She threw a great robe netlike over his head, tangled him in its
      rich folds,
520   And cut him down.
That is how a great man died,
Pious, a good husband, loved by those he commanded.
I have described the woman's deed in naked terms,
Shown her to you for what she was,
525   To awaken righteous anger in you who will judge this case.

CHORUS. You claim that Zeus gives precedence to the rights of a
      father.
But did not Zeus put his own father Kronos in chains?[11]

---

11. **Kronos in chains:** Kronos was a god, the son of Uranus (the sky) and Gaea (the earth). He
    fathered five children, all of whom he swallowed. The sixth, Zeus, was hidden from him and
    escaped the fate of the others through trickery. Zeus later rescued his brothers and sisters and
    waged war on Kronos, whom he defeated.

Your argument contradicts itself.
I call upon the court to take note of this.

530 APOLLO. Filthy animals, creatures that sicken the gods,
Chains can be loosened, such a wrong can be set right
And no one is the worse.
But once the dust has drunk up a man's blood,
Once life has left him, there is no raising him to his feet again.
535 That is one thing for which my father Zeus devised no cure,
Though otherwise he can turn the world over
Without a labored breath.

CHORUS. Well: consider the implications of your argument.
This man spilled his mother's blood into the dust.
540 Is he then to rest untroubled in his father's estate in Argos?
What fellowship of worshipers will welcome him?
What altar is he to touch and not pollute?

APOLLO. I shall explain this too,
And you will see that right is on my side.
545 The mother is not the parent of what is called her child,
She is only the nurse, the matrix, the incubator of the seed
That is sown in her by the true parent, the man.
She is the stranger host who receives a stranger guest,
Shelters and feeds him for a time, and then,
550 If no god blight the seed,
Speeds him upon his way.
There can be fatherhood without a mother,
And as living proof of this I call to witness
Pallas Athena herself, daughter of Zeus,
555 Never nurtured in the darkness of the womb,
The goddess whom no goddess bore.

ATHENA. Apollo, you have made my task of blameless and
impartial justice no easier.
Shall I assume now that enough has been said
And bid the jury render its verdict?

560 CHORUS. Our arrows have been shot. We wait for the decision.

APOLLO. You have heard what you have heard.
Cast your votes accordingly,
And keep in your hearts the oath that you have taken.

ATHENA. Listen now to my ordinance, people of Athens,
565 In this first trial for the act of blood.
On this hill, the Areopagus,[12]
Shall succeeding generations assemble to see justice done,

-----

12. **the Areopagus:** a hill west of the Acropolis, where the Athenian court met.

And the authority of this court shall be passed on
To the end of all time.

570 Respect and devotion and healthy fear
Shall keep the hands of the citizens from evil
As long as justice and law remain uncorrupt;
For once the clear fountain is tainted with mire
Never more will its waters be quite fit to drink.

575 Let neither anarchy nor dictatorship be cherished among you,
And do not banish fear entirely from the state,
For a man who fears nothing knows no law but his own
    passion.
The power of judgment is passed to the hands of men,
But that man who uses it unwisely will be judged by the gods.

580 I institute this court
Impersonal, incorruptible, severe,
A watcher in the night, an open eye in darkness.
I have spoken at length that all may hear
And take to heart these words when this day is over

585 And for all days to come.
Now must each man take his ballot, remember his oath,
And record his honest judgment.
I have said my say.

One at a time, the jurors scratch their votes on potshards and drop
them in a single urn.

CHORUS. Do not take our sisterhood lightly.
590   We can be a heavy weight on your land.

APOLLO. Remember the word of my oracle reflects the will of
    Zeus.
I advise you to let it come to fruition.

CHORUS. You honor acts of blood and meddle beyond your place.
The word of your oracle is corrupt and no longer valid.

595 APOLLO. Then my father Zeus was in the wrong
In receiving as suppliant Ixion,[13] the first murderer?

CHORUS. Talk. But if justice is denied me
This land will never shake me from its back.

APOLLO. No one pays any heed to you,
600   Either among the elder gods or the younger. I shall win.

CHORUS. And abuse your victory, no doubt, as once before
When you tricked the Fates into letting a man escape death.

---

13. Ixion: A king who murdered his father-in-law. Zeus purified him of the crime. Ixion later
abused this favor by trying to seduce Zeus's wife. He was then condemned to the underworld.

APOLLO. When a suppliant comes to me,
    I believe in doing the right thing by him.

605 CHORUS. Especially when it gives you a chance
    To mock the dignity of time-honored authority.
    I remember how you muddled the wits of the ancient goddesses
      with strong wine.

APOLLO. And I look forward to watching *you*,
    Drunk with impotent rage, harmlessly puking your poison
610   When the verdict has gone against you.

CHORUS. Because I am old and you are young
    You enjoy riding roughshod over me.
    But I will await the verdict, and then I will know
    Whether or not to let loose my rage upon this city.

615 ATHENA. The final judgment is mine,
    And I shall explain how it will be made.
    It is true that I was not born of woman,
    And thus in all things I am the child of my father
    And see things, admittedly, in the man's way.
620   A woman's natural loyalty is to her blood kin,
    And she feels herself subject only to the law of her own heart.
    But a man must move not only in the home but in the world,
    And is responsible not only to his own kind but to strangers.
    His choices are not so easily made,
625   And since the woman in this case was not loyal even to her own
      children,
    I cannot find in her favor.
    If the votes are equal, Orestes shall go on living.
    Let the ballots be counted.

ORESTES. O bright Apollo, how will this end?

630 CHORUS. Black Night, my mother, are you watching this?

ORESTES. My hour has come: the noose or the light.

CHORUS. The end, or vindication of our dark powers.

APOLLO. Shake out the votes attentively, my friends,
    And count them out with a painstaking care.
635   A lapse of judgment may bring disaster,
    And one single vote save a great house from ruin,

ATHENA. The number of votes is equal on both sides.
    I acquit this man of blood-guilt.

ORESTES. Pallas Athena, you have saved my house.
640   My country was lost to me and you have brought me home.
    Now in Hellas men will say
    "He is an Argive again,

And has returned to the estate of his father,
Thanks to wise Pallas and mighty Apollo
645 And that great Third[14] who determines all things."
I go now, but first I pledge an oath
To you and your people, to endure for all time:
Never shall a ruler of Argos
Lead forth his armed men against Athens;
650 For if, as may be, we lie in the tomb of a hero-king,
We shall reach out our hand to strew their path
With evil omens, despair, and confusion.
But if they keep our covenant with the people of Athens
As friends in peace and companions in arms,
655 We shall touch them with grace from beyond the grave.
Farewell then, to you and to your people.
May you wrestle to a fall all those who come against you,
And may the wreath of victory crown your spears.

Exit ORESTES.

CHORUS. Aah, you upstart generation of gods,
660 You have crushed underfoot the laws of old time
And ripped my honored powers from my hands.
Now it is I who am disinherited, frustrated, abused;
But from my heart, sodden with anger,
As from a black cloud, I will rain poison on this land.
665 A crawling contagion—Justice! Justice!
White leprous foulness furring flesh,
Death to children and green leaves,
And ruin sweeping houses and fields like a broom.
I am mad with sorrow and mocked in my misery:
670 Daughters of darkness, what shall we do?

ATHENA. Listen to me, and restrain your anger.
You have not been as deprived of honor as you think.
A fair trial was held, and the balance of votes was equal.
The decision made came by the bright-burning word of Zeus,
675 Interpreted through me and through Apollo,
That Orestes should not be only another drop to feed the ocean
      of blood.
Let me persuade you not to visit your wrath upon poor men
Who have given you the respect and honor that is your due, if
      you would only think about it,
As will *I,* if you will hear me.

680 CHORUS. That they could treat me so!
I, the ancient wisdom of the dark earth
Cast out like so much filth!

---

14. Third: Zeus

I shall do such things—
My rage chokes me, my breath hot and thick with anger—
685   Earth! Earth!
What agony crawls beneath my ribs?
O Night, mother Night, hear me:
They have made me a thing of scorn;
They, the clever tricksters, the new gods,
690   They who know nothing of honor have taken my honors away!

ATHENA. I am remaining patient with you, because you are my elders
    And know many things that I will never know.
    But I would not have you despise *my* wisdom altogether;
    Nor my power—for Zeus has given me the keys to his dreadful treasuries of thunder,
695   Which I am unwilling but not unable to use.
    You may find, in the fullness of time,
    That you love this land better than you know,
    And that it can be a hospitable home to you.
    Why, then, gnaw its heart with fury and resentment,
700   Poisoning the blood of its young men with the wine of violence
    Till they senselessly tear each other's flesh,
    Fighting cocks of the same brood locked in a circled wall?
    Let the spirit of war be turned outward, against the pride-drunk man
    Who has fallen into the horrible love of glory.
705   There is room for both of us in this land;
    For my shrine that towers in the light
    And for yours in the caverns beneath the earth.
    For each of us there will be shining thrones
    Before a hearthside where the people come
710   To offer the first fruits of the harvest
    And to pray for blessings on the seed that grows in the womb.

CHORUS. Let me understand this. What is this place you offer me?

ATHENA. A place where sorrow is never heard of. Please accept it.

CHORUS. And if I do accept it, is this mouth-honor, or shall I have some power?

715 ATHENA. There will be life and joy in no house that is not touched by your grace.

CHORUS. Do you mean this? Would you give me so important a place?

ATHENA. Both of us have our place in the lives of men.

CHORUS. You will remember this tomorrow, and the day after?

ATHENA. I would not promise what I do not mean to perform.

720 CHORUS. Your persuasion is strong. I feel a little less angry already.

ATHENA. Stay here, then. You shall win other friends besides.

World Literature
Greek Theater

Dionysia-

Dithyrambs

Dionysus- "the force that through the green fuse drives the flower" Dylan Thomas

Communal dance

Theater-

Masks

Three Great Tragedians

Contest- 3 days, 3 tragedies, voting, ten Judges, Sophicles won most often.

Question- What does competition do for art?

Three tragedies and a comedy-

Question- Does comedy have the same staying power as tragedy? What modern day equivalents can you think of for the Greek Comedies? Tragedy lasts longer. Stand up

Tragedies- Shakespeare wrote that the role of the dramatist is to "hold ...the mirror up to nature, to show...the very age and body of the time his form and pressure"

CHORUS. I am still of a mind to put a spell on this country.
    What shall it be?

ATHENA. A spell of victories never arrived at by evil means;
725   A blessing that rises out of the soil like the gray olive tree,
    Leaps in blinding silver out of the sun-fired water,
    Crosses the land with the breathing wind
    Over the fat sleek beasts feeding in the meadow,
    And circles the child growing beneath the mother's heart.
730   Let your power bring decay only to strangling and parasitic
        weeds,
    For like the gardener who works in love
    I would bring to fruition the lives of the just and gentle.
    This shall be your place. For me,
    I shall see that the name of this city is held in honor
735   Throughout the world of men.

CHORUS. Then my home shall be here, beside you,
    And my prayers for the good of your town:
    That joy befall weddings and life attend birth
    As the great sun to the ancient earth
740   Sends roots of radiance down.

ATHENA. It is indeed for the good of my people
    That I give a place among them
    To these goddesses, so violent and so difficult to reconcile.
    For their workings are to be seen in the heart of every human act,
745   And the man who denies them will be torn by forces beyond his
        understanding
    And the sins of his parents against them
    May encircle him unperceived
    Until, too late, he cries, "What have I done?" and they,
    Not dignifying him with an answer, batter him to dust.

750 CHORUS. Great Pan,[15] against the black wind
    Protect the young green leaves
    While the double wealth of herd and vine
    And the glowing yield of the deep mine
    Athena's city receives.

755 ATHENA. Guardians of this city, hear these words
    And the promise they convey.
    Great is the power of these, the Furies,
    Both among the gods and among the nations of the dead,
    But among men their power is absolute
760   And as they dispose, so must it be;
    Singing for some, for others, the eye dimmed with tears.

---

15. Pan: god of woods and pastures. Pan had the upper body of a man and the lower body of a
  goat.

CHORUS. I pray for no more youth
　　　To perish before its prime;
　　　That Revenge and iron-hearted War
765　　May fade with all that has gone before
　　　Into the night of time.

ATHENA. Why, now you speak good words,
　　　Words of life and peace,
　　　And I salute the power of patient Persuasion, by which this has
　　　　come about.
770　　I see in these once terrible faces
　　　Great good, great blessing for all who give them due honor
　　　And deal justly with them, as I have done.

CHORUS. Long be your city's years
　　　And wisdom and joy your part.
775　　Farewell: your destiny is great
　　　If you can learn to love and hate
　　　With a united heart.

ATHENA. Farewell, ancient children of Night. Go now to your
　　　　home,
　　　Led by me and guided by the people of this land,
780　　Purple-robed, bearing the dancing fire
　　　Of ceremonial torches.
　　　To the primal caverns under the holy hill,
　　　With solemn sacrifice, blessed and blessing,
　　　With praise and great honor, go to your home.

785 CHORUS. Farewell. Farewell.

ATHENA. And you, people of my city:
　　　For the good of all men a compact has been made
　　　Between the power of Zeus and the power of Fate,
　　　Between the light of the mind and the voices of the blood.
790　　Think of these things in silence.

CHORUS OF ATHENIAN CITIZENS. Now to the caverns of night,
　　　Honored and praised, by the fire of the torches,
　　　Daughters of Earth
　　　Whose name is mystery,
795　　Blessed and blessing
　　　Go to your homes.

　　　Lead them with singing and light,
　　　Honor and praise to their mercy and justice;
　　　Men of the earth,
800　　Think on this mystery:
　　　Blessed and blessing
　　　Go to your homes.

Exit All

DISCUSSION QUESTIONS

1. In many Greek tales, the gods are portrayed as childish and irresponsible individuals who play games with human lives. Do Apollo and Athena, as they are shown in *The Furies*, fit this description? How would you characterize them?

2. Who are the individuals making up the chorus in this final play? What concept or idea do they represent?

3. There is a sharp distinction made in this play between the older traditions represented by the Furies and the new ideas being proposed by the younger gods, such as Apollo and Athena. What are these new ideas?

4. Persuasion plays a large role in *The House of Atreus* trilogy. Clytemnestra uses her persuasive skills to entice Agamemnon to walk the purple carpet and later tries to use those skills to convince Orestes to spare her life. How is the role of persuasion different in this final play?

5. Starting with Tantalus at the top, make a genealogy tree showing the members of the House of Atreus down to the children of Agamemnon. Circle the individuals who were either murderers or victims of murder. How many such individuals are there? For how many generations did the curse run?

6. In the closing lines of the play, Athena speaks of an agreement that has been made "between the light of the mind and the voices of the blood." What kind of agreement is she talking about? How does it help to end the curse on the House of Atreus?

SUGGESTIONS FOR WRITING

1. Imagine that you are a defense attorney assigned to the task of defending either Agamemnon, Clytemnestra, or Orestes. Write a brief script of your defense. Feel free to include the testimony of any character witnesses who might speak on behalf of your client.

2. In *The Furies* Athena establishes a new and radically different way to deal with accused criminals. She plans to set forth "new ordinances" (line 455) that will "endure to the end of all being." Imagine that she has given you the assignment of writing down these ordinances for the new court system. She wants the finished document to contain a mission statement explaining the purpose of the Athenian court system and a list of specific procedures to be followed during trials. This document should reflect the ideas and procedures established by Athena during Orestes' trial.

AESOP

(6th century B.C.)

The assumed creator of innumerable animal fables, Aesop was thought to have been a Greek slave who lived during the sixth century B.C. and who got himself out of tight spots by inventing these amusing tales. Nothing factual is known about Aesop, and his very existence may be a fable. These famous stories were spread by word of mouth for several centuries until they were written down by Valerius Babrius, who probably lived during the second century A.D. ■

from THE FABLES

Translated by Denison B. Hull

THE CRANES AND THE FARMER

    Cranes occupied a farmer's place
    Seeded with wheat. So to give chase
    The farmer shook an empty sling
    That seemed to them a fearsome thing.
5   But as they faced him while he threw
    The breezes at them, they soon knew
    That they would never need to flee
    Again in future; until he,
    As he had never done before,
10   Threw stones, and beat them hard and sore.
    They left his field behind with screams:
    "Flee to the Pygmies' lands![1] It seems
    This man's not satisfied to scare—
    He's starting now to act. Beware!"

THE FIELD MOUSE AND THE HOUSE MOUSE

    Among the mice was one who led
    A simple field mouse life; instead
    The other lurked in hole and bin
    And storeroom which were rich within.

---

1. **the Pygmies' lands:** southern Egypt. Homer refers in the *Iliad* to the battles between the pygmies and migrating cranes.

5   They held their lives up to compare,
And see which had the better share.
Now first the house mouse came to dine
When fields were blooming green and fine.
He nibbled slender roots of grain

10   In lumps all black and wet from rain.
He said, "The life you revel in
Is like an ant's; your loaves are thin,
And you must eat them in a ditch
But as for me, I'm truly rich;

15   The horn of Amalthea's[2] mine
In contrast with the way you dine.
If you will only come with me,
You'll see what luxury can be
Without this digging like a mole."

20   Persuading him to see his hole
Beneath the wall of some man's house,
He led away the farmer mouse.
He showed him barley piled in heaps,
And all the pulse[3] the master keeps;

25   He showed him jars of figs and honey,
All sticky, sweet, and rather runny;
And dates in baskets in a pile.
Rejoicing in these things a while
He dragged a cheese across the floor

30   When someone opened up the door.
He leaped away at once to race
From danger in such narrow space
Down in the mousehole taking flight,
And screamed and jabbered, mad with fright,

35   Making his host feel most distressed
At what had happened to his guest.
He paused a minute; then peeked out,
And gaining courage was about
To touch a Camirean fig

40   When someone else—and also big—
Came to pick up some other thing
Out of the storeroom; cowering,
The mice kept hidden well inside.
The field mouse said, "You may abide,

45   Rejoice, and feel that you are rich,

---

2. **The horn of Amalthea:** a horn of plenty. Amalthea was the goat whose milk nourished the infant Zeus. He later borrowed one of her horns and gave it to the nymphs who had cared for him. This horn would supply whatever food or drink its possessor desired.

3. **pulse:** the seeds of legumes (peas, beans, lentils, and so forth) used as food.

And revel in these dinners which
You have alone. I'm leaving you.
For there are many dangers too,
And I myself shall not refrain
50   From simple clods of earth, and grain
From which to gnaw the loaves I've made.
And not forever be afraid."

THE NORTH WIND AND THE SUN

Between the North Wind and the Sun
A quarrel rose as to which one
Could strip the mantle from a man
Walking the road. The wind began,
5   And blew, for in his Thracian[4] way
He thought that he would quickly lay
The wearer bare by force. But still
The man, shivering with the chill,
Held fast his cloak, nor let it go
10   The more the North Wind tried to blow,
But drew the edges close around,
Sat himself down upon the ground,
And leaned his back against a stone.
And then the Sun peeped out, and shone,
15   Pleasant at first, and set him free
From the cold blowing bitterly,
And next applied a little heat.
Then suddenly, from head to feet,
By burning fire the man was gripped,
20   Cast off his cloak himself, and stripped.

THE OLD MAN AND HIS CHILDREN

Among the ancients was a man
Who'd lived a very goodly span,
And who had children numberless.
And when he made his last address
5   (For death was near him where he stood),
He urged them bring some rods of wood
If there were any anywhere;
And someone found, and brought some there.

---

4. **Thracian:** rough or violent. Boreas, the North Wind, was supposed to have his home in Thrace,
a region to the north of Greece known for its harsh climate and barbarous inhabitants.

"Now try for me with all your might
10   To break rods bound together tight."
They could not do so. "Now try one,"
And that was very quickly done.
He said, "Now children, as you see,
When all of you alike agree,
15   No one, it matters not how strong,
Can ever do you any wrong.
But surely if you're separated,
You'll be, like this, annihilated."

THE TWO PACKS

Among the gods when time began
Prometheus[5] lived. He made a man
All molded out of earth and plaster,
And thus produced for beasts a master.
5   He hung on him two packs to wear,
Filled with the woes that men must bear,
With strangers' woes the one before,
But that in back, which carried more,
Was filled with evils all his own.
10   Hence many men, I think, are prone
To see the ills some other bears
But still be ignorant of theirs.

––––––

5. **Prometheus:** a Titan who was supposed to have created man by forming an image from clay and
water into which the goddess Athena breathed life.

DISCUSSION QUESTIONS

1. On the chalkboard, make a quick list of familiar proverbs such as "All
that glitters is not gold" and "Don't count your chickens before they
hatch." Try to list at least ten. When the list is complete, count the
number of proverbs that express the idea in symbolic language like
the two given above. How many state the idea directly? ("Don't put
off until tomorrow what you can do today," for example.) Why do
you think advice is often presented in an indirect, symbolic way?

2. A fable is a story, often with animals as characters, that offers moral
instruction or advice. Sometimes the moral is even tagged on at the
end for those who might have missed the point. What is the moral of
each of the first three fables? Try to express it in a single sentence.

3. How do the last two fables, "The Old Man and His Children" and "The Two Packs," differ from the first three fables? In your opinion, are they more or less successful? Why?

4. In "The Field Mouse and the House Mouse," the house mouse tells his field companion, "But as for me, I'm truly rich." In what way is the house mouse rich? Why might the field mouse be considered richer?

SUGGESTION FOR WRITING

Choose one of the following sayings and create a fable that dramatizes it:

- Nothing ventured, nothing gained.
- Necessity is the mother of invention.
- Haste makes waste.
- United we stand, divided we fall.

If time permits, read each fable to the rest of the class and see if they can assign the right "moral" to it.

ARISTOTLE

(384–322 B.C.)

One of the world's greatest philosophers, Aristotle studied with Plato and had Alexander the Great as one of his students. He placed strong emphasis on direct observation and systematic, logical thinking. His works consist mostly of notes made on his lectures by students. Among them are the *Rhetoric*, *Poetics*, *Ethics*, *Physics*, and *Metaphysics*.

Aristotle's *Poetics*, from which the following selection is taken, was largely responsible for the recognition of literature as a legitimate and important discipline. Prior to Aristotle, literary works were generally viewed as harmless lies. Aristotle, however, revealed the difference between literary truth and factual truth and established drama and poetry as respectable disciplines. ■

from THE POETICS

Translated by Ingram Bywater

A tragedy is the imitation of an action that is serious and also, as having magnitude, complete in itself; in language with pleasurable accessories, each kind brought in separately in the parts of the work; in a dramatic, not in a narrative form; with incidents arousing pity and fear, wherewith to accomplish its catharsis of such emotions. Here by "language with pleasurable accessories" I mean that with rhythm and harmony or song superadded; and by "the kinds separately" I mean that some portions are worked out with verse only, and others in turn with song.

As they act the stories, it follows that in the first place the Spectacle (or stage-appearance of the actors) must be some part of the whole; and in the second Melody and Diction, these two being the means of their imitation. Here by "Diction" I mean merely this, the composition of the verses; and by "Melody," what is too completely understood to require explanation.[1] But further: the subject represented also is an action; and the action involves agents, who must necessarily have their distinctive qualities both of character and thought, since it is from these that we ascribe certain qualities to their actions. There are in the natural order of things, therefore, two causes, Character and Thought, of their actions, and consequently of their success or failure in their lives. Now the action (that which was done) is represented in the play by the Fable or Plot. The Fable, in our present sense of the term, is simply this, the combination of

---

1. **"Melody" . . . explanation:** The musical accompaniment to Greek drama was provided by either of two harp-like stringed instruments, the lyre or the cithara, and a flute-like wind instrument, the aulos.

the incidents, or things done in the story; whereas Character is what makes us ascribe certain moral qualities to the agents; and Thought is shown in all they say when proving a particular point or, it may be, enunciating a general truth. There are six parts consequently of every tragedy.

The most important of the six is the combination of the incidents of the story. Tragedy is essentially an imitation not of persons but of action and life, of happiness and misery. All human happiness or misery takes the form of action; the end for which we live is a certain kind of activity, not a quality. Character gives us qualities, but it is in our actions—what we do—that we are happy or the reverse. In a play accordingly they do not act in order to portray the Characters; they include the Characters for the sake of the action. So that it is the action in it, i.e. its Fable or Plot, that is the end and purpose of the tragedy; and the end is everywhere the chief thing. Besides this, a tragedy is impossible without action, but there may be one without Character. And again: one may string together a series of characteristic speeches of the utmost finish as regards Diction and Thought, and yet fail to produce the true tragic effect; but one will have much better success with a tragedy which, however inferior in these respects, has a Plot, a combination of incidents, in it. A further proof is in the fact that beginners succeed earlier with the Diction and Characters than with the construction of a story; and the same may be said of nearly all the early dramatists. We maintain, therefore, that the first essential, the life and soul, so to speak, of Tragedy is the Plot; and that the Characters come second—compare the parallel in painting, where the most beautiful colors laid on without order will not give one the same pleasure as a simple black-and-white sketch of a portrait. We maintain that Tragedy is primarily an imitation of action, and that it is mainly for the sake of the action that it imitates the personal agents. Third comes the element of Thought, i.e. the power of saying whatever can be said, or what is appropriate to the occasion. One must not confuse it with Character. Character in a play is that which reveals the moral purpose of the agents, i.e. the sort of thing they seek or avoid, where that is not obvious—hence there is no room for Character in a speech on a purely indifferent subject. Thought, on the other hand, is shown in all they say when proving or disproving some particular point, or enunciating some universal proposition. Fourth among the literary elements is the Diction of the personages, i.e. as before explained, the expression of their thoughts in words, which is practically the same thing with verse as with prose. As for the two remaining parts, the Melody is the greatest of the pleasurable accessories of Tragedy. The Spectacle, though an attraction, is the least artistic of all the parts, and has least to do with the art of poetry. The tragic effect is quite possible without a public performance and actors; and besides, the getting-up of the Spectacle is more a matter for the costumier than the poet.

. . . . .

Having thus distinguished the parts, let us now consider the proper construction of the Fable or Plot, as that is at once the first and the most important thing in Tragedy. We have laid it down that a tragedy is an imitation of an action that is complete in itself, as a whole of some magnitude; for a whole may be of no magnitude to speak of. Now a whole is that which has beginning, middle, and end. A beginning is that which is not itself necessarily after anything else, and which has naturally something else after it; an end is that which is naturally after something itself, either as its necessary or usual consequent, and with nothing else after it; and a middle, that which is by nature after one thing and has also another after it. A well-constructed Plot, therefore, cannot either begin or end at any point one likes; beginning and end in it must be of the forms just described.

. . . . .

The Unity of a Plot does not consist, as some suppose, in its having one man as its subject. An infinity of things befall that one man, some of which it is impossible to reduce to unity; and in like manner there are many actions of one man which cannot be made to form one action. One sees, therefore, the mistake of all the poets who have written a *Heracleid,* a *Theseid,* or similar poems; they suppose that, because Heracles was one man, the story also of Heracles must be one story. Homer, however, evidently understood this point quite well, whether by art or instinct, just in the same way as he excels the rest in every other respect. In writing an *Odyssey,* he did not make the poem cover all that ever befell his hero—it befell him, for instance, to get wounded on Parnassus and also to feign madness at the time of the call to arms, but the two incidents had no probable or necessary connection with one another—instead of doing that, he took an action with a Unity of the kind we are describing as the subject of the *Odyssey,* as also of the *Iliad.* The truth is that the story, as an imitation of action, must represent one action, a complete whole, with its several incidents so closely connected that the transposal or withdrawal of any one of them will disjoin and dislocate the whole. For that which makes no perceptible difference by its presence or absence is no real part of the whole.

. . . . .

From what we have said it will be seen that the poet's function is to describe, not the thing that has happened, but a kind of thing that might happen, i.e. what is possible as being probable or necessary. The distinction between historian and poet is not in the one writing prose and the other verse—you might put the work of Herodotus into verse, and it would still be a species of history; it consists really in this, that the one describes the thing that has been, and the other a kind of thing that might be. Hence poetry is something more philosophic and of graver import than history, since its statements are of the nature rather of universals, whereas those of history are singulars. By a universal statement I mean one as to what such or such a kind of man will probably or necessarily say or do—which is the aim of poetry, though it affixes proper names to the characters; by a singular statement, one as to what, say, Alcibiades[2] did or

---

2. **Alcibiades:** Athenian politician and general (c.450–404 B.C.), pupil and friend of Socrates.

had done to him. In Comedy this has become clear by this time; it is only when their plot is already made up of probable incidents that they give it a basis of proper names, choosing for the purpose any names that may occur to them, instead of writing like the old iambic poets about particular persons. In Tragedy, however, they still adhere to the historic names; and for this reason: what convinces is the possible; now whereas we are not yet sure as to the possibility of that which has not happened, that which has happened is manifestly possible, else it would not have come to pass. Nevertheless even in Tragedy there are some plays with but one or two known names in them, the rest being inventions; and there are some without a single known name, e.g. Agathon's *Antheus*,[3] in which both incidents and names are of the poet's invention; and it is no less delightful on that account. So that one must not aim at a rigid adherence to the traditional stories on which tragedies are based. It would be absurd, in fact, to do so, as even the known stories are only known to a few, though they are a delight none the less to all.

It is evident from the above that the poet must be more the poet of his stories or Plots than of his verses, inasmuch as he is a poet by virtue of the imitative element in his work, and it is actions that he imitates. And if he should come to take a subject from actual history, he is none the less a poet for that; since some historic occurrences may very well be in the probable and possible order of things; and it is in that aspect of them that he is their poet.

Of simple Plots and actions the episodic are the worst. I call a Plot episodic when there is neither probability nor necessity in the sequence of its episodes. Actions of this sort bad poets construct through their own fault, and good ones on account of the players. His work being for public performance, a good poet often stretches out a Plot beyond its capabilities, and is thus obliged to twist the sequence of incident.

Tragedy, however, is an imitation not only of a complete action, but also of incidents arousing pity and fear. Such incidents have the very greatest effect on the mind when they occur unexpectedly and at the same time in consequence of one another; there is more of the marvelous in them then than if they happened of themselves or by mere chance. Even matters of chance seem most marvelous if there is an appearance of design as it were in them; as for instance the statue of Mitys at Argos killed the author of Mitys' death by falling down on him when a looker-on at a public spectacle; for incidents like that we think to be not without a meaning. A Plot, therefore, of this sort is necessarily finer than others.

. . . . .

Plots are either simple or complex, since the actions they represent are naturally of this twofold description. The action, proceeding in the way defined, as one continuous whole, I call simple, when the change in the

---

3. **Agathon's *Antheus*:** Agathon (c. 450–400 B.C.) was a tragic poet and a friend of Plato. Plato commemorated Agathon's victory at a dramatic festival in 416 in his *Symposium;* none of Agathon's works survive.

hero's fortunes takes place without Peripety[4] or Discovery; and complex, when it involves one or the other, or both. These should each of them arise out of the structure of the Plot itself, so as to be the consequence, necessary or probable, of the antecedents. There is a great difference between a thing happening *propter hoc* and *post hoc.*[5]

. . . . .

A Peripety is the change from one state of things within the play to its opposite of the kind described, and that too in the way we are saying, in the probable or necessary sequence of events; as it is for instance in *Oedipus:*[6] here the opposite state of things is produced by the Messenger, who, coming to gladden Oedipus and to remove his fears as to his mother, reveals the secret of his birth. A Discovery is, as the very word implies, a change from ignorance to knowledge, and thus to either love or hate, in the personages marked for good or evil fortune. The finest form of Discovery is one attended by Peripeties, like that which goes with the Discovery in *Oedipus.* There are no doubt other forms of it; what we have said may happen in a way in reference to inanimate things, even things of a very casual kind; and it is also possible to discover whether some one has done or not done something. But the form most directly connected with the Plot and the action of the piece is the first-mentioned. This, with a Peripety, will arouse either pity or fear—actions of that nature being what Tragedy is assumed to represent; and it will also serve to bring about the happy or unhappy ending.

Two parts of the Plot, then, Peripety and Discovery, are on matters of this sort. A third part is Suffering; which we may define as an action of a destructive or painful nature, such as murders on the stage, tortures, woundings, and the line. The other two have been already explained.

. . . . .

The next points after what we have said above will be these: (1) What is the poet to aim at, and what is he to avoid, in constructing his Plots? and (2) What are the conditions on which the tragic effect depends?

We assume that, for the finest form of Tragedy, the Plot must be not simple but complex; and further, that it must imitate actions arousing pity and fear, since that is the distinctive function of this kind of imitation. It follows, therefore, that there are three forms of Plot to be avoided. (1) A good man must not be seen passing from happiness to misery, or (2) a bad man from misery to happiness. The first situation is not fear-inspiring or piteous, but simply odious to us. The second is the most untragic that can be; it has no one of the requisites of Tragedy; it does not appeal either to the human feeling in us, or to our pity, or to our fears. Nor, on the other hand, should (3) an extremely bad man be seen falling from happiness into

---

4. **Peripety** (pə rip′ ə tē): reversal of fortune, usually for the worse.

5. *propter hoc* **and** *post hoc:* Latin phrases meaning "because of this" and "after this." The difference is between an event that is a result of an action and one that merely follows it in time.

6. *Oedipus:* *Oedipus the King,* a famous play by Sophocles. See p. 181.

misery. Such a story may arouse the human feeling in us, but it will not move us to either pity or fear; pity is occasioned by undeserved misfortune, and fear by that of one like ourselves; so that there will be nothing either piteous or fear-inspiring in the situation. There remains, then, the intermediate kind of personage, a man not pre-eminently virtuous and just, whose misfortune, however, is brought upon him not by vice and depravity but by some error of judgment, of the number of those in the enjoyment of great reputation and prosperity; e.g. Oedipus, Thyestes,[7] and the men of note of similar families. The perfect Plot, accordingly, must have a single, and not (as some tell us) a double issue; the change in the hero's fortunes must be not from misery to happiness, but on the contrary from happiness to misery; and the cause of it must lie not in any depravity, but in some great error on his part; the man himself being either such as we have described, or better, not worse, than that. Fact also confirms our theory. Though the poets began by accepting any tragic story that came to hand, in these days the finest tragedies are always on the story of some few houses, on that of Alcmeon,[8] Oedipus, Orestes,[9] Meleager,[10] Thyestes, Telephus,[11] or any others that may have been involved, as either agents or sufferers, in some deed of horror. The theoretically best tragedy, then, has a Plot of this description. The critics, therefore, are wrong who blame Euripides for taking this line in his tragedies, and giving many of them an unhappy ending. It is, as we have said, the right line to take. The best proof is this: on the stage, and in the public performances, such plays, properly worked out, are seen to be the most truly tragic; and Euripides, even if his execution be faulty in every other point, is seen to be nevertheless the most tragic certainly of the dramatists.

. . . . .

The tragic fear and pity may be aroused by the Spectacle; but they may also be aroused by the very structure and incidents of the play—which is the better way and shows the better poet. The Plot in fact should be so framed that, even without seeing the things take place, he who simply hears the account of them shall be filled with horror and pity at the incidents; which is just the effect that the mere recital of the story in *Oedipus* would have on one. To produce this same effect by means of the Spectacle is less artistic, and requires extraneous aid. Those, however, who make use of the Spectacle to put before us that which is merely monstrous and not productive of fear, are wholly out of touch with

---

7. **Thyestes:** brother of Atreus, who killed and boiled Thyestes' children and served them to him in a stew.

8. **Alcmeon:** one of the Seven against Thebes. Following the expedition, he returned home and avenged his father's death on his mother Eriphyle and then, driven by the Furies, wandered from place to place.

9. **Orestes:** the son of Agamemnon, who avenged his father's murder by killing his mother, Clytemnestra.

10. **Meleager:** hero who slew the Calydonian boar.

11. **Telephus:** son of Heracles and Auge.

Tragedy; not every kind of pleasure should be required of a tragedy, but only its own proper pleasure.

The tragic pleasure is that of pity and fear, and the poet has to produce it by a work of imitation; it is clear, therefore, that the causes should be included in the incidents of his story. Let us see, then, what kinds of incident strike one as horrible, or rather as piteous. In a deed of this description the parties must necessarily be either friends, or enemies, or indifferent to one another. Now when enemy does it on enemy, there is nothing to move us to pity either in his doing or in his meditating the deed, except so far as the actual pain of the sufferer is concerned; and the same is true when the parties are indifferent to one another. Whenever the tragic deed, however, is done within the family—when murder or the like is done or meditated by brother on brother, by son on father, by mother on son, or son on mother—these are the situations the poet should seek after. The traditional stories, accordingly, must be kept as they are, e.g., the murder of Clytemnestra by Orestes and of Eriphyle by Alcmeon. At the same time even with these there is something left to the poet himself; it is for him to devise the right way of treating them. Let us explain more clearly what we mean by "the right way." The deed of horror may be done by the doer knowingly and consciously, as in the old poets, and in Medea's murder of her children in Euripides.[12] Or he may do it, but in ignorance of his relationship, and discover that afterwards, as does the Oedipus in Sophocles. Here the deed is outside the play; but it may be within it. A third possibility is for one meditating some deadly injury to another, in ignorance of his relationship, to make the discovery in time to draw back. These exhaust the possibilities, since the deed must necessarily be either done or not done, and either knowingly or unknowingly.

The worst situation is when the personage is with full knowledge on the point of doing the deed, and leaves it undone. It is odious and also (through the absence of suffering) untragic; hence it is that no one is made to act thus except in some few instances, e.g. Haemon and Creon in *Antigone*.[13] Next after this comes the actual perpetration of the deed meditated. A better situation than that, however, is for the deed to be done in ignorance, and the relationship discovered afterwards, since there is nothing odious in it, and the Discovery will serve to astound us. But the best of all is the last; what we have in *Cresphontes*,[14] for example, where

---

12. **Medea . . . Euripides:** Medea, abandoned by the hero Jason, kills their children and flees from Corinth. The story is the subject of a famous play by Euripides.

13. *Antigone:* a play by Sophocles.

14. *Cresphontes:* a play about the king of Messenia, who was killed by Polyphontes in a rebellion. His son Aepytus escaped because Aepytus' mother Merope sent him away. Merope was then forced to marry Polyphontes. Years later Aepytus returned, claiming to be his own murderer in order to gain entrance into the palace of Polyphontes. He narrowly escaped death at the hands of his mother, who wanted revenge on the man who supposedly killed her son. She recognized him just in time, however, and together they brought about the death of Polyphontes. Aepytus then claimed his rightful place as king.

Merope, on the point of slaying her son, recognizes him in time; in *Iphigenia,*[15] where sister and brother are in a like position; and in *Helle,*[16] where the son recognizes his mother, when on the point of giving her up to her enemy.

This will explain why our tragedies are restricted (as we said just now) to such a small number of families. It was accident rather than art that led the poets in quest of subjects to embody this kind of incident in their Plots. They are still obliged, accordingly, to have recourse to the families in which such horrors have occurred.

On the construction of the Plot, and the kind of Plot required for Tragedy, enough has now been said.

. . . . .

In the Characters there are four points to aim at. First and foremost, that they shall be good. There will be an element of character in the play, if (as has been observed) what a personage says or does reveals a certain moral purpose; and a good element of character, if the purpose so revealed is good. Such goodness is possible in every type of personage, even in a woman or a slave, though the one is perhaps an inferior, and the other a wholly worthless being. The second point is to make them appropriate. The Character before us may be, say, manly; but it is not appropriate in a female Character to be manly, or clever. The third is to make them like the reality, which is not the same as their being good and appropriate, in our sense of the term. The fourth is to make them consistent and the same throughout; even if inconsistency be part of the man before one for imitation as presenting that form of character, he should still be consistently inconsistent. We have an instance of inconsistency in *Iphigenia in Aulis,*[17] where Iphigenia the suppliant is utterly unlike the later Iphigenia. The right thing, however, is in the Characters just as in the incidents of the play to endeavor always after the necessary or the probable; so that whenever such-and-such a personage says or does such-and-such a thing, it shall be the probable or necessary outcome of his character; and whenever this incident follows on that, it shall be either the necessary or the probable consequence of it. From this one sees (to digress for a moment) that the Denouement also should arise out of the plot itself, and not depend on a stage-artifice. The artifice must be reserved for matters outside the play—for past events beyond human knowledge, or events yet to come, which require to be foretold or announced; since it is the privilege of the Gods to know everything. There should be nothing improbable among the actual incidents. If it be unavoidable, however, it should be outside the tragedy, like the improbability in the *Oedipus* of Sophocles. But to return to the Characters. As Tragedy is an imitation of personages better than the ordinary man, we in our way should follow the example of good

---

15. *Iphigenia: Iphigenia in Tauris,* a play by Euripides.

16. *Helle:* a play by an unknown author.

17. *Iphigenia in Aulis:* a play by Euripides. See p. 89.

portrait-painters, who reproduce the distinctive features of a man, and at the same time, without losing the likeness, make him handsomer than he is. The poet in like manner, in portraying men quick or slow to anger, or with similar infirmities of character, must know how to represent them as such, and at the same time as good men, as Agathon and Homer have represented Achilles.

DISCUSSION QUESTIONS

1. If Aristotle were alive today, he might be interested in evaluating several types of movies that involve "undeserved misfortune." One type is the disaster movie, in which people perish because of tornadoes, floods, earthquakes, airplane crashes, and sinking ships. The other type is the horror movie, in which a non-human or depraved human figure attacks and kills people randomly. Do you think Aristotle would consider these to be genuine tragedies? Why or why not?

2. What two emotions are aroused by a successful tragedy? In general, how is each of these emotions aroused?

3. A tragic plot always involves a reversal of fortune, but many kinds of reversals are not appropriate. Give some examples of plots that are inappropriate to tragedy. What is the ideal tragic plot?

4. According to Aristotle, which is more important, history or poetry? Why?

5. Of the six parts of tragedy (character, plot, diction, spectacle, thought, and melody), which did Aristotle consider most important? Which did he regard as least important? What do you think he would say about modern dramas or movies that rely strongly on special effects to make an impact?

SUGGESTION FOR WRITING

Aristotle is famous for being a precise thinker who examines every possibility. (Note how he is likely to sum up an argument: "These [examples] exhaust the possibilities, since the deed must necessarily be either done or not done, and either knowingly or unknowingly.")

Select a type of art or literature that you admire. It could be science fiction, horror movies, musicals, detective fiction, or anything else you are familiar with. Explain the goal of these works and which features are likely to make them successful. Try to explore every possibility, both good and bad, as Aristotle does.

EURIPIDES

(480–406 B.C.)

The youngest of the great tragic playwrights of ancient Greece, Euripides is the most modern in outlook and, for many people, the most accessible. He was critical of convention, sensitive to suffering, appalled by injustice, and skeptical of the gods. ("If gods do evil, then they are not gods.") His questioning attitudes made him enormously unpopular during his own lifetime, but his reputation skyrocketed shortly after his death. Since that time he has been revered as one of the greatest writers of all time, and his compassionate eloquence has spoken to every generation for 25 centuries.

Euripides wrote between 80 and 90 plays, of which 18 tragedies remain. Filled with psychological insight, many of these plays retell familiar Greek myths in a down-to-earth way, emphasizing the human side of heroes and gods rather than making them grand and aloof. Euripides' compassion extended to such individuals as the women of an "enemy nation" (*Trojan Women*) and to figures usually depicted as evil (*Medea*). Euripides was fond of putting a new slant on traditional stories, and the following selection is no exception. Here Euripides offers a sympathetic view of one of the blackest villains of mythology, Clytemnestra, and an unheroic view of one of the most famous Greek heroes, Agamemnon. (See the headnote for Aeschylus on page 3 if you are unfamiliar with the story of Agamemnon and Clytemnestra.)

Unlike Aeschylus' play, the one that follows opens before the Trojan War has begun.

Euripides assumes that his audiences knows the legendary cause of the war and therefore makes many references to it. The modern reader, however, may need some background information to understand these references, and so a brief account is given below:

The trouble started when the goddess of discord rolled a golden apple into a banquet of the gods with the message, "For the fairest." Athena, Hera, and Aphrodite each wanted the apple and asked Zeus to decide who was the fairest. Zeus wisely declined to be the judge and told the three goddesses to go to Mount Ida near Troy and find Paris, the son of King Priam, who was an expert judge of beauty. The goddesses appeared before Paris, who was tending sheep, and offered him various bribes. Aphrodite, the goddess of love and beauty, offered him the love of the most beautiful woman in the world, and Paris accepted this bribe, awarding Aphrodite the golden apple.

As it turned out, the most beautiful woman in the world was Helen, wife of Menelaus. With the help of Aphrodite, Paris successfully enticed her away from her husband. When Menelaus realized what had happened, he called upon all of Greece to come to his aid. Under the leadership of Agamemnon, a thousand ships from all over Greece met at the town of Aulis to launch an expedition against Troy. This was the legendary cause of a war that lasted ten years and destroyed the splendid ancient civilization of Troy. ■

IPHIGENIA IN AULIS

Translated by F. M. Stawell

CHARACTERS

AGAMEMNON, *Commander-in-Chief of the Greek army*

MENELAUS, *his brother*

CLYTEMNESTRA, *his Queen*

IPHIGENIA, *his daughter*

ORESTES, *his little son*

ACHILLES

AN OLD SERVANT

A MESSENGER

CHORUS OF WOMEN FROM CHALCIS, *a city near Aulis*

in the Epilogue, ANOTHER MESSENGER

Scene: *The quarters of the Greek army at Aulis.*[1] *Before the King's tent.*
Between midnight and dawn. AGAMEMNON *enters from the tent.*

AGAMEMNON. Come out, old man, out from the tent to me!

OLD SERVANT (*entering*). Coming, my lord!
    What new plan is afoot,
    King Agamemnon?

5   AGAMEMNON. O, make haste, make haste!

OLD SERVANT. All that you will, my lord.
    I'm a light sleeper yet.

AGAMEMNON. What star is yonder, traveling in the sky?

OLD SERVANT.   Sirius;
    Close to the sevenfold voyaging Pleiades,
10   Still high overhead.

AGAMEMNON. No sound from the birds;
    No sound from the sea
    The hush of the winds
    Broods over Euripus.[2]

---

1. Aulis: a town on the eastern coast of Greece.

2. Euripus: the strait dividing Greece from the island of Euboea.

15   OLD SERVANT. Why did you hasten out of the tent,
        Lord Agamemnon?
        No one is stirring in Aulis yet:
        Nothing has roused
        The guards on the ramparts.
20   Let us go in.

      AGAMEMNON. O, you are fortunate,
        Fortunate, all of you humble men,
        Unknown, unhonored, and free from fear!
      Leaders may envy your lot.

25   OLD SERVANT. Ay, but glory is theirs.

      AGAMEMNON. And in that glory lies their grief.
        Suddenly, full in their pride of place
        The wrath of the high gods shatters their life,
        Or the quarrels of men
30   Mock them and thwart them.

      OLD SERVANT. Are those the words of a chief? For shame!
        You were not born for a life of ease,
        Lord Agamemnon!
        Joy and grief are a mortal's lot,
35   And the will of the high gods stronger than we.
        But what has troubled you
        All through the night? You kindled a torch,
        Wrote on that tablet you hold in your hand,
        Wrote and rewrote, sealed it, unsealed,
40   Dashed out the torch and burst into tears,
        As though you were crazed.
        Tell me, trust me, a faithful man,
        Who came with your queen from her father's home,
        One of the guard for the bride.

45   AGAMEMNON. Here lie our men, all banded against Troy
        To win back Helen for her rightful lord,
        My brother Menelaus. I lead the host—
        Doubtless they chose me for my brother's sake—
        This glorious host of men and steeds and ships.
50   Would I had not been chosen! Here we lie,
        Becalmed at Aulis, helpless! In our need
        We asked the prophet Calchas, and he said
        That I must sacrifice my own dear child,
        Iphigenia, to soften Artemis,[3]
55   The Goddess of this plain. Then, only then,
        The fleet could sail, and we should conquer Troy.

---

3. Artemis: goddess of the hunt and of the moon.

When I heard that,
I told my herald to dismiss the host:—
I could not be my daughter's murderer.
60   But then my brother came and plied me hard,
And I, I yielded. A letter went from me
To the queen my wife, bidding her send our girl
To wed Achilles, for he was too proud,—
Or so I said,—to sail with me to Troy
65   Unless he had a child of ours to wife.
I thought this tale would work upon the queen
To send the girl. None knew of it but four,
Menelaus, Calchas, Odysseus, and myself.
But I have changed, I have repented me.
70   I wrote this other letter in the night,
The one you see here. Take it.—
Go with it straight to Argos. Stay. I'll read
What I have written. You're my faithful man.

OLD SERVANT. Do so: I'll speak the better to the queen.

75   AGAMEMNON. "Daughter of Leda,[4] do not send our girl,
As I wrote first, unto this wide-winged gulf,
Where no waves dash on the deep-bosomed shore.
The marriage-feast
We must hold later."

80   OLD SERVANT. But, Achilles, sire,—
What of his anger if he lose his bride?
Will it not flame against you and your lady?

AGAMEMNON. O, that was dreadful too!

OLD SERVANT.   What can you mean?

AGAMEMNON. I only used his name. He has not heard
85   Aught of our plans nor any word of marriage.

OLD SERVANT. Ill done, O king, using him for a lure
To make your child the victim for the army.

AGAMEMNON. Alas, some madness seized me, I was lost!
But hasten now, old man! Forget your age!

OLD SERVANT. Trust me, my lord.

90   AGAMEMNON.   Let nothing make you loiter:
No cool spring in the shade, no drowsiness.

---

4. **Daughter of Leda:** Clytemnestra. Leda was the mother of Clytemnestra by her husband
Tyndareus and of Helen by Zeus, who appeared to her in the shape of a swan.

OLD SERVANT. O, do not say such things!

AGAMEMNON. Scan all the crossways on your road, for fear
The chariot pass you bringing the maid to us.
95 And if you meet her, quick, turn back the steeds,
Drive with loose rein to Argos!

OLD SERVANT. So I will.

AGAMEMNON.   Undo the barriers, go.

OLD SERVANT. What sign is there to show I come from you?

AGAMEMNON. The seal upon this tablet. Guard it! Quick!
100 The dawn is whitening in the sky, the sun's bright car
Will soon be here.—

The OLD SERVANT *hurries out.*

Woe's me for mortal men!
None have been happy yet.

AGAMEMNON *goes into the tent. Enter the* CHORUS, *Greek
women from Chalcis in the island opposite Aulis.*

CHORUS (*singing*).
To the sands of the bay
105 Where the salt waves run
Over the narrows
We come, we come,
From Chalcis our harbor-town,—
Nurse of the Naiad
110 Whose waters neighbor the sea,
Arethusa⁵ of all renown,—
To gaze on our chivalry.

Ten thousand sail
Across the sea to Troy,—
115 Our husbands have told us the tale,—
They follow their far-famed, fair-haired kings
For the sake of that queen
Whom the Herdsman⁶ beguiled
By the reedy Spartan springs,
120 Whom the Cyprian⁷ gave,
When Hera and Pallas and she
Met by the dews of the mountain-lake,

---

5. the Naiad . . . Arethusa: Arethusa, a naiad or water-nymph, was a companion of Artemis. The goddess changed her into a fountain to save her from the pursuit of the river-god Alpheus.

6. the Herdsman: Paris.

7. the Cyprian: Aphrodite, the goddess of love, was often called *Cyprian* because Cyprus was sacred to her.

Met in their rivalry.

Up through the grove,—
125   The victim-place
That Artemis hallows,—
We sped apace;
Blushed at our boldness,
A new shy red in our cheeks
130   For all that we longed to see,
Aflame to see
Bulwark and buckler and cavalry,
Camp of our fighters,
Armed host of our horses and men.

        Enter MENELAUS *and the* OLD SERVANT, *struggling together.*

135   OLD SERVANT. Shame on you, Menelaus! You have no right.

MENELAUS. Off! You are far too faithful to your lord.

OLD SERVANT. That sneer's my boast.

MENELAUS.   You'll soon repent your zeal.

OLD SERVANT. You had no right to read the words I bore.

MENELAUS. Nor you to bear what would destroy the Greeks.

140   OLD SERVANT. Argue that out with others! Give me the letter.

MENELAUS. I will not.

OLD SERVANT. Then I will not let you go.

MENELAUS. You'll bleed for that! Your head shall feel my scepter.

OLD SERVANT. Fair fame is his who dies to serve his lord.

MENELAUS. Let go! How the slave chatters!

OLD SERVANT.   Master, help!
145   Help, Agamemnon! Thieves!—This man has stolen
The letter that you gave me.

                    Enter AGAMEMNON.

AGAMEMNON. Ha! What's this?
  What means this brawling at my very gate?

MENELAUS. Hear me! I am the one to speak, not he.

150   AGAMEMNON. Menelaus struggling with my man? How's this?

MENELAUS. First look me in the face and then I'll speak.

AGAMEMNON. You think I dare not? I, King Atreus' son?

MENELAUS. You see this tablet, you know its shameful words?

                                          Euripides   **93**

AGAMEMNON. It's mine. Give it to me.

MENELAUS.   No, not until
155   I show the army what you've written there.

AGAMEMNON. You broke the seal, then, read what was not yours?

MENELAUS. Yes, to lay bare your guilt.

AGAMEMNON.   Have you no shame?
   Where did you get it?

MENELAUS.   On the road to Argos,
   Watching to see if they would send your girl.

160   AGAMEMNON. And who set you to watch and spy on me?

MENELAUS. My own will set me. I'm no slave of yours.

AGAMEMNON. You dare? Can I not rule my house myself?

MENELAUS. No, for you change and veer with every wind.

AGAMEMNON. Well argued! But the wit of cruel men
   Is hateful.

165   MENELAUS. And the purpose of weak men
   Contemptible, and treacherous to boot.
   O, you're the same man still! I'll show you that.
   Hush, no more raging! I'll be fair enough.
   Do you remember when your heart was set,
170   Though you concealed it, on this high command?
   How suave you were, how friendly to each clown,
   Doors open to the world, so affable,
   Ready to talk with all, even when they would not!
   And so you bought your power. But power won,
175   My lord was changed. He scarcely could be seen,
   His old friends friends no more. Yet a true man
   Will use his power most to help his friends.
   So much for that. We sailed to Aulis then,
   And lay becalmed, until the other lords
180   Bade you dismiss the fleet, nor linger here.
   You came to me; you cried, "What can I do?
   How keep the army, my command, my fame?"
   Then Calchas bade you sacrifice your child
   To Artemis, and she would send the wind.
185   And you were glad; you promised all he asked.
   You wrote for her yourself,—you cannot say
   Any man forced you,—bidding the queen your wife
   Send her, to wed Achilles, so you feigned;
   The eternal heavens hearkened to your words.
190   Now you betray us, writing fine new things;
   You cannot be your daughter's murderer!

O, the trick's not uncommon! Many a chief
Endures at first, then fails; some through the fault
Of foolish citizens, but some because
195   They have not wit to keep their own land safe.
Alas for Hellas! I mourn most for her.
Equipped for glory, she must leave her foes,
Barbarians, to mock her,—through your girl and you.
Choose no man leader for his name, say I,
200   In peace or war. A general should have brains,
And it's the man of sense who rules the land.

LEADER OF THE CHORUS. Bitter are brothers when they fall to strife.

AGAMEMNON. Now I'll speak in my turn and show your faults
Frankly and plainly, yes, but soberly,
205   More like a brother. A good man should not rail.
Why are you fierce and your eyes full of blood?
How have I wronged you? What is it you want?
A lovely wife? I cannot help you there.
You could not rule the one you had. Must I
210   Suffer for you? Is my ambition blamed?
No, no, it's that fair woman you desire,
Careless of honor or of righteousness.
If I repent the evil thought I had,
Do you call me mad? Why, you are mad yourself,
215   Seeking a wicked wife, once rid of her.
Enough! I will not slay my child to win
Unjust success for you, and for myself
Long nights and days of weeping bitter tears
For monstrous crime against my own dear children.
220   Do as you like; I will not do this deed.
There is my answer, short and clear enough.

LEADER OF THE CHORUS. Ah, he has changed, repented! It is well.

MENELAUS. Woe's me! I have no friends.

AGAMEMNON.   Not if you slay them.

MENELAUS. Are you my brother?

AGAMEMNON.   In good deeds, not in vile.

MENELAUS. Brothers should share their griefs.

225   AGAMEMNON.   Exhort me not
    To death and ruin.

MENELAUS.   Will you not help Greece?

AGAMEMNON. Some god has sent Greece mad and you with her.

MENELAUS. Guard your king's scepter, traitor to your kin!
    I'll turn to other means and other friends.

230   MESSENGER. Leader of Hellas,[8] Agamemnon, Lord!
        I come to tell you I have brought your child,
        Iphigenia, and her mother too,
        The queen herself, your lady Clytemnestra,
        And young Orestes, that you should have joy
235   Seeing them now, so far away from home.
        Even while I speak they are resting by the stream
        In a smooth, grassy meadow, taking food
        While I come to prepare you. But already
        The army knows they are here. Rumor runs quick.
240   And all the people throng to see your daughter,
        For all men worship splendor. And they ask,
        "Is it a marriage, or her father's love
        That brings the maiden?" Or I hear some say,
        "They mean to give the girl to Artemis,
245   Lady of Aulis." Who's to lead her here?
        Tell me, prepare the rites, and crown yourselves,
        You and lord Menelaus. The marriage-song,
        The sound of flutes and dancing feet should fill
        King's tent and camp.—
250   It is a day of glory for the girl.

    AGAMEMNON. I thank you. Get you in. All shall go well.

The MESSENGER *goes into the tent.*

        Woe, woe is me, unhappy, caught by fate,
        Outwitted by the cunning of the gods!
        O that I were base-born! Then I could weep.
255   What can I do, a king? Our dignity
        Still rules our lives, and still we serve the mob.
        I shame to weep, and yet I shame to weep not,
        In this sore strait. What shall I tell my wife?
        How can I greet her, look her in the face?
260   She has undone me, coming now, uncalled,
        Coming to wed her daughter, full of love,
        To find me thus, a murderer. And she,
        Poor hapless maiden, now the bride of Death!
        The pity of it! I hear her call to me,
265   "Father, O father, would you slay your child?
        A bitter bridal have you made for me:
        I would you had the like!" And he, the boy,
        Little Orestes, he will cry with her,
        Knowing and knowing not. Accursed Paris,
270   Thy rape of Helen hath destroyed me!

---

8. Hellas: Greece.

LEADER OF THE CHORUS. I am a stranger to these lords, and yet
    My heart is sick to feel the sorrow here.

MENELAUS. Brother, give me your hand.

AGAMEMNON.   There.—You have won,
    And I must suffer.

MENELAUS.   No, it shall not be!
275   I swear by Pelops, grandsire of us both,
    And by our father Atreus, I will speak
    The very truth, out of my heart of hearts.
    I saw you weep, I pitied you, and now
    Unsay my words. I cannot torture you.
280   I cannot bid you slay your child for me.
    Why should you mourn and I have joy thereby?
    Your dear ones fall and mine have light and life?
    There are more women if I lost this one.
    Why should I slay my brother, my own flesh,
285   And take back Helen, an ill gift for a good?
    I was mad, blinded, till I looked and saw
    What this thing meant. Yes, and I pity her,
    Poor maid, my brother's child, if she should die
    To win my wife. What's Helen to your daughter?
290   Disband the army: send the host away.
    Dry your eyes, brother; do not make me weep.
    That prophecy you heard about your child,
    I'll none of it: I leave it all to you.
    My cruel thoughts have gone, and it is well
295   That love and pity for my own have changed me.

LEADER OF THE CHORUS. Gallantly spoken! You do not shame your
    sires.

AGAMEMNON. I thank you, Menelaus, for this change,
    Sudden and worthy of yourself. But I,
    I am compelled to that dread slaughter now.

300 MENELAUS. How so? Who'll force you now to kill your child?

AGAMEMNON. The army: this great concourse of the Greeks.

MENELAUS. Not if you send her back again to Argos.

AGAMEMNON. That we could hide: there's more cannot be hid.

MENELAUS. And what? We should not shrink before the mob.

305 AGAMEMNON. Calchas will tell them all the prophecy.

MENELAUS. Not if we stop his mouth, and that's soon done.

AGAMEMNON. He's base, ambitious, like every prophet born.

MENELAUS. They do no good: they are never any use.

AGAMEMNON. But there's another danger, is there not?

310 MENELAUS. How can I say? What danger do you mean?

AGAMEMNON. The son of Sisyphus[9] knows everything.

MENELAUS. Odysseus? He's no match for you and me.

AGAMEMNON. He's full of cunning, and he rules the mob.

MENELAUS. Yes,—he's ambitious.—Curse on that curse of men!

315 AGAMEMNON. Can you not hear him, risen in his place,
 Telling the army all that Calchas said
 And how I promised I would give my child
 And then drew back?—Thus he'll goad on the men
 To kill us, and then sacrifice the girl.
320 Or if we fled to Argos they would follow,
 Conquer the land, and lay the great walls low.
 See how the gods have compassed us about
 With suffering,—no escape now! O, my brother,
 Do this one thing for me! Go to the army
325 And see that Clytemnestra shall not learn
 What must be, till I give my child to Death.
 Let my tears be enough. And you, my friends,
 Strangers, yet friends too,—keep the secret safe.

MENELAUS *goes to the camp*, AGAMEMNON *and the* OLD SERVANT
into the king's tent.

CHORUS (*singing*). Thrice blest the calmer natures, the stronger
  hearts of passion,
330 Peace-possessed, though the god,
 Gold-haired, twin-souled, should smite them.
 Keen are his darts for rapture, and keen, keen for ruin!
 O Cyprian, grant us rest,
 Come not for our undoing!
335 But send us holy love,
 Thou dearest, loveliest,
 All madness far above.

 The ways of man are many, and changeful all their fashion;
 The true Good still shines fair,
340 And souls that are schooled
 Shall still draw nigh to her.
 Reverence shall sit in Wisdom's place,

---

9. **son of Sisyphus:** Odysseus. Sisyphus, king of Corinth, revenged himself on Autolycus for stealing his cattle by raping Autolycus' daughter Ariticlea, the wife of Laertes. She bore Odysseus,
who was raised as Laertes' son.

Hers is the high, compelling grace
To find, thought-led, the right,
345 Whence glories flow,
Failing not in this life.
Seek virtue, for the search is great,
Where woman's hidden love may grow,
A splendor in the soul of man,
350 Strengthening thousand-fold the State.

The king's son[10] herded cattle,
A lad alone on Ida,
Playing tunes on his pipe, strange melodies,
Like the airs Olympus sang,
355 Suddenly called from sleek white herds at pasture
To judge the goddesses
And sent forthwith to Hellas.
Beneath pearl-carver portals
His eyes looked deep in Helen's,
360 A long and answered look.
Love he gave, love he took,
Paris, athrob and trembling. But from that joy rose war, war
    that will not yield,
All Hellas sailing for Troy
With sword and spear and shield.

The royal car appears with CLYTEMNESTRA, IPHIGENIA,
ORESTES, *and their attendants.*

365 LEADER OF THE CHORUS. See, O see!
Iphigenia the young princess,
Clytemnestra the queen!
Great are the joys of the great,
Born from kings and for long renown!
370 Like gods in their splendor they seem
To us, weak mortals and poor.
Gather round, daughters of Chalcis,
Help the queen from her car
Courteously, gently! Disturb not the child
375 Nor startle the stranger princesses.

CLYTEMNESTRA. I thank you, women, for your kindly words,
Words of good omen, for I come, I hope,
To a good marriage, bringing the young bride.
Take out the dowries I have brought for her.
380 Carry them in, right carefully. And now,
My darling child, here we must leave the car.
Lift her down, maidens, take her in your arms;

10. **The king's son:** Paris.

She's a frail flower. Give me a hand too, some one,
The chariot-step is high. Carry the child,
385 Orestes: he's a babe. What, fast asleep
With all the driving? Wake up, little lad,
Wake for your sister's wedding! Chieftain's child,
Brother-in-law to Thetis' godlike son![11]
Put him here, Iphigenia, at my feet,
390 And stand beside me there yourself. The strangers
Will envy me for my rich motherhood.

Enter AGAMEMNON.

CLYTEMNESTRA. There comes your father! Let us greet him, girl!
Most honored lord, King Agamemnon, hail!
We come at your behest.

395 IPHIGENIA. O mother, blame me not! Let me go first
And put my arms about my father's neck.

CLYTEMNESTRA. Go, go, my girl. You always loved your father
More than the other children.

IPHIGENIA. Father, how glad it makes my heart to see you!
400 It is so long since you have been away!

AGAMEMNON. Yes, and mine too; your words are for us both!

IPHIGENIA. How good it was of you to send for me!

AGAMEMNON. No, child, not good; and yet there's good in it.

IPHIGENIA. Why, what is it? There's trouble in your face,
405 Your eyes are sad. You are not glad to see me!

AGAMEMNON. A general and a king has many cares.

IPHIGENIA. O, stay with me now; send your cares away!

AGAMEMNON. Why, all my cares are only for your sake.

IPHIGENIA. Then smooth your face, unknit your brows, and smile!

410 AGAMEMNON. I am as glad as I can be, my child.

IPHIGENIA. And all the while the tears are in your eyes!

AGAMEMNON. The parting that must come will be for long.

IPHIGENIA. O, father dear, I do not understand.

AGAMEMNON. Had you the sense I should but suffer more.

415 IPHIGENIA. Then I'll talk nonsense, if that pleases you.

AGAMEMNON. I cannot bear this. But I thank you, child.

---

11. **Thetis' godlike son:** the Greek hero Achilles, son of the sea-goddess Thetis.

IPHIGENIA. Stay with your children, father, stay at home.

AGAMEMNON. I would I could; I cannot have my will.

IPHIGENIA. Ruin take the army and my uncle's wrongs!

420 AGAMEMNON. They will ruin others. They have ruined me.

IPHIGENIA. How long you have been here in Aulis Bay!

AGAMEMNON. And something holds me still from setting out.

IPHIGENIA. Father, where is it that the Phrygians[12] live?

AGAMEMNON. Where Paris never should have found a home.

425 IPHIGENIA. Will it be long till you return to me?

AGAMEMNON. As long for me as you, my darling child.

IPHIGENIA. If you could take me on the journey too!

AGAMEMNON. There is another journey you must take—
  And you will not forget your father there.

430 IPHIGENIA. Shall I go with my mother, or alone?

AGAMEMNON. Alone, alone, severed from both of us.

IPHIGENIA. Father, it is not to another home?

AGAMEMNON. Hush, hush! A maiden must not know such things.

IPHIGENIA. Well, conquer Troy and come back soon to me.

435 AGAMEMNON. I have a sacrifice to offer first.

IPHIGENIA. We ask God's will, I know, in solemn rites.

AGAMEMNON. Yes. You will stand beside the bowl and learn.

IPHIGENIA. And lead the dances round the altar too?

AGAMEMNON. O, you are happy, for you do not know!
440   Go to the tent, my child. It is not fit
      For maidens to be seen—
      Give me the bitter sweetness of your kiss,
      Give me your hand,—you will be long away.
      O face, dear face, O breast, O golden hair!
445   A heavy burden has been laid on you
      By Troy and Helen! I must speak no more,
      I must not touch you: the tears fill my eyes.
      Now go within.

IPHIGENIA *goes into the tent.*

---

12. **the Phrygians:** the Trojans.

> Forgive me, O my queen,
> If I seem too much moved, wedding our child
450 To young Achilles. 'Tis a goodly match,
> But fathers feel it when they lose their girls.

CLYTEMNESTRA. I have my feelings too. I shall shed tears,
> I know, like you. But all such things must be,
> And time will help us. Tell me of the groom:
455 His name I know, but tell me of his race.[13]

AGAMEMNON. Aegina was the daughter of Asopus.

CLYTEMNESTRA. Who was her husband? A mortal or a god?

AGAMEMNON. Zeus. Aeacus their child, Oenone's lord.

CLYTEMNESTRA. What son of Aeacus succeeded him?

460 AGAMEMNON. Peleus, and Peleus won the Nereid.[14]

CLYTEMNESTRA. By the gods' grace, or in the gods' despite?

AGAMEMNON. Zeus gave her, Zeus, the best of guarantors.

CLYTEMNESTRA. Where was the bridal? Not in the ocean-surge?

AGAMEMNON. Where Cheiron[15] dwelt among the solemn hills.

465 CLYTEMNESTRA. Ah, where they say the Centaurs had their haunts?

AGAMEMNON. Ay, there the high gods held the marriage-feast.

CLYTEMNESTRA. Did Thetis rear Achilles or his sire?

AGAMEMNON. Neither of them. They sent him unto Cheiron
> To train him up far from the sins of men.

CLYTEMNESTRA. Wise teacher, wiser parents.

470 AGAMEMNON.   And a fine son-in-law.

CLYTEMNESTRA. He's not unworthy. Where has he his home?

AGAMEMNON. In Phthia,[16] by the river.

CLYTEMNESTRA.   Will you take her there?

AGAMEMNON. That we must leave to him.

CLYTEMNESTRA.   Well, good go with them!—
> When is the bridal?

AGAMEMNON.   When the moon is full.

---

13. **his race:** his ancestors

14. **the Nereid:** the sea-goddess Thetis, Achilles mother.

15. **Cheiron** (kī´ ron): a Centaur, the tutor of Achilles.

16. **Phthia** (thī´ ə): a town and district in northern Greece.

475 CLYTEMNESTRA. And have you slain the victim for the goddess?

AGAMEMNON. I shall do so: I must.

CLYTEMNESTRA. The marriage-feast,
You hold it later?

AGAMEMNON. When I have sacrificed
What the gods call for.

CLYTEMNESTRA. And we women, where
Hold we our banquet?

AGAMEMNON. There, beside the ships.

480 CLYTEMNESTRA. Among the ropes and anchors? Well, so be it.

AGAMEMNON. Listen to me, wife: bear with me in this.

CLYTEMNESTRA. Do I not do so always? What's your wish?

AGAMEMNON. To give the bride myself.

CLYTEMNESTRA. Without her mother?
And where will you send me?

AGAMEMNON. Why, home to Argos
To guard our unwed daughters.

485 CLYTEMNESTRA. Leaving her?
My eldest child? Who'll hold the marriage-torch?

AGAMEMNON. I will.

CLYTEMNESTRA. Unheard-of! You think naught of that?

AGAMEMNON. A naval camp is no fit place for you.

CLYTEMNESTRA. But fitting, and most fitting, I should be
At my own daughter's bridal.

490 AGAMEMNON. Nor should our girls
Be left alone at Argos.

CLYTEMNESTRA. Oh, for that,
They are well cared for in their maiden-halls.

AGAMEMNON. Good wife, be counseled.

CLYTEMNESTRA. Now, by Hera, husband,
Do your man's work and leave the home to me.

CLYTEMNESTRA *goes into the tent with her escort.*

495 AGAMEMNON. All's vain! I cannot rid myself of her.
Ah! how I twist and turn, how fruitlessly,
Plotting against my dearest every way!
It is for Hellas. I go to Calchas now

And plan with him what best will please the goddess
500 Although it crush me. Ah, the prudent man
Will choose for wife a helpmeet, or choose none.

He goes out towards the camp.

CHORUS (*singing*)
They shall come to the streams
Silver-swift on Apollo's shores,[17]
Our host of Greeks, our ships, our warriors.
505 There the wild Cassandra[18]
Will loose her laureled hair,
Bright hair tossed wide on a wind of dreams,
And cry aloud when God
Cries to men through her.
510 Right well must Troy be manned
When our war, ocean-borne, full in flood
Sweeps their land.
Lords of the air are Helen's brothers,[19]
Twins enskied,
515 But Greeks bring home the bride,
Home with shield and spear.
Towered Troy shall be taken
In a closed ring of blood,
Red whelming waters;
520 Her women wail for horror,
The queen and all her train
Of weeping daughters,
When our stroke smites their city,
Spares not, has no pity.
525 All Lydia's golden dames reproach the bride,
The bride of error,
Weaving their webs, lamenting, terrified:—
(O far from me or mine that terror!)
One to another they say,—
530 Whispering, shaken:—
"Which of the foemen will drag me away,
Making grim spoil of the long bright hair,
When our city is taken?"
Through thee, through thee, thou fair-faced child of the
Swan![20]

---

17. **Apollo's shores:** Troy. The god Apollo was a patron of the Trojans.

18. **Cassandra:** a daughter of Priam, king of Troy, famous for her prophecies of doom.

19. **Helen's brothers:** Castor and Pollux, called Gemini, the Twins. They were placed by Zeus in the heavens after death.

20. **child of the Swan:** Helen. Her father was Zeus, who took the shape of a swan when he sired Helen, which probably accounts for her grace and beauty.

535   Of the Swan, if it be
       That the tale is sooth,
       Not only the idle song
       Of a singer laughing at truth.

Enter ACHILLES.

ACHILLES. Where is the captain of the hosts of Greece?
540   Tell him Achilles stands without the door,
       The son of Peleus, asking speech of him.
       I have left my home Pharsalus[21] and my sire
       To linger here along Euripus' beach
       And wait upon these winds that will not blow.
545   My Myrmidons[22] grow restless: day by day
       Their murmur swells: "More waiting! How much more
       Before we launch upon our voyage for Troy!
       Act, son of Peleus, if to act at all
       Be your intent: else take us home, and leave
550   The sons of Atreus to their own delays."

Enter CLYTEMNESTRA *from the tent.*

CLYTEMNESTRA. Son of the Nereid, we were in the tent
    And heard your voice, and now come forth to greet you.

ACHILLES. How's this? A woman? So stately and so fair!

CLYTEMNESTRA. You are amazed because you know us not,
    Never have seen us yet.

555 ACHILLES.   Who are you, lady?
    How have you come, a woman, to the camp?

CLYTEMNESTRA. My name is Clytemnestra, Leda's daughter
    And Agamemnon's wife.

ACHILLES.   All thanks, great queen,
    For your high courtesy. But I must go:
    I should not talk with women.

560 CLYTEMNESTRA.   Why should you go?
    Stay here: give me your hand, and may the clasp
    Be pledge of happy married days to come!

ACHILLES. I? Clasp your hand? Agamemnon would be wroth!
    I have no right.

CLYTEMNESTRA. Surely the best of rights,
    Wedding my daughter.

---

21. **Pharsalus:** a city in northern Greece.
22. **Myrmidons:** the followers of Achilles.

565 ACHILLES.   Wedding your daughter? How?
       Lady, I cannot speak. What dream is this?

     CLYTEMNESTRA. I know it must be strange to meet new friends
       Speaking of marriage on your wedding-eve.

     ACHILLES. I was no suitor for your daughter, lady;
570   The sons of Atreus never spoke of her.

     CLYTEMNESTRA. What can this mean? My words are strange to
         you,
       But even so strange to me is all you say.

     ACHILLES. We both must wonder: both have cause for wonder,
       For surely both speak truth.

     CLYTEMNESTRA.   Am I deceived, then?
575   Have I been made to woo you for my daughter
       Against your will? O, I am all abashed.

     ACHILLES. Someone, it seems, has played upon us both.
       But let it pass, and care not overmuch.

     CLYTEMNESTRA. Farewell. I cannot look you in the face,
580   Thus put to shame and made to speak a lie.

     ACHILLES. I am shamed too, O queen! But I will go
       Into the tent and ask your husband all.

                    The OLD SERVANT *appears at the tent-door.*

     OLD SERVANT. Wait, son of Aeacus! Wait, Leda's daughter!

     ACHILLES. Who calls? Some frightened man, opening the door!

     OLD SERVANT. A slave: I'll own that now.

585 ACHILLES.   Whose? None of mine:
       My men and Agamemnon's keep apart.

     OLD SERVANT. I am the queen's: her sire gave me to her.

     ACHILLES. Speak, we are waiting: tell us what you want.

     OLD SERVANT. Are you alone? Is no one near the gates?

590 CLYTEMNESTRA. We are alone. Come out and speak with us.

     OLD SERVANT. O luck and wits of mine! Save those I love!

     ACHILLES. He'll not speak till tomorrow. He's afraid.

     CLYTEMNESTRA. Surely you trust me? Tell me: have no fear.

     OLD SERVANT. You know that I have served you faithfully.

595 CLYTEMNESTRA. Long years, I know, you have served my house
       and me.

OLD SERVANT. Agamemnon only got me with your dower.

CLYTEMNESTRA. Yes, yes.
   You came with me to Argos on my marriage.

OLD SERVANT. So I am yours, and Agamemnon's less.

600 CLYTEMNESTRA. Come, come, your secret! Out with it at last!

OLD SERVANT. He means to kill your child, his child!

CLYTEMNESTRA. What? Are your wits turning, man?

OLD SERVANT.   I say the steel
   Is sharpening now for that white neck of hers.

CLYTEMNESTRA. What horror's here? Or is my husband mad?

605 OLD SERVANT. O, sane enough, except for you and her.

CLYTEMNESTRA. But what's his purpose? What devil drives him on?

OLD SERVANT. The prophet Calchas, that the fleet may sail.

CLYTEMNESTRA. And whither?—O, my child, my child!—

OLD SERVANT.   To Troy,
   So Menelaus get his wife again.

610 CLYTEMNESTRA. And so for Helen's sake my girl is doomed?

OLD SERVANT. Even as you say. He'll sacrifice the maid
   To Artemis.

CLYTEMNESTRA.   Then it was all a lie,
   That marriage?

OLD SERVANT. Yes; to lure you from your home.

CLYTEMNESTRA. O, we are lost, my child and I! Lost, lost!

615 OLD SERVANT. Most piteously, and Agamemnon damned.

CLYTEMNESTRA. Utterly lost! I cannot stop my tears.

OLD SERVANT. What mother could? Let your tears have their way.

CLYTEMNESTRA. You say it's true, old man,—how do you know?

OLD SERVANT. He sent me to you with another letter.

620 CLYTEMNESTRA. Bidding us come, that he might murder her?

OLD SERVANT. No, stopping you. He had relented then.

CLYTEMNESTRA. But how was it you did not give it me?

OLD SERVANT. Menelaus seized it. He's the cause of all.

CLYTEMNESTRA. Son of the Nereid, do you hear these words?

625 ACHILLES. Dread words for you, and grim enough for me.

CLYTEMNESTRA. They used your name to lure my child to death.

ACHILLES. Ill done, by Heaven, ill done!

CLYTEMNESTRA.   O goddess-born!
    You see a wretched woman at your knees!
    All pride has left me. What should I care for now
630   Except my daughter? Help me, Thetis' son!
    Pity my need, and pity your poor bride,
    Bride but in name, I know, yet none the less
    I decked her for you, dreamed she would be yours,
    Brought her to you,—and brought her to her death.
635   You will be shamed if you desert her now,
    Poor hapless maid, not yours, and yet called yours!
    Now by your right hand and your mother's soul
    Your name destroyed us,—save it and save us!
    This is my only altar, at your knees!
640   I have no friend here else: you heard yourself
    Lord Agamemnon's cruelty—I stand
    Alone, a helpless woman, as you see,
    Among a crowd of sailors, lawless men,
    Fierce men, if goaded, yet much good in them,
645   When they're so minded. If you champion me,
    You save us: if you stand aside, we die.

LEADER OF THE CHORUS. There speaks a mother's heart, the thrall
    of love;
    She will dare all things for her children's sake.

ACHILLES. My blood's on fire. All tyrants I detest,
650   Though I yield gladly to a tempered rule.
    Noble old Cheiron taught me to love truth,
    And I'll obey our chiefs when they lead well,
    Not when they counsel crimes. Here and in Troy
    I'll keep my spirit free, my sword unstained.
655   Lady, indeed you have been foully used,
    Even at the hands where you should look for love;
    And all the pity that a soldier can
    I give you freely. Fear not for your child,
    Mine she was called, and to the sacrifice
660   I will not yield her. I'll not play decoy
    To lure the victim to the net of death.
    My name it was, though I touched not the steel,
    Mine which should slay your daughter. True, the cause
    Is Agamemnon: yet I needs must bear
665   The stain of murder if she perish thus,
    Betrayed and cheated through her trust in me,
    Outraged, dishonored. I must count myself
    The meanest man in all the host of Greece,

Viler than Menelaus, child of hell,
670   Not son of Peleus, should I lend my name
To be the accomplice of your husband's deed.
Now by the sea-born founder of my line,
Nereus, the sire of Thetis, who gave me birth,
Never shall Agamemnon touch your child—
675   No, not the merest fringes of her robe.
The steel shall answer, red with clots of gore,
Long before Troy is reached, if any man
Should drag your daughter from me. Be at rest:
I seem a god to you and I am none,
680   Yet will I play this part you choose for me.

LEADER OF THE CHORUS. Fit words, O son of Peleus, for yourself
And for your mother, the sea-pure Nereid!

CLYTEMNESTRA. I have no words—my words would seem too wild
And yet too poor where so great thanks are due.
685   A generous heart, I know, will turn from praise—
How dare I praise you, sick with my own griefs
And you a stranger with no part in them?
Yet a true man will help a stranger's need.
O pity us, for pitiable we are!
690   I took you for my son, an empty hope,
Yes, and an evil omen for yourself
If she must die who once was called your bride,
My daughter. Never let that omen be!
But you have answered nobly, first and last,
695   And through your help my daughter will be saved.
Or should I bring her here to clasp your knees?
No maiden's part, yet if you will she'll come,
Her eyes still brave and free in her shy face.
But, would you grant us all without her coming,
700   I'd keep her back. I know the girl is proud,
Too proud,—though modesty becomes a maid.

ACHILLES. I would not have you bring her to me thus,
For we must shun the gossip of the crowd:
Scandal's the joy of an idle army.
705   Nor do I need more prayers to help you now;
It is my pride to save you and my joy.
And of one thing be sure: I keep my pledge.
If I play false and make but idle boast,
Death be my lot: but if I save her, life.

710   CLYTEMNESTRA. Heaven help you for your help in our distress!

ACHILLES. Now hear my plan, and all may yet be well.

CLYTEMNESTRA. Say what you wish: in all I will obey.

ACHILLES. Let us persuade your lord to better thoughts.

CLYTEMNESTRA. He is a coward, and he fears the army.

715   ACHILLES. Yet reasons good may conquer reasons bad.

CLYTEMNESTRA. Small hope of that! Yet say what I should do.

ACHILLES. Plead with the father for the daughter's life:
    If he should still refuse you, turn to me.
    But should he listen, good; I need not act.
720   You are safe without it. And I'd treat a friend
    More fairly thus, nor could the army blame me
    If I had won by reason, not by force,
    While you yourself would have more peace at home
    If all seemed done without me and done well.

725   CLYTEMNESTRA. Wise are your words. I will do all you say.
    Yet if we not accomplish what we hope,
    Where shall I find you, whither turn to reach
    Your hand, your succor, in our desperate need?

ACHILLES. I will keep watch myself, and wait for you,
730   That none may see you hurrying through the host
    Alone in all your grief, a great man's daughter.

CLYTEMNESTRA. So let it be! Surely one day the gods
    Will bless you for your generous help to me,—
    If gods there are: if not, what use our toil?

        CLYTEMNESTRA *goes into the tent,* ACHILLES *towards the camp.*

735   CHORUS (*singing*). Who knows the marriage-song that once so
        proudly rang
    To the flute and the pipe and the dancer's lyre,
    The song the Muses[23] sang?
    Up Pelion's[24] glades they danced,
    The bright Pierian choir:[25]
740   Their golden sandals glanced,
    Their tresses gleamed as they made their way,
    Chanting the names, the names of bride and bridegroom,
    Through woods where Centaurs lay
    To the god-given feast
745   For Thetis and her lover.
    Page Ganymede,[26] the Phrygian boy,

---

23. **the Muses:** the nine goddesses, daughters of Zeus and Mnemosyne (Memory), who inspired poets, musicians, and scholars.

24. **Pelion:** a mountain in northern Greece.

25. **Pierian choir:** the Muses from Pieria, a region in northern Greece.

26. **Ganymede:** a Trojan boy taken to Olympus by Zeus to be his cupbearer.

Darling of Zeus, his luxury's toy,
Poured wine in golden beakers.
Far down on white-lit sand
750   Beside Aegean waters
Danced, circling hand-in-hand,
The Nereid maids,
The Sea-king's fifty daughters.
With green grass crowned and pine
755   Did the reveling Centaurs race
To the bowl of the Bacchanal[27] wine,
Their horse-hoofs thudding apace,
And one, the prophet, Apollo's friend,
Cheiron, shouted and sang of what should be in the end:—
760   "Hearken, child of the sea!
Thou shalt bear a son, a son to be
Light and glory for Thessaly.
Shield and spear shall he send to destroy
The land of Priam, sack
765   The far-famed town of Troy,
Gold-helmed, gold harness on his back,
Harness a god had wrought,
Harness his mother brought."
High rose that revelry
770   When gods made cheer for bride and groom,
For Peleus and the Nereid,
The first-born of the sea.
Ah, but thou! Thou shalt be crowned for thy doom,
Thy fair hair garlanded,
775   Like a dappled heifer ensnared
On lone hills in a cavern's gloom.
Blood will the Argives[28] draw from thy throat,
Though no pipe drew thee, no herdsman's cord;
Nay, but thy mother to be the bride
780   Of a Grecian lord.
Honor hath vanished and faithfulness fled,
Their faces faint as the face of the dead.
Sin grows strong, crime bears rule,
Lost is the loyal endeavor, the school
785   Of holy dread.

CLYTEMNESTRA *hurries out from the tent.*

CLYTEMNESTRA. Where is my lord? I come to look for him.
    He has been long away, and my poor child

---

27. **Bacchanal:** pertaining to the Bacchanalia, the festival of the wine-god Bacchus.

28. **the Argives:** the Greeks. The term was originally applied to the Greeks of Argos.

Is all in tears, learning the cruel death
Her father means for her. Ah, there he comes,
790   His children's murderer!—as I shall prove.

Enter AGAMEMNON *from the camp.*

AGAMEMNON. Well met, my wife, alone! I have things to say
Not fit for brides to hear.

CLYTEMNESTRA.   And what is it
For which you seize the chance?

AGAMEMNON.   Send out the girl
Here to her father. All is ready now,
795   The lustral water,[29] the flour, the cleansing fire,
The heifers that must fall to please the goddess
Before the marriage.

CLYTEMNESTRA.   Truly, your words are fair;
Your deeds, how shall I name them?

(She goes to the tent-door.)

                        Come, my girl;
You know your father's will. Come, bring with you
The child, Orestes.

IPHIGENIA *and* ORESTES *come from the tent.*

800   Here is your daughter, sire,
At your command. Now will I speak for her.

AGAMEMNON. Why do you weep, my girl? No smile for me?
Your eyes fixed on the ground? Your sweet face hid?

CLYTEMNESTRA. O, which of all my wrongs shall I take first?
805   For first and last and midmost, all are first.

AGAMEMNON. What is it? What has happened to you all?
Sad, drooping faces, trouble-darkened eyes?

CLYTEMNESTRA. Speak truth, my husband, in what I ask you now.

AGAMEMNON. No need bid me: ask what you will.

810   CLYTEMNESTRA. Your daughter, yours and mine, you mean to kill
    her?

AGAMEMNON. Hold!
You dare ask that? There's something you suspect?

CLYTEMNESTRA. Rage not, my lord:
Answer my question.

29: **lustral water:** water used in the lustrum, the ancient rite of purification.

AGAMEMNON.   Such questions are not fit.

CLYTEMNESTRA. I have no others.

815 AGEMEMNON.   O, my wretched fate!

CLYTEMNESTRA. And mine and hers, all three thrice miserable.

AGAMEMNON. Whom have I injured?

CLYTEMNESTRA.   You ask that of me?

AGAMEMNON. Betrayed, betrayed! My secret has been sold.

CLYTEMNESTRA. I know, I have learned, all that you mean to do.
820   Your silence and your groanings,—they confess,
       They speak for you. O, weary not yourself!

AGAMEMNON. See, I am silent: I'll not add lies to grief.

CLYTEMNESTRA. Then hear me now. I'll speak the naked truth,
       No dark hints now! By force you wedded me,
825   I never loved you! Tantalus you slew,
       My first dear husband; and my little son,
       You tore him from my breast. And when my brothers,
       The sons of God, flashed to me on their steeds,
       My father pitied you, his suppliant,
830   Gave me to you for wife. And a true wife I was,
       Yes, chaste and true, and cared well for your home.
       Such wives are not so common!—
       Three girls I bore you and a son, and now
       You rob me of the first! Your reason, pray,
835   If men should ask it? O, I'll answer that,—
       To win back Helen! Your own child for a wanton,
       Your dearest for a foe! A proper bargain!
       If you do this, if you are long at Troy,
       What will my heart be like, think you, at home,
840   When I look on my daughter's empty chair,
       And empty room, sitting there all alone,
       Companied by my tears, still muttering,
       "Your father killed you, child, killed you himself!"
       What will your wages be when you come back?
845   We who are left, we shall not want much urging
       To greet you with the welcome you deserve!
       O, by the gods, drive me not thus to sin,
       Nor sin yourself!
       If once you killed your child, how could you pray?
850   What good thing ask for? Rather for defeat,
       Disgrace, and exile! Nor could I pray for you:
       We make fools of the gods if we suppose
       They can love murderers. If you come home,
       Will you dare kiss your girls? Or they dare come,

855   That you may choose another for the knife?
     Have you once thought of this? Are you a man?
     Or nothing but a scepter and a sword?
     You should have gone among the Greeks and said,
     "You wish to sail for Troy? Good, then draw lots,
860   And see whose child must die." That had been fair;
     Or Menelaus should have slain his own,—
     Hermione[30] for Helen. But I, the chaste,
     I must be robbed, and she come home in triumph
     To find her daughter! Answer, if I am wrong!
865   If not, give up this murder! Sin no more!

LEADER OF THE CHORUS. O listen, listen! Help to save your child!
     Yield, Agamemnon! Not a man will blame you.

IPHIGENIA. Had I the voice of Orpheus,[31] O my father,
     If I could sing so that the rocks would move,
870   If I had words to win the hearts of all,
     I would have used them. I have only tears.
     See, I have brought them! They are all my power.
     I clasp your knees, I am your suppliant now,
     I, your own child; my mother bore me to you.
875   O, kill me not untimely! The sun is sweet!
     Why will you send me into the dark grave?
     I was the first to sit upon your knee,
     The first to call you father, first to give
     Dear gifts and take them. And you used to say,
880   "My darling, shall I see you safely wed,
     In some good husband's home, a happy wife,
     As I would have you?" Then I'd answer you,
     Stroking your beard, the beard that I touch now,
     "What shall I do for you, O father mine?
885   Welcome you, a loved guest, in my own house,
     Pay you for all your nursing-care of me?
     Oh, I remember every word we said,
     But you forget them, and you wish my death.
     Have pity, for your father Atreus' sake
890   And for my mother's; she has suffered once
     When I was born, and she must suffer now.
     What can I have to do with Helen's love?
     How is it she has come to ruin me?
     My father, look at me, and kiss me once,
895   That I may take this memory at least
     Unto the grave with me, if I must die.

———

30. Hermione: daughter of Menelaus and Helen.

31. Orpheus: the great musician and poet in Greek mythology.

(She turns to the child ORESTES.)

O, brother, you are young to help your friends,
Yet come and cry with me, kneel down and pray
For your poor sister's life. O father, see!
900   Even children understand when sorrow comes!
He asks for mercy though he cannot speak;
Yes, we two children touch your beard and pray,
We, your grown daughter and your little son.
Now will I gather all prayers into one
905   And that must conquer. Life is sweet, is sweet!
The dead have nothing. Those who wish to die
Are out of reason. Life, the worst of lives,
Is better than the proudest death can be!

LEADER OF THE CHORUS. Accursed Helen! Through your love and
        you
910   Torture has come upon this royal house!

AGAMEMNON. I know the touch of pity, know it well:
I love my children,—I am no madman, wife.
It is a fearful thing to do this deed,
Yet fearful not to do it: I am bound.

(He turns to IPHIGENIA.)

915   You see this host of ships and mail-clad men,—
They cannot reach the towers of Ilium,[32]
They cannot take the far-famed steep of Troy,
Unless I sacrifice you as he bids,
Calchas, the prophet. And our Greeks are hot
920   To smite the foe, nor let them steal our wives.
If I refuse the Goddess, they will come
To Argos, kill your sisters, you and me!
I am no slave of Menelaus, child;
I do not bow to him, I bow to Hellas,
925   As bow I must, whether I will or no.
She is the greater. For her we live, my child,
To guard her freedom. Foreigners must not rule
Our land, nor tear our women from their homes.

                                    He goes out to the camp.

CLYTEMNESTRA. O, my child! O, my friends!
930   You must die! You must die!
Your father has fled,
He has flung you to death!

---

32. Ilium: Troy.

IPHIGENIA. Mother, mother! O, mourn with me!
  The daylight has died,
935 I have lost the light of the sun!

(*She flings herself in her mother's arms.*)

CHORUS (*singing*). Far snow-bound glens of Phrygia's lonely moun-
    tains,
  Where Priam's babe[33] was left, left by his father,
  Cast out to die, hapless unmothered boy,
  Paris the shepherd-lad, born prince of Troy!
940 Would he had died there, left lone by his father,
  Lone by the lake-side, the nymph-haunted fountains,
  Meadows of hyacinth, starry with roses
  The goddesses gather!
  Pallas came, Hera came, came Beauty's queen,—
945 Hermes the messenger led,—
  Pallas, proud of her lance,
  Hera, vaunting the royal bed,
  Beauty, guile-hearted, waked love with her glance.
  Ah, the prize, fraught with hate,
950 For Beauty's lovely head!

IPHIGENIA. Fraught with my fate, for the glory of Greece.

LEADER OF THE CHORUS. Artemis orders your sacrifice,
  Maiden, for Ilium.

IPHIGENIA (*chanting*). Mother, my father has gone,
955 Left me, betrayed and alone!
  I have seen Helen, her face was death.
  And I am hunted to my doom,
  A cruel doom, by a cruel father.
  O that they never had come,
960 The bronze-beaked, pine-oared ships,
  To the shores of Aulis Bay!
  O that God had not sent
  Contrary winds on the sea,
  Gentle breezes for some,
965 Sailing and harbor for some,
  Sorrow and doom for us!
  Yes, we are children of sorrow, of sorrow, who live for the space
    of a day:
  Trouble must rise up afresh for the race of man evermore
  Helen, O Helen, the woe thou hast wrought, the grief and the
    suffering!

------

33. **Priam's babe:** When Paris was a baby, he was sent away by his father, Priam, to live with a shepherd because Priam had learned from an oracle that his son would bring about the ruin of Troy.

970   LEADER OF THE CHORUS. I pity you and your unhappy fate.
Alas, it never should have come on you!

ACHILLES *enters with a small band of armed men.*

IPHIGENIA. O mother, mother! Armed men are coming here!

CLYTEMNESTRA. Our friend the hero, child, for whom you came.

IPHIGENIA. Open the door! Quick! Let me hide myself.

CLYTEMNESTRA. Why so?

975   IPHIGENIA.   I cannot meet Achilles now.

CLYTEMNESTRA. Why not, I pray you?

IPHIGENIA.   My marriage—I am shamed.

CLYTEMNESTRA. No time this for such whimsies! Stay here, girl!
Let all pride go, if only—

ACHILLES.   Leda's child!
Daughter of sorrow.

CLYTEMNESTRA.   Sorrow? True enough!

980   ACHILLES. A cry goes through the army, a dread cry.

CLYTEMNESTRA. What for?

ACHILLES.   Your daughter—

CLYTEMNESTRA.   O, that means worst!

ACHILLES. It means her murder.

CLYTEMNESTRA.   No man took her part?

ACHILLES. I did: I faced their mob.

CLYTEMNESTRA.   What did they do?

ACHILLES. Do? Tried to stone me.

CLYTEMNESTRA.   Because you'd save my girl?

ACHILLES. Even so.

985   CLYTEMNESTRA.   Who'd dare to lay a hand on you?

ACHILLES. Who? All the army.

CLYTEMNESTRA.   You had your Myrmidons?

ACHILLES. The first to turn against me.

CLYTEMNESTRA.   Child, we are lost!

ACHILLES. They called me lovesick, sneered—

CLYTEMNESTRA.   You answered them?

ACHILLES. No slaughter for my bride!

CLYTEMNESTRA.   You answered well.

ACHILLES. Her father promised me—

990   CLYTEMNESTRA.   Brought her from Argos.

ACHILLES. But I was shouted down—

CLYTEMNESTRA.   The cursed mob!

ACHILLES. Yet I will save you.

CLYTEMNESTRA.   One man against a host?

ACHILLES. You see these men-at-arms behind me?

CLYTEMNESTRA.   Ay!
    Now bless you for your thought!

ACHILLES.   And blest we shall be.

995   CLYTEMNESTRA. There's hope then, and my girl need not be slain?

ACHILLES. Not while I live.

CLYTEMNESTRA.   They come to seize her here?

ACHILLES. Ten thousand strong: Odysseus leads them.

CLYTEMNESTRA.   He?
    That son of Sisyphus?

ACHILLES.   The very man.

CLYTEMNESTRA. Self-chosen was he, or elected? Which?

ACHILLES. Why, both at once.

1000   CLYTEMNESTRA.   Elected murderers!

ACHILLES. I'll keep him off.

CLYTEMNESTRA.   Ah, would he drag the girl
    Against her will?

ACHILLES.   What else can you expect?
    Seizing those long fair tresses.

CLYTEMNESTRA.   O, and I?
    What can I do?

ACHILLES.   Hold her, and hold her fast.

1005   CLYTEMNESTRA. O God, if that can save her, she is safe!

ACHILLES. It's come to that now.

IPHIGENIA.   Mother, let me speak!

This anger with my father is in vain,
Vain to use force for what we cannot win.
Thank our brave friend for all his generous zeal,
1010 But never let us broil[34] him with the host,
No gain to us, and ruin for himself.
I have been thinking, mother,—hear me now!—
I have chosen death: it is my own free choice.
I have put cowardice away from me.
1015 Honor is mine now. O, mother, say I am right!
Our country—think, our Hellas—looks to me,
On me the fleet hangs now, the doom of Troy,
Our women's honor all the years to come.
My death will save them, and my name be blest,
1020 She who freed Hellas! Life is not so sweet
I should be craven. You who bore your child,
It was for Greece you bore her, not yourself.
Think! Thousands of our soldiers stand to arms,
Ten thousand man the ships, and all on fire
1025 To serve their outraged country, die for Greece:
And is my one poor life to hinder all?
Could we defend that? Could we call it just?
And, mother, think! How could we let our friend
Die for a woman, fighting all his folk?
1030 A thousand women are not worth one man!
The goddess needs my blood: can I refuse?
No: take it, conquer Troy! This shall be
My husband, and my children, and my fame.
Victory, mother, victory for the Greeks!
1035 The foreigner must never rule this land,
Our own land! They are slaves and we are free.

LEADER OF THE CHORUS. O maiden, all is generous in your heart,
But fortune and the goddess are to blame.

ACHILLES. Agamemnon's daughter, I had been thrice blest
1040 If you could be my bride. Hellas and you,
Ye are happy in each other! All your words
Are grandly spoken, worthy of your land.
I see your nature now, see what you are,
And thirst to win you, soul of nobleness!
1045 Come, I would help you, serve you all I can,
And take you to my home. I count it ill,
By Thetis! if I may not fight the Greeks
And save you. Think; death is a fearful thing.

---

34. broil: embroil, throw into disorder.

IPHIGENIA. I will say one word, without fear of shame.
1050   The face of Helen has roused war enough,
    Battles of men and murders. O my friend,
    Die not because of me, slay none for me.
    Let me save Hellas if I have the power.

ACHILLES. O glorious heart! What is there I can say
1055   Against your purpose? O, your soul is great!
    Why should I not speak truth? Yet, none the less,
    For it may be this thought of yours will change,
    Hear what I have resolved. I will go hence,
    And set my men about the altar's side,
1060   That I may save you, and not let you die.
    Even you may find a meaning in my words
    When the sharp steel is close upon your neck.
    Your rashness must not bring you to your death.
    These men of mine shall take their stand with me
1065   Hard by the temple, and await you there.

ACHILLES goes out.

IPHIGENIA. Mother, why are you weeping silently?

CLYTEMNESTRA. Have I not cause enough to be heart-sick?

IPHIGENIA. Hush! Do not weaken me; grant what I ask.

CLYTEMNESTRA. Ask on, my child; I cannot do you wrong.

1070 IPHIGENIA. I would not have you cut your hair for me
    Nor wear black raiment—

CLYTEMNESTRA.   What is it you say?
    When you are lost—

IPHIGENIA.   O, never speak like that!
    I am saved, saved! You will be proud of me.

CLYTEMNESTRA. I must not mourn?

IPHIGENIA.   No place for mourning here,
    No tomb.

1075 CLYTEMNESTRA. Surely the slain have burial?

IPHIGENIA. The holy altar is my monument.

CLYTEMNESTRA. I will obey you, child; your words are good.

IPHIGENIA. My lot is good, and I do good to Greece.

CLYTEMNESTRA. What shall I tell your sisters of all this?

1080 IPHIGENIA. Ah, do not dress them, either, in black robes!

CLYTEMNESTRA. Shall I not take some message to the girls,
    Some loving word from you?

IPHIGENIA.   Yes, my farewell.
And Orestes—O, take care of him for me,
And bring him up to manhood.

CLYTEMNESTRA.   Hold him now,
1085   Draw him to you, look your last look on him.

IPHIGENIA (*to* ORESTES). Darling, you gave me all the help you
     could.

CLYTEMNESTRA. Is there no more that I can do to please you?

IPHIGENIA. O, hate him not,—my father, and your husband!

CLYTEMNESTRA. He has an evil course to run for you.

1090 IPHIGENIA. He offers me to Greece against his will.

CLYTEMNESTRA. By treachery, unworthy of his house.

IPHIGENIA. Who will go with me, lead me to the place,
Before they drag me thither by the hair?

CLYTEMNESTRA. I will, beside you.

IPHIGENIA.   No . . . it is not fit.

CLYTEMNESTRA. Clutching your garments.

1095 IPHIGENIA.   Listen, mother dear.
Stay here; that is far better for us both.
One of my father's men will go with me
To the field of Artemis, where I must die.

CLYTEMNESTRA. Child, are you going?

IPHIGENIA.   Yes, I will not come back.

CLYTEMNESTRA. You leave your mother?

1100 IPHIGENIA.   Yes, not as I would.

CLYTEMNESTRA. O, leave me not!

             CLYTEMNESTRA *falls fainting and is carried into the tent.*

IPHIGENIA.   I will not shed a tear.

(*She turns to the women.*)

Now sing the paean for my destiny!
Sing to the child of Zeus, to Artemis;
Let the glad sound be heard by all the Greeks.
1105   Let them lift up the baskets, light the fire,
And fling the barley; bid my father come
And touch the altar. I will bring this day
Victory and salvation unto Greece.

Follow me now, the victor,
1110   Follow the taker of Troy!

Crown my head with a garland,
Wash my hands for the rite.
Dance!
On to the shrine of the Maiden,
1115 Artemis the blest!
She calls me, and I,
I come as the victim, I give my blood,
Fulfill the seer's command.

LEADER OF THE CHORUS. O sovereign Lady, O Queen and Mother,
1120 Now we may give you our tears.
No tears must be shed at the rite.

IPHIGENIA. Sing, O sing unto Artemis,
Queen of the Aulis-land
And the harbor-mouth,
1125 Where the swords are athirst for me.
Farewell Pelasgia, motherland of mine!
Farewell my nurse, Mycenae!

LEADER OF THE CHORUS. You call on the city where Perseus[35]
    dwelt,
Where the Cyclops built the walls?

1130 IPHIGENIA. You bare me for a light to Greece.
In death I will remember you.

LEADER OF THE CHORUS. Ah, your glory will not die!

IPHIGENIA. Hail! All hail!
Torch-bearer! Giver of brightness! Day!
1135 O flame of God! I leave you, I go
To another life, to another world!
Dear sunlight, farewell, farewell!

IPHIGENIA *goes out, with one attendant, followed by the*
    CHORUS *chanting solemnly.*

CHORUS. Behold!
Behold the conqueror of Troy!
1140 She is crowned and made pure for a goddess's joy.
She goes to the dead.
Her white neck pierced, her blood running red.

The lustral waters wait,
Her father and the army wait
1145 For the wind that shall waft them to high-towered Troy.
Come, let us call on Artemis,
Goddess of all gods great,

---

35. Perseus: the Greek hero who founded Argos.

Virgin, huntress and queen,
That she bless them in this!

1150 O Maiden, glad of maiden's blood,
Send our Greeks like a flood on the treacherous town!
Let their leader be crowned by his warriors' spears
For the glory of Greece
With undying renown,
1155 Unforgotten throughout the years.

EPILOGUE[36]

Enter a MESSENGER.

MESSENGER. Daughter of Tyndarus, Clytemnestra, Queen,
Come from the tent and listen to my tidings.

CLYTEMNESTRA. I hear your voice and come, but come in dread,
Trembling and shattered, fearful of more woe
And I have woes enough.

1160 MESSENGER.   My tidings, queen,
Are of your daughter, strange and marvelous.

CLYTEMNESTRA. O, tell me, tell me! Make no more delay!

MESSENGER. Dear mistress, I will tell you everything
From first to last, unless my tongue should stumble
1165 Through my heart's haste. Soon as we reached the grove
And flowered fields of Artemis the blest
Where lay the host, bringing the maid with us,
Straightway they flocked about us. And the king,
Seeing his daughter coming for her death,
1170 Groaned bitterly and turned his head away
Holding his cloak to hide the falling tears.
But she came up and stood beside him, saying,
"My father, I am here, to give my life
Willingly for my country, for our Greece.
1175 Now lead me to the altar of the goddess
And sacrifice me as the seer bids.
For me, I pray now for your victory
And safe return unto our native land.
Therefore let no man lay a hand on me.
1180 I will stand quietly; I will not flinch."
Such were her words and all the army wondered
At her great heart. And then the herald rose,
Stood in the midst, calling aloud for silence
And Calchas took the golden basket up,

---

36. **Epilogue:** It is the translator's opinion that Euripides concluded his work with the departure of
Iphigenia to the sacrificial altar and that the epilogue is a later addition written to make the
play conform with the version of the legend Euripides relied on in his *Iphigenia in Tauris*.

1185	Laying the sharp sword naked in the barley,
	And crowned the maiden. Then Achilles came,
	Lifted the basket, sprinkling all the shrine,
	And made libation, crying, "Artemis,
	Daughter of Zeus and huntress, queen of shades,
1190	Guiding the light in darkness, now receive
	The victim that we soldiers bring to thee,
	The Achaean army and their lord and king,
	This unstained body of a perfect maid.
	And may there be no failing of the fleet:
1195	Send us to Troy and let us take the town."
	He spoke and all the host stood motionless,
	Their eyes fixed on the ground. And the priest prayed,
	Lifting the knife and gazing at her neck
	To see where he should strike. Then my heart failed me,
1200	I dropped my eyes, when lo, a sudden wonder!
	All might have heard the thud, but no man saw
	Where the maid vanished. Calchas cried aloud
	And all the army, marking a miracle,
	Unhoped-for, not to be believed, though seen.
1205	A panting hind lay in the victim's place,
	Most beautiful, and deer's blood stained the altar.
	Think of the joy for Calchas! He turned and cried,
	"Lords of the Argives and this gathered host,
	Behold the victim that the goddess chose
1210	For her own altar, a wild doe of the hills.
	She will not stain her shrine with generous blood,
	Gladly she takes the substitute and grants
	Passage to you and swift attack on Troy.
	Now let all sailors' hearts be high and now
1215	Go to the ships. For on this very day
	We leave the Aulis hollows for the sea
	And cross the open waters." Then they burned
	The sacrifice to ashes and all prayed
	For safe return. The king has sent me here
1220	To tell you of the lot the gods have given
	Unto your daughter and her deathless fame.
	And I who saw it tell you. She has risen
	Straight to the gods. So shall you lay aside
	Your grief and all your anger with your lord.
1225	The ways of the gods no mortal can foresee:
	They save the souls they love. And this one day
	Has known your daughter's death, your daughter's life.

LEADER OF THE CHORUS. O, joy has filled us now we hear these
    tidings!
Your daughter lives, he tells us, with the gods.

1230 CLYTEMNESTRA. Stolen, my child, by the gods?
       What gods?
       Where shall I call you?
       What shall I say?
       An idle story to cheat my sorrow!

1235 LEADER OF THE CHORUS. And here Lord Agamemnon comes him-
         self
       To tell you the same tale.

                      Enter AGAMEMNON *from the camp.*

AGAMEMNON.   Glad may we be,
       Wife, for our daughter, she is with the gods.
       Now take this youngling steer, and home again.
       The army looks to sea. Farewell. From Troy
1240   I will send word. May all go well with you.

     CHORUS. Rejoice, O king, go forth in joy,
       In joy return to us, bringing rich booty,
       Home again from captured Troy.

DISCUSSION QUESTIONS

1. If you have read Aeschylus' play, *The House of Atreus*, discuss how your impressions of Agamemnon and Clytemnestra differ in this play. Which of these two characters do you tend to side with in Euripides' play? Why?

2. Euripides' plays often present characters that are torn by inner conflicts. At one point in the play, the chorus acknowledges this human tendency by chanting: "The ways of man are many, and changeful all their fashion" (line 338). Which of the main characters in *Iphigenia in Aulis* are "changeful" about the sacrifice of Iphigenia? Are there any characters that never change their minds about this proposed deed?

3. Early in the play Menelaus suggests that Agamemnon give up his plan to sacrifice Iphigenia and call off the whole military plan. Agamemnon, however, responds by saying that he is "compelled to that dread slaughter now." What reasons does he give for pursuing this plan? What other, unspoken motives does he have? What do these motives suggest about his character?

4. What details about Clytemnestra's past relationship with Agamemnon are revealed in this play? What effect is this new knowledge likely to have on the audience?

5. At first Iphigenia pleads for her life, but she later changes her mind and willingly offers herself as a sacrifice. How do you account for this change?

6. Euripides often takes characters who are traditionally shown as great heroes and lowers them to a more human level. Agamemnon's human failings have already been discussed. How does Euripides humanize the other Greek hero of the Trojan War, Achilles?

7. Euripides makes frequent references to the legendary cause of the Trojan War—the beauty contest among the three goddesses and Paris' relationship with Helen—even though his Greek audience already knew the story. Why do you think the author refers to these past events so often in the course of the play?

SUGGESTION FOR WRITING

Euripides often creates characters who delude themselves into thinking that they are motivated by high moral principles when they are actually motivated by personal desires. Select a character from *Iphigenia in Aulis* who you think might be deluded in this way. Pretend that you are a respected psychologist who is writing a letter to that character in hopes of stopping the sacrifice of Iphigenia. Explain to your chosen character what you think his or her true motives are. End your letter with some constructive advice.

THE GREEK ANTHOLOGY

The Greek Anthology is a collection of about four thousand poems covering a wide variety of themes, moods, styles, and poetic forms. The poems were written between the seventh century B.C. and the tenth century A.D., when they were first collected by a Byzantine scholar. The eight short poems that appear below all deal with the subject of death or loss. Even for a subject as serious as this one, however, the poems exhibit an amazing variety of moods, ranging from humorous to bitterly somber. ■

Anonymous

A GRAVESTONE AT CORINTH

Translated by Kenneth Rexroth

This little stone, dear Sabinos,
Is all the memorial
Of our great love. I miss you
Always, and I hope that you
5   Did not drink forgetfulness
Of me when you drank the waters
Of death[1] with the new dead.

Antipatros (1st or 2nd century B.C.)

NEVER AGAIN, ORPHEUS

Translated by Kenneth Rexroth

Never again, Orpheus,[2]
Will you lead the enchanted oaks,
Nor the rocks, nor the beasts
That are their own masters.
5   Never again will you sing to sleep
The roaring wind, nor the hail,
Nor the drifting snow, nor the boom

---

1. **the waters of death:** Upon entering the Underworld, the dead drank from the river Lethe, which caused them to forget their former lives.

2. **Orpheus:** son of the muse Calliope and a king of Thrace, the greatest poet and musician in Greek legend. He was given the lyre by Apollo and played so beautifully that the beasts and even the rocks and trees danced to his music.

Of the sea wave.
You are dead now.
10   Led by your mother, Calliope,
The Muses shed many tears
Over you for a long time.
What good does it do us to mourn
For our sons when the immortal
15   Gods are powerless to save
Their own children from death?

WHERE IS YOUR FAMOUS BEAUTY?

Translated by Kenneth Rexroth

Where is your famous beauty,
Corinth[3] of the Dorians?[4]
Where is your crown of towers?
Where are your ancient treasures?
5   Where are the temples of the
Immortals, and where are the
Houses and the wives of the
Lineage of Sisyphos,[5]
All your myriad people?
10   Most unhappy city, not
A trace is left of you. War[6]
Has seized and eaten it all.
Only the inviolate
Sea nymphs, the daughters of the
15   Ocean,[7] remain, crying like
Sea birds over your sorrows.

Nikarchos (1ˢᵗ century A.D.)

A PHYSICIAN'S TOUCH

Translated by Willis Barnstone

Only yesterday the good Dr. Markos
laid his sure hand on a statue of Zeus.
Although he was Zeus and made of marble
we're burying him today.

---

3. **Corinth:** an ancient city in southern Greece.

4. **Dorians:** one of the traditional branches of the Greek people. They invaded southern Greece about 1100 B.C.

5. **Sisyphos:** traditional founder of Corinth.

6. **War:** Corinth was destroyed by the Romans in 146 B.C. It was rebuilt by Julius Caesar in 46 B.C.

7. **Ocean:** the eldest of the Titans, the father of all the river-gods and sea-nymphs.

Praxilla (5th century B.C.)

OF THE SENSUAL WORLD
Translated by Willis Barnstone

> Most beautiful of things I leave is sunlight;
> then come glazing stars and the moon's face;
> then ripe cucumbers and apples and pears.

Solon (640 B.C.–560 B.C.)

TEN AGES IN THE LIFE OF MAN
Translated by Willis Barnstone

> A boy who is still a child grows baby teeth
>   and loses them all in seven years.
> When God makes him fourteen, the signs of
>   maturity begin to shine on his body.
> 5   In the third seven, limbs growing, chin bearded,
>   his skin acquires the color of manhood.
> In the fourth age a man is at a peak in
>   strength—a sign in man of excellence.
> The time is ripe in the fifth for a young man
> 10   to think of marriage and of offspring.
> In the sixth the mind of man is trained in all
>   things; he doesn't try the impossible.
> In the seventh and eighth, that is, fourteen years,
>   he speaks most eloquently in his life.
> 15   He can still do much in the ninth but his speech
>   and thought are discernibly less keen;
> and if he makes the full measure of ten sevens,
>   when death comes, it will not come too soon.

Semonides (556 B.C.–468 B.C.)

THE DARKNESS OF HUMAN LIFE
Translated by Willis Barnstone

> My child, deep-thundering Zeus controls the end
> of all that is, disposing as he wills.
> We who are mortals have no mind; we live like cattle,
> day to day, knowing nothing of god's plans
> 5   to end each one of us. Yet we are fed
> by hope and faith to dream impossible plans.
> Some wait for a day to come, others watch
> the turning of years. No one among the mortals
> feels so broken as not to hope in coming time
> 10   to fly home rich to splendid goods and lands.

Yet before he makes his goal, odious old age
lays hold of him first. Appalling disease
consumes another. Some are killed in war
where death carries them under the dark earth.

15 Some drown and die under the myriad waves
when a hurricane slams across the blue salt water
cracking their cargo ship. Others rope a noose
around their wretched necks and choose to die,
abandoning the sun of day. A thousand black spirits

20 waylay man with unending grief and suffering.
If you listen to my counsel, you won't want
the good things of life; nor batter your heart
by torturing your skull with cold remorse.

Anonymous

THE LAST UTTERANCE OF THE DELPHIC ORACLE

Translated by Kenneth Rexroth

*Apollo's shrine at Delphi was the home of the most famous oracle in Greece
and drew pilgrims from all over the Mediterranean world. (See article on page
xiii.) The oracle's power waned after the coming of Christianity. Julian the
Apostate (A.D. 331–363) attempted to restore the influence of the oracle as
part of his revival of paganism, but received in response to his efforts "The
Last Utterance" given below.*

Go tell the King: The daedal[8]
Walls have fallen to the earth
Phoibos[9] has no sanctuary,
No prophetic laurel, no

5 Speaking spring. The garrulous
Water has dried up at last.

———

8. daedal: skillfully made.

9. Phoibos: Apollo in his aspect as sun-god.

DISCUSSION QUESTIONS

1. Most of these poems were written over 2,000 years ago. In what way
are they relevant to readers of today? What details mark them as
ancient poems?

2. Verses on tombstones are not intended for publication, but they
sometimes become famous if they are moving or amusing. Why do
you think the engraving on the Corinthian tomb ("A Gravestone at
Corinth") gained fame as a poem?

3. In what ways do the two poems "Never Again, Orpheus" and "Where Is Your Famous Beauty?" share the same attitude toward their subject?

4. In "A Physician's Touch," the poet describes the doctor's hand as a "sure hand"? What does the term "sure hand" usually mean? What does it mean in this poem?

5. In the poem titled "Of the Sensual World," Praxilla offers six images that characterize her view of the world as she prepares to leave it. How are the three images in the last line different from the previous images? What is the effect of this unusual combination of images? How would you describe the general mood of this poem?

6. "Ten Ages in the Life of Man" reveals a great deal about social expectations in ancient Greece. What was the expected age for marriage for men? What types of skills were most valued? What was the average age of death, according to Solon?

7. The word *hope* is used twice in Semonides' poem, "The Darkness of Human Life." What is the poet's attitude toward hope? Why does he feel this way?

8. How would you describe the mood of "The Last Utterance of the Delphic Oracle"? Would you say that the poet is pleased or sorry that the oracle's shrine is gone?

SUGGESTION FOR WRITING

Select a poem from this collection that presents a positive view of human existence and one that presents a negative view. Compare the ways in which the two poets try to persuade the reader to share their views. (For instance, what aspects of life does each poet focus on? What images and details are used to influence the reader's responses?)

HERODOTUS

(c. 484–c. 424 b.c.)

Herodotus is usually credited with being the "father of history," and probably no man was better qualified to write about events and individuals than he was. Intensely interested in the customs and ideas of all people, he traveled widely, observing, listening, weighing evidence, and carefully trying to separate fact from fiction. He was a born investigator and was the first person to use the Greek word *historia*, which means "inquiry," to describe his activities. Skeptical and careful in his method, Herodotus was also kind, tolerant, and about as unprejudiced as a person could be, neither rejecting practices just because they were foreign nor accepting practices just because they were familiar. His historical accounts are fascinating mixtures of anecdotes, observations on social and religious customs, and speculations about the thoughts and feelings of important historical figures.

Very little is known about Herodotus' own life, beyond the fact that he was born in Halicarnassus in Asia Minor and traveled to Mesopotamia, Babylon, Persia, Greece, and probably Egypt. His only work to survive is his history of the struggle of Greece to maintain its freedom against the powerful Persian invaders who wished to enslave them. The selection that follows is part of that work. ■

from THE HISTORY

Translated by George Rawlinson

On the death of Alyattes, Croesus,[1] his son, who was thirty-five years old, succeeded to the throne. Of the Greek cities,[2] Ephesus was the first that he attacked. The Ephesians, when he laid siege to the place, made an offering of their city to Diana, by stretching a rope from the town wall to the temple of the goddess, which was distant from the ancient city, then besieged by Croesus, a space of seven furlongs. They were, as I said, the first Greeks whom he attacked. Afterwards, on some pretext or other, he made war in turn upon every Ionian and Aeolian state, bringing forward, where he could, a substantial ground of complaint; where such failed him, advancing some poor excuse.

   In this way he made himself master of all the Greek cities in Asia, and forced them to become his tributaries; after which he began to think of building ships, and attacking the islanders. Everything had been got ready for this purpose, when Bias of Priêné, or as some say, Pittacus the Mytilenean, put a stop to the project. The king had made inquiry of this

---

1. **Croesus:** (c. 595–546 b.c.), king of Lydia, a country in Asia Minor.

2. **Greek cities:** Many cities of Asia Minor were founded by Greek colonists.

person, who was lately arrived at Sardis,[3] if there were any news from Greece; to which he answered, "Yes, sire, the islanders are gathering ten thousand horses, designing an expedition against thee and against thy capital." Croesus, thinking he spake seriously, broke out, "Ah, might the gods put such a thought into their minds as to attack the sons of the Lydians with cavalry!" "It seems, oh! king," rejoined the other, "that thou desirest earnestly to catch the islanders on horseback upon the mainland,—thou knowest well what would come of it. But what thinkest thou the islanders desire better, now that they hear thou art about to build ships and sail against them, than to catch the Lydians at sea, and there revenge on them the wrongs of their brothers upon the mainland, whom thou holdest in slavery?" Croesus was charmed with the turn of the speech; and thinking there was reason in what was said, gave up his shipbuilding and concluded a league of amity with the Ionians of the isles.

Croesus afterwards, in the course of many years, brought under his sway almost all the nations to the west of the Halys.[4] The Lycians and Cilicians alone continued free; all the other tribes he reduced and held in subjection. They were the following: the Lydians, Phrygians, Mysians, Mariandynians, Chalybians, Paphlagonians, Thynians and Bithynians, Thracians, Carians, Ionians, Dorians, Aeolians and Pamphylians.[5]

When all these conquests had been added to the Lydian empire, and the prosperity of Sardis was now at its height, there came thither, one after another, all the sages of Greece living at the time, and among them Solon,[6] the Athenian. He was on his travels, having left Athens to be absent ten years, under the pretense of wishing to see the world, but really to avoid being forced to repeal any of the laws which, at the request of the Athenians, he had made for them. Without his sanction the Athenians could not repeal them, as they had bound themselves under a heavy curse to be governed for ten years by the laws which should be imposed on them by Solon.

On this account, as well as to see the world, Solon set out upon his travels, in the course of which he went to Egypt to the court of Amasis, and also came on a visit to Croesus at Sardis. Croesus received him as his guest, and lodged him in the royal palace. On the third or fourth day after, he bade his servants conduct Solon over his treasuries, and show him all their greatness and magnificence. When he had seen them all, and, so far as time allowed, inspected them, Croesus addressed this question to him. "Stranger of Athens, we have heard much of thy wisdom and of thy travels through many lands, from love of knowledge and a

---

3. **Sardis:** capital of Lydia.

4. **the Halys:** a river of Asia Minor, now called Kizil Irmik.

5. **Lydians . . . Pamphylians:** peoples of Asia Minor and its adjacent islands.

6. **Solon:** Athenian statesman and poet (c. 638–559 B.C.). Since Croesus did not become king until 560 B.C., by which time Solon had long since returned from his travels, the story of his interview with Solon is probably fictional.

wish to see the world. I am curious therefore to inquire of thee, whom, of all the men that thou hast seen, thou deemest the most happy?" This he asked because he thought himself the happiest of mortals: but Solon answered him without flattery, according to his true sentiments, "Tellus of Athens, sire." Full of astonishment at what he heard, Croesus demanded sharply, "And wherefore dost thou deem Tellus happiest?" To which the other replied, "First, because his country was flourishing in his days, and he himself had sons both beautiful and good, and he lived to see children born to each of them, and these children all grew up; and further because, after a life spent in what our people look upon as comfort, his end was surpassingly glorious. In a battle between the Athenians and their neighbors near Eleusis, he came to the assistance of his countrymen, routed the foe, and died upon the field most gallantly. The Athenians gave him a public funeral on the spot where he fell, and paid him the highest honors."

Thus did Solon admonish Croesus by the example of Tellus, enumerating the manifold particulars of his happiness. When he had ended, Croesus inquired a second time, who after Tellus seemed to him the happiest, expecting that at any rate, he would be given the second place. "Cleobis and Bito," Solon answered; "they were of Argive race;[7] their fortune was enough for their wants, and they were besides endowed with so much bodily strength that they had both gained prizes at the Games. Also this tale is told of them:—There was a great festival in honor of the goddess Juno at Argos, to which their mother must needs be taken in a car. Now the oxen did not come home from the field in time: so the youths, fearful of being too late, put the yoke on their own necks, and themselves drew the car in which their mother rode. Five and forty furlongs did they draw her, and stopped before the temple. This deed of theirs was witnessed by the whole assembly of worshippers, and then their life closed in the best possible way. Herein, too, God showed forth most evidently, how much better a thing for man death is than life. For the Argive men, who stood around the car, extolled the vast strength of the youths; and the Argive women extolled the mother who was blessed with such a pair of sons; and the mother herself, overjoyed at the deed and at the praises it had won, standing straight before the image, besought the goddess to bestow on Cleobis and Bito, the sons who had so mightily honored her, the highest blessing to which mortals can attain. Her prayer ended, they offered sacrifice and partook of the holy banquet, after which the two youths fell asleep in the temple. They never woke more, but so passed from the earth. The Argives, looking on them as among the best of men, caused statues of them to be made, which they gave to the shrine at Delphi."

When Solon had thus assigned these youths the second place, Croesus broke in angrily, "What, stranger of Athens, is my happiness, then, so

---

7. **Argive race:** the Greeks of Argolis, a district of the Peloponnesus Peninsula in southern Greece.

utterly set at nought by thee, that thou dost not even put me on a level with private men?"

"Oh! Croesus," replied the other, "thou askedst a question concerning the condition of man, of one who knows that the power above us is full of jealousy, and fond of troubling our lot. A long life gives one to witness much, and experience much oneself, that one would not choose. Seventy years I regard as the limit of the life of man. In these seventy years are contained, without reckoning intercalary months,[8] twenty-five thousand and two hundred days. Add an intercalary month to every other year, that the seasons may come round at the right time, and there will be, besides the seventy years, thirty-five such months, making an addition of one thousand and fifty days. The whole number of the days contained in the seventy years will thus be twenty-six thousand two hundred and fifty, whereof not one but will produce events unlike the rest. Hence man is wholly accident. For thyself, oh! Croesus, I see that thou art wonderfully rich, and art the lord of many nations; but with respect to that whereon thou questionest me, I have no answer to give, until I hear that thou hast closed thy life happily. For assuredly he who possesses great store of riches is no nearer happiness than he who has what suffices for his daily needs, unless it so hap that luck attend upon him, and so he continue in the enjoyment of all his good things to the end of life. For many of the wealthiest men have been unfavored of fortune, and many whose means were moderate have had excellent luck. Men of the former class excel those of the latter but in two respects; these last excel the former in many. The wealthy man is better able to content his desires, and to bear up against a sudden buffet of calamity. The other has less ability to withstand these evils, from which, however, his good luck keeps him clear, but he enjoys all these following blessings: he is whole of limb, a stranger to disease, free from misfortune, happy in his children, and comely to look upon. If, in addition to all this, he end his life well, he is of a truth the man of whom thou art in search, the man who may rightly be termed happy. Call him, however, until he die, not happy but fortunate. Scarcely, indeed, can any man unite all these advantages: as there is no country which contains within it all that it needs, but each, while it possesses some things, lacks others, and the best country is that which contains the most; so no single human being is complete in every respect—something is always lacking. He who unites the greatest number of advantages, and retaining them to the day of his death, then dies peaceably, that man alone, sire, is, in my judgment, entitled to bear the name of 'happy.' But in every matter it behooves us to mark well the end: for oftentimes God gives men a gleam of happiness, and then plunges them into ruin."

---

8. **intercalary months:** The ancient Greeks reckoned time in terms of lunar months and solar years. Very early they realized that while twelve of these months were approximately equal to one solar year—354 or 355 days compared to 365¼—the difference was sufficient to cause their calendar to be about three months short in a period of eight years. To correct this, they began the practice of putting the years in groups of eight and inserting three extra months.

Such was the speech which Solon addressed to Croesus, a speech which brought him neither largess nor honor. The king saw him depart with much indifference, since he thought that a man must be an arrant fool who made no account of present good, but bade men always wait and mark the end.

After Solon had gone away a dreadful vengeance, sent of God, came upon Croesus, to punish him, it is likely, for deeming himself the happiest of men. First he had a dream in the night which foreshowed him truly the evils that were about to befall him in the person of his son. For Croesus had two sons, one blasted by a natural defect, being deaf and dumb; the other, distinguished far above all his co-mates in every pursuit. The name of the last was Atys. It was this son concerning whom he dreamt a dream, that he would die by the blow of an iron weapon. When he woke, he considered earnestly with himself, and, greatly alarmed at the dream, instantly made his son take a wife and whereas in former years the youth had been wont to command the Lydian forces in the field, he now would not suffer him to accompany them. All the spears and javelins, and weapons used in the wars, he removed out of the male apartments, and laid them in heaps in the chambers of the women, fearing lest perhaps one of the weapons that hung against the wall might fall and strike him.

Now it chanced that while he was making arrangements for the wedding, there came to Sardis a man under a misfortune, who had upon him the stain of blood. He was by race a Phrygian, and belonged to the family of the king. Presenting himself at the palace of Croesus, he prayed to be admitted to purification according to the customs of the country. Now the Lydian method of purifying is very nearly the same as the Greek. Croesus granted the request, and went through all the customary rites, after which he asked the suppliant of his birth and country, addressing him as follows—"Who art thou, stranger, and from what part of Phrygia fleddest thou to take refuge at my hearth? And whom, moreover, what man or what woman, hast thou slain?" "Oh! king," replied the Phrygian, "I am the son of Gordias, son of Midas. I am named Adrastus. The man I unintentionally slew was my own brother. For this my father drove me from the land, and I lost all. Then fled I here to thee." "Thou art the offspring," Croesus rejoined, "of a house friendly to mine, and thou art come to friends. Thou shalt want for nothing so long as thou abidest in my dominions. Bear thy misfortune as easily as thou mayest, so will it go best with thee." Thenceforth Adrastus lived in the palace of the king.

It chanced that at this very same time there was in the Mysian Olympus a huge monster of a boar, which went forth often from this mountain-country, and wasted the corn-fields of the Mysians. Many a time had the Mysians collected to hunt the beast, but instead of doing him any hurt, they came off always with some loss to themselves. At length they sent ambassadors to Croesus, who delivered their message to him in these words: "Oh! king, a mighty monster of a boar has appeared in our parts, and destroys the labor of our hands. We do our best to take him, but in vain. Now therefore we beseech thee to let thy son accompany us back, with some chosen youths and hounds, that we may rid our country of the animal." Such was the tenor of their prayer.

But Croesus bethought him of his dream, and answered, "Say no more of my son going with you; that may not be in any wise. He is but just joined in wedlock, and is busy enough with that. I will grant you a picked band of Lydians, and all my huntsmen and hounds; and I will charge those whom I send to use all zeal in aiding you to rid your country of the brute."

With this reply the Mysians were content; but the king's son, hearing what the prayer of the Mysians was, came suddenly in, and on the refusal of Croesus to let him go with them, thus addressed his father: "Formerly, my father, it was deemed the noblest and most suitable thing for me to frequent the wars and hunting-parties, and win myself glory in them; but now thou keepest me away from both, although thou hast never beheld in me either cowardice or lack of spirit. What face meanwhile must I wear as I walk to the forum or return from it? What must the citizens, what must my young bride think of me? What sort of man will she suppose her husband to be? Either, therefore, let me go to the chase of this boar, or give me a reason why it is best for me to do according to thy wishes."

Then Croesus answered, "My son, it is not because I have seen in thee either cowardice or aught else which has displeased me that I keep thee back; but because a vision which came before me in a dream as I slept, warned me that thou wert doomed to die young, pierced by an iron weapon. It was this which first led me to hasten on thy wedding, and now it hinders me from sending thee upon this enterprise. Fain would I keep watch over thee, if by any means I may cheat fate of thee during my own lifetime. For thou art the one and only son that I possess; the other, whose hearing is destroyed, I regard as if he were not."

"Ah! father," returned the youth, "I blame thee not for keeping watch over me after a dream so terrible; but if thou mistakest, if thou dost not apprehend the dream aright, 'tis no blame for me to show thee wherein thou errest. Now the dream, thou saidst thyself, foretold that I should die stricken by an iron weapon. But what hands has a boar to strike with? What iron weapon does he wield? Yet this is what thou fearest for me. Had the dream said that I should die pierced by a tusk, then thou hadst done well to keep me away; but it said a weapon. Now here we do not combat men, but a wild animal. I pray thee, therefore, let me go with them."

"There thou hast me, my son," said Croesus, "thy interpretation is better than mine. I yield to it, and change my mind, and consent to let thee go."

Then the king sent for Adrastus, the Phrygian, and said to him, "Adrastus, when thou wert smitten with the rod of affliction—no reproach, my friend—I purified thee, and have taken thee to live with me in my palace and have been at every charge. Now, therefore, it behooves thee to requite the good offices which thou hast received at my hands by consenting to go with my son on this hunting party, and to watch over him, if perchance you should be attacked upon the road by some band of daring robbers. Even apart from this, it were right for thee to go where thou mayest make thyself famous by noble deeds. They are the heritage of thy family, and thou too art so stalwart and strong."

Adrastus answered, "Except for thy request, Oh! king, I would rather have kept away from this hunt; for methinks it ill beseems a man under a misfortune such as mine to consort with his happier compeers; and besides, I have no heart to it. On many grounds I had stayed behind; but, as thou urgest it, and I am bound to pleasure thee, for truly it does behoove me to requite thy good offices, I am content to do as thou wishest. For thy son, whom thou givest into my charge, be sure thou shalt receive him back safe and sound, so far as depends upon a guardian's carefulness."

Thus assured, Croesus let them depart, accompanied by a band of picked youths, and well provided with dogs of chase. When they reached Olympus, they scattered in quest of the animal; he was soon found, and the hunters, drawing round him in a circle, hurled their weapons at him. Then the stranger, the man who had been purified of blood, whose name was Adrastus, he also hurled his spear at the boar, but missed his aim, and struck Atys. Thus was the son of Croesus slain by the point of an iron weapon, and the warning of the vision was fulfilled. Then one ran to Sardis to bear the tidings to the king, and he came and informed him of the combat and of the fate that had befallen his son.

If it was a heavy blow to the father to learn that his child was dead, it yet more strongly affected him to think that the very man whom he himself once purified had done the deed. In the violence of his grief he called aloud on Jupiter Catharsius, to be a witness of what he had suffered at the stranger's hands. Afterwards he invoked the same god as Jupiter Ephistius and Hetaereus—using the one term because he had unwittingly harbored in his house the man who had now slain his son; and the other, because the stranger, who had been sent as his child's guardian, had turned out his most cruel enemy.

Presently the Lydians arrived, bearing the body of the youth, and behind them followed the homicide. He took his stand in front of the corpse, and, stretching forth his hands to Croesus, delivered himself into his power with earnest entreaties that he would sacrifice him upon the body of his son—"his former misfortune was burden enough; now that he had added to it a second, and had brought ruin on the man who purified him, he could not bear to live." Then Croesus, when he heard these words, was moved with pity towards Adrastus, notwithstanding the bitterness of his own calamity; and so he answered, "Enough, my friend; I have all the revenge that I require, since thou givest sentence of death against thyself. But in sooth it is not thou who hast injured me, except so far as thou hast unwittingly dealt the blow. Some god is the author of my misfortune, and I was forewarned of it a long time ago." Croesus after this buried the body of his son, with such honors as befitted the occasion. Adrastus, son of Gordias, son of Midas, the destroyer of his brother in time past, the destroyer now of his purifier, regarding himself as the most unfortunate wretch whom he had ever known, so soon as all was quiet about the place slew himself upon the tomb. Croesus, bereft of his son, gave himself up to mourning for two full years.

At the end of this time the grief of Croesus was interrupted by intelligence from abroad. He learnt that Cyrus,[9] the son of Cambyses, had destroyed the empire of Astyages, the son of Cyaxares; and that the Persians were becoming daily more powerful. This led him to consider with himself whether it were possible to check the growing power of that people before it came to a head. With this design he resolved to make instant trial of the several oracles in Greece, and of the one in Libya. So he sent his messengers in different directions, some to Delphi,[10] some to Abae in Phocis, and some to Dodôna; others to the oracle of Amphiaraüs; others to that of Trophonius; others, again, to Branchidae in Milesia. These were the Greek oracles which he consulted. To Libya he sent another embassy, to consult the oracle of Ammon. These messengers were sent to test the knowledge of the oracles, that, if they were found really to return true answers, he might send a second time, and inquire if he ought to attack the Persians.

The messengers who were dispatched to make trial of the oracles were given the following instructions: they were to keep count of the days from the time of their leaving Sardis, and, reckoning from that date, on the hundredth day they were to consult the oracles, and to inquire of them what Croesus the son of Alyattes, king of Lydia, was doing at that moment. The answers given them were to be taken down in writing, and brought back to him. None of the replies remain on record except that of the oracle at Delphi. There, the moment that the Lydians entered the sanctuary, and before they put their questions, the Pythoness[11] thus answered them in hexameter verse:—

> I can count the sands, and I can measure the ocean;
> I have ears for the silent, and know what the dumb man meaneth;
> Lo! on my sense there striketh the smell of a shell-covered tortoise,
> Boiling now on a fire, with the flesh of a lamb, in a cauldron,—
> Brass is the vessel below, and brass the cover above it.

These words the Lydians wrote down at the mouth of the Pythoness as she prophesied, and then set off on their return to Sardis. When all the messengers had come back with the answers which they had received, Croesus undid the rolls, and read what was written in each. Only one approved itself to him, that of the Delphic oracle. This he had no sooner heard than he instantly made an act of adoration, and accepted it as true,

---

9. **Cyrus:** Cyrus the Great (?–529 B.C.), who ruled Persia after he overthrew his grandfather, Astyages.

10. **Delphi:** the famous shrine of Apollo's oracle. (See article, page xiii.) The others mentioned in this paragraph are less famous oracles.

11. **the Pythoness:** the oracular priestess of Apollo at Delphi.

declaring that the Delphic was the only really oracular shrine, the only one that had discovered in what way he was in fact employed. For on the departure of his messengers he had set himself to think what was most impossible for any one to conceive of his doing, and then, waiting till the day agreed on came, he acted as he had determined. He took a tortoise and a lamb, and cutting them in pieces with his own hands, boiled them both together in a brazen cauldron, covered over with a lid which was also of brass.

Such then was the answer returned to Croesus from Delphi. What the answer was which the Lydians who went to the shrine of Amphiaraüs and performed the customary rites, obtained of the oracle there, I have it not in my power to mention, for there is no record of it. All that is known is, that Croesus believed himself to have found there also an oracle which spoke the truth.

After this Croesus, having resolved to propitiate the Delphic god with a magnificent sacrifice, offered up three thousand of every kind of sacrificial beast, and besides made a huge pile, and placed upon it couches coated with silver and with gold, and golden goblets, and robes and vests of purple; all which he burnt in the hope of thereby making himself more secure of the favor of the god. Further he issued his orders to all the people of the land to offer a sacrifice according to their means. When the sacrifice was ended, the king melted down a vast quantity of gold, and ran it into ingots, making them six palms long, three palms broad, and one palm in thickness. The number of ingots was a hundred and seventeen, four being of refined gold, in weight two talents[12] and a half; the others of pale gold, and in weight two talents. He also caused a statue of a lion to be made in refined gold, the weight of which was ten talents. At the time when the temple of Delphi was burnt to the ground, this lion fell from the ingots on which it was placed; it now stands in the Corinthian treasury, and weighs only six talents and a half, having lost three talents and a half by the fire.

On the completion of these works Croesus sent them away to Delphi, and with them two bowls of an enormous size, one of gold, the other of silver, which used to stand, the latter upon the right, the former upon the left, as one entered the temple.

The messengers who had the charge of conveying these treasures to the shrine, received instructions to ask the oracles whether Croesus should go to war with the Persians, and if so, whether he should strengthen himself by the forces of an ally. Accordingly, when they had reached their destinations and presented the gifts, they proceeded to consult the oracles in the following terms:—"Croesus, king of Lydia and other countries, believing that these are the only real oracles in all the world, has sent you such presents as your discoveries deserved, and now inquires of you whether he shall go to war with the Persians, and if so, whether he shall strengthen himself by the forces of a confederate." Both the oracles agreed

---

12. **talent:** around sixty pounds.

in the tenor of their reply, which was in each case a prophecy that if Croesus attacked the Persians, he would destroy a mighty empire, and a recommendation to him to look and see who were the most powerful of the Greeks, and to make alliance with them.

At the receipt of these oracular replies Croesus was overjoyed, and feeling sure now that he would destroy the empire of the Persians, he sent once more to Pytho, and presented to the Delphians, the number of whom he had ascertained, two gold staters[13] apiece. In return for this the Delphians granted to Croesus and the Lydians the privilege of precedency in consulting the oracle, exemption from all charges, the most honorable seat at the festivals, and the perpetual right of becoming at pleasure citizens of their town.

After sending these presents to the Delphians, Croesus a third time consulted the oracle, for having once proved its truthfulness, he wished to make the constant use of it. The question whereto he now desired an answer was—"Whether his kingdom would be of long duration?" The following was the reply of the Pythoness:—

Wait till the time shall come when a mule is monarch of Media;

Then, thou delicate Lydian, away to the pebbles of Hermus;[14]

Haste, oh! haste thee away, nor blush to behave like a coward.

Of all the answers that had reached him, this pleased him far the best, for it seemed incredible that a mule should ever come to he king of the Medes, and so he concluded that the sovereignty would never depart from himself or his seed after him. Afterwards he turned his thoughts to the alliance which he had been recommended to contract, and sought to ascertain by inquiry which was the most powerful of the Grecian states. His inquiries pointed out to him two states as pre-eminent above the rest. These were the Lacedaemonians[15] and the Athenians, the former of Doric, the latter of Ionic blood.[16]

On inquiring into the condition of these two nations, Croesus found that one, the Athenian, was in a state of grievous oppression and distraction under Pisistratus, the son of Hippocrates, who was at that time tyrant of Athens. Proceeding to seek information concerning the Lacedaemonians, he learnt that, after passing through a period of great depression, they had lately been victorious in a war with the people of Tegea.[17]

Croesus, informed of all these circumstances, sent messengers to Sparta, with gifts in their hands, who were to ask the Spartans to enter into alliance with him. They received strict injunctions as to what they should say, and on their arrival at Sparta spake as follows:—

---

13. **staters:** coins of ancient Greece and Persia.

14. **Hermus:** a river of Asia Minor upon which Sardis was located; the modern Gedis.

15. **Lacodaemonians:** the Spartans.

16. **Doric . . . Ionic blood:** The Dorians were northern tribesmen who invaded and conquered Greece about 1100 B.C., destroying the Mycenean civilization. The Ionians were earlier invaders occupying Attica and Euboea, the islands of the Aegean Sea and western Asia Minor.

17. **Tegea:** a city in the center of the Peloponneus.

"Croesus, king of the Lydians and of other nations, has sent us to speak thus to you; 'Oh! Lacedaemonians, the god has bidden me to make the Greek my friend; I therefore apply to you, in conformity with the oracle, knowing that you held the first rank in Greece, and desire to become your friend and ally in all true faith and honesty.'"

Such was the message which Croesus sent by his heralds. The Lacedaemonians, who were aware beforehand of the reply given him by the oracle, were full of joy at the coming of the messengers, and at once took the oaths of friendship and alliance: this they did the more readily as they had previously contracted certain obligations towards him. They had sent to Sardis on one occasion to purchase some gold, intending to use it on a statue of Apollo—the statue, namely, which remains to this day at Thornax in Laconia, when Croesus, hearing of the matter, gave them as a gift the gold which they wanted.

This was one reason why the Lacedaemonians were so willing to make the alliance: another was, because Croesus had chosen them for his friends in preference to all the other Greeks. They therefore held themselves in readiness to come at his summons, and not content with so doing, they further had a huge vase made in bronze, covered with figures of animals all round the outside of the rim, and large enough to contain three hundred amphoras,[18] which they sent to Croesus as a return for his presents to them.

The vase, however, never reached Sardis. Its miscarriage is accounted for in two quite different ways. The Lacedaemonian story is, that when it reached Samos,[19] on its way towards Sardis, the Samians having knowledge of it, put to sea in their ships of war and made it their prize. But the Samians declare, that the Lacedaemonians who had the vase in charge, happening to arrive too late, and learning that Sardis had fallen and that Croesus was a prisoner, sold it in their island, and the purchasers, who were they say private persons, made an offering of it at the shrine of Juno: the sellers were very likely on their return to Sparta to have said that they had been robbed of it by the Samians. Such, then, was the fate of the vase.

Meanwhile Croesus, taking the oracle in a wrong sense, led his forces into Cappadocia,[20] fully expecting to defeat Cyrus and destroy the empire of the Persians. While he was still engaged in making preparations for his attack, a Lydian named Sandanis, who had always been looked upon as a wise man, but who after this obtained a very great name indeed among his countrymen, came forward and counseled the king in these words:

"Thou art about, oh! king, to make war against men who wear leathern trousers, and have all their other garments of leather; who feed not on what they like, but on what they can get from a soil that is sterile and unkindly; who do not indulge in wine, but drink water; who possess no

---

18. **amphoras:** tall, slender, two-handled jars for storing grain, oil, wine, etc.

19. **Samos:** an island in the Aegean Sea off the west coast of Asia Minor.

20. **Cappadocia:** a country in south central Asia Minor.

figs nor anything else that is good to eat. If, then, thou conquerest them, what canst thou get from them, seeing that they have nothing at all? But if they conquer thee, consider how much that is precious thou wilt lose: if they once get a taste of our pleasant things, they will keep such hold of them that we shall never be able to make them loose their grasp. For my part, I am thankful to the gods, that they have not put it into the hearts of the Persians to invade Lydia."

Croesus was not persuaded by this speech, though it was true enough; for before the conquest of Lydia, the Persians possessed none of the luxuries or delights of life.

There were two motives which led Croesus to attack Cappadocia: firstly, he coveted the land, which he wished to add to his own dominions; but the chief reason was, that he wanted to revenge on Cyrus the wrongs of Astyages, and was made confident by the oracle of being able so to do: for Astyages, son of Cyaxares and king of the Medes, who had been dethroned by Cyrus, son of Cambyses, was Croesus' brother by marriage.

Cyrus had captured this Astyages, who was his mother's father, and kept him prisoner, for a reason which I shall bring forward in another part of my history. This capture formed the ground of quarrel between Cyrus and Croesus, in consequence of which Croesus sent his servants to ask the oracle if he should attack the Persians; and when an evasive answer came, fancying it to be in his favor, carried his arms into the Persian territory. When he reached the river Halys, he transported his army across it, as I maintain, by the bridges which exist there at the present day; but, according to the general belief of the Greeks, by the aid of Thales the Milesian.[21] The tale is, that Croesus was in doubt how he should get his army across, as the bridges were not made at that time, and that Thales, who happened to be in the camp, divided the stream and caused it to flow on both sides of the army instead of on the left only. This he effected thus:—Beginning some distance above the camp, he dug a deep channel, which he brought round in a semicircle, so that it might pass to rearward of the camp; and that thus the river, diverted from its natural course into the new channel at the point where this left the stream, might flow by the station of the army, and afterwards fall again into the ancient bed. In this way the river was split into two streams, which were both easily fordable. It is said by some that the water was entirely drained off from the natural bed of the river. But I am of a different opinion; for I do not see how, in that case, they could have crossed it on their return.

Having passed the Halys with the forces under his command, Croesus entered the district of Cappadocia which is called Pteria. It lies in the neighborhood of the city of Sinope upon the Euxine, and is the strongest position in the whole country thereabouts. Here Croesus pitched his

---

21. **Thales the Milesian:** pre-Socratic philosopher (c. 640–c. 546 B.C.). Miletus was a city on the coast of Asia Minor.

camp, and began to ravage the fields of the Syrians. He beseiged and took the chief city of the Pterians, and reduced the inhabitants to slavery: he likewise made himself master of the surrounding villages. Thus he brought ruin on the Syrians, who were guilty of no offense towards him. Meanwhile, Cyrus had levied an army and marched against Croesus, increasing his numbers at every step by the forces of the nations that lay in his way. Before beginning his march he had sent heralds to the Ionians, with an invitation to them to revolt from the Lydian king: they, however, had refused compliance. Cyrus, notwithstanding, marched against the enemy, and encamped opposite them in the district of Pteria, where the trial of strength took place between the contending powers. The combat was hot and bloody, and upon both sides the number of the slain was great; nor had victory declared in favor of either party, when night came down upon the battle-field. Thus both armies fought valiantly.

Croesus laid the blame of his ill success on the number of his troops, which fell very short of the enemy; and as on the next day Cyrus did not repeat the attack, he set off on his return to Sardis, intending to collect his allies and renew the contest in the spring. He meant to call on the Egyptians to send him aid, according to the terms of the alliance which he had concluded with Amasis,[22] previously to his league with the Lacedaemonians. He intended also to summon to his assistance the Babylonians, under their king Labynetus, for they too were bound to him by treaty: and further, he meant to send word to Sparta, and appoint a day for the coming of their succors. Having got together these forces in addition to his own, he would, as soon as the winter was past and springtime come, march once more against the Persians. With these intentions Croesus, immediately on his return, dispatched heralds to his various allies, with a request that they would join him at Sardis in the course of the fifth month from the time of the departure of his messengers. He then disbanded the army—consisting of mercenary troops—which had been engaged with the Persians and had since accompanied him to his capital, and let them depart to their homes, never imagining that Cyrus, after a battle in which victory had been so evenly balanced, would venture to march upon Sardis.

While Croesus was still in this mind, all the suburbs of Sardis were found to swarm with snakes, on the appearance of which the horses left feeding in the pasture-grounds, and flocked to the suburbs to eat them. The king, who witnessed the unusual sight, regarded it very rightly as a prodigy. He therefore instantly sent messengers to the soothsayers of Telmessus,[23] to consult them upon the matter. His messengers reached the city, and obtained from the Telmessians an explanation of what the prodigy portended, but fate did not allow them to inform their lord; for

22. **Amasis:** a pharaoh of Egypt who allied himself with various Greek city-states in the face of the Persian threat.

23. **Telmessus:** a town on the coast of Asia Minor noted for its oracle of Apollo.

ere they entered Sardis on their return, Croesus was a prisoner. What the Telmessians had declared was, that Croesus must look for the entry of an army of foreign invaders into his country, and that when they came they would subdue the native inhabitants; since the snake, said they, is a child of earth, and the horse a warrior and a foreigner. Croesus was already a prisoner when the Telmessians thus answered his inquiry, but they had no knowledge of what was taking place at Sardis, or of the fate of the monarch.

Cyrus, however, when Croesus broke up so suddenly from his quarters after the battle at Pteria, conceiving that he had marched away with the intention of disbanding his army, considered a little, and soon saw that it was advisable for him to advance upon Sardis with all haste, before the Lydians could get their forces together a second time. Having thus determined, he lost no time in carrying out his plan. He marched forward with such speed that he was himself the first to announce his coming to the Lydian king. That monarch, placed in the utmost difficulty by the turn of events which had gone so entirely against all his calculations, nevertheless led out the Lydians to battle. In all Asia there was not at that time a braver or more warlike people. Their manner of fighting was on horseback; they carried long lances, and were clever in the management of their steeds.

The two armies met in the plain before Sardis. It is a vast flat, bare of trees, watered by the Hyllus and a number of other streams, which all flow into one larger than the rest, called the Hermus. This river rises in the sacred mountain of the Dindymenian Mother,[24] and falls into the sea near the town of Phocaea.

When Cyrus beheld the Lydians arranging themselves in order of battle on this plain, fearful of the strength of their cavalry, he adopted a device which Harpagus, one of the Medes, suggested to him. He collected together all the camels that had come in the train of his army to carry the provisions and the baggage, and taking off their loads, he mounted riders upon them accoutered as horsemen. These he commanded to advance in front of his other troops against the Lydian horse; behind them were to follow the foot soldiers, and last of all the cavalry. When his arrangements were complete, he gave his troops orders to slay all the other Lydians who came in their way without mercy, but to spare Croesus and not kill him, even if he should be seized and offer resistance. The reason why Cyrus opposed his camels to the enemy's horse was, because the horse has a natural dread of the camel, and cannot abide either the sight or the smell of that animal. By this stratagem he hoped to make Croesus's horse useless to him, the horse being what he chiefly depended on for victory. The two armies then joined battle, and immediately the Lydian war-horses, seeing and smelling the camels, turned round and galloped off; and so it came to pass that all Croesus's hopes withered away. The Lydians, however, behaved manfully. As soon as they understood what was happening, they

---

24. **Dindymenian Mother:** the earth-goddess Cybele, also called Dindymene.

leaped off their horses, and engaged with the Persians on foot. The combat was long; but at last, after a great slaughter on both sides, the Lydians turned and fled. They were driven within their walls, and the Persians laid siege to Sardis.

Thus the siege began. Meanwhile Croesus, thinking that the place would hold out no inconsiderable time, sent off fresh heralds to his allies from the beleaguered town. His former messengers had been charged to bid them assemble at Sardis in the course of the fifth month, they whom he now sent were to say that he was already besieged, and to beseech them to come to his aid with all possible speed. Among his other allies Croesus did not omit to send to Lacedemon.

The following is the way in which Sardis was taken. On the fourteenth day of the siege Cyrus bade some horsemen ride about his lines, and make proclamation to the whole army that he would give a reward to the man who should first mount the wall. After this he made an assault, but without success. His troops retired, but a certain Mardian, Hyroeades by name, resolved to approach the citadel and attempt it at a place where no guards were ever set. On this side the rock was so precipitous, and the citadel, as it seemed, so impregnable, that no fear was entertained of its being carried in this place. Here was the only portion of the circuit round which their old king Meles did not carry the lion which his leman[25] bore to him. For when the Telmessians had declared that if the lion were taken round the defenses, Sardis would be impregnable, and Meles, in consequence, carried it round the rest of the fortress where the citadel seemed open to attack, he scorned to take it round this side, which he looked on as a sheer precipice, and therefore absolutely secure. It is on that side of the city which faces Mount Tmolus. Hyroeades, however, having the day before observed a Lydian soldier descend the rock after a helmet that had rolled down from the top, and having seen him pick it up and carry it back, thought over what he had witnessed, and formed his plan. He climbed the rock himself, and other Persians followed in his track, until a large number had mounted to the top. Thus was Sardis taken, and given up entirely to pillage.

With respect to Croesus himself, this is what befell him at the taking of the town. He had a son, of whom I made mention above, a worthy youth, whose only defect was that he was deaf and dumb. In the days of his prosperity Croesus had done the most that he could for him, and among other plans which he had devised, had sent to Delphi to consult the oracle on his behalf. The answer which he had received from the Pythoness ran thus:—

> Lydian, wide-ruling monarch, thou wondrous simple Croesus,
> Wish not ever to hear in thy palace the voice thou hast prayed for,
> Uttering intelligent sounds. Far better thy son should be silent!
> Ah! woe worth the day when thine ear shall first list to his accents.

---

25. **leman:** sweetheart; mistress.

When the town was taken, one of the Persians was just going to kill Croesus, not knowing who he was. Croesus saw the man coming, but under the pressure of his affliction, did not care to avoid the blow, not minding whether or no he died beneath the stroke. Then this son of his, who was voiceless, beholding the Persian as he rushed towards Croesus, in the agony of his fear and grief burst into speech, and said, "Man, do not kill Croesus." This was the first time that he had ever spoken a word, but afterwards he retained the power of speech for the remainder of his life.

Thus was Sardis taken by the Persians, and Croesus himself fell into their hands, after having reigned fourteen years, and been besieged in his capital fourteen days; thus too did Croesus fulfill the oracle, which said that he should destroy a mighty empire,—by destroying his own. Then the Persians who had made Croesus prisoner brought him before Cyrus.[26] Now a vast pile had been raised by his orders, and Croesus, laden with fetters, was placed upon it, and with him twice seven of the sons of the Lydians. I know not whether Cyrus was minded to make an offering of the first-fruits to some god or other, or whether he had vowed a vow and was performing it, or whether, as may well be, he had heard that Croesus was a holy man, and so wished to see if any of the heavenly powers would appear to save him from being burnt alive. However it might be, Cyrus was thus engaged, and Croesus was already on the pile, when it entered his mind in the depth of his woe that there was a divine warning in the words which had come to him from the lips of Solon, "No one while he lives is happy." When this thought smote him he fetched a long breath, and breaking his deep silence, groaned out aloud, thrice uttering the name of Solon. Cyrus caught the sounds, and bade the interpreters inquire of Croesus who it was he called on. They drew near and asked him, but he held his peace, and for a long time made no answer to their questionings, until at length, forced to say something, he exclaimed, "One I would give much to see converse with every monarch." Not knowing what he meant by this reply, the interpreters begged him to explain himself; and as they pressed for an answer, and grew to be troublesome, he told them how, a long time before, Solon, an Athenian, had come and seen all his splendor, and made light of it; and how whatever he had said to him had fallen out exactly as he foreshowed, although it was nothing that specially concerned him, but applied to all mankind alike, and most to those who seemed to themselves happy. Meanwhile, as he thus spoke, the pile was lighted, and the outer portion began to blaze. Then Cyrus, hearing from the interpreters what Croesus had said,

---

26. **Cyrus:** The oracle who said that Croesus' kingdom would endure until "a mule is monarch of Media" was referring to Cyrus, who can be compared to a mule. His grandfather Astyages, king of Media, dreamed that his daughter's son would dethrone him. Therefore he did not marry her to a Median but to a Persian, a member of a subject nation. Cyrus was born from this union, the offspring of two different nations, just as a mule is the offspring of two different species, a horse and a donkey.

relented, bethinking himself that he too was a man, and that it was a fellow-man, and one who had once been as blessed by fortune as himself, that he was burning alive; afraid, moreover, of retribution, and full of the thought that whatever is human is insecure. So he bade them quench the blazing fire as quickly as they could, and take down Croesus and the other Lydians, which they tried to do, but the flames were not to be mastered.

Then, the Lydians say that Croesus, perceiving by the efforts made to quench the fire that Cyrus had relented, and seeing also that all was in vain, and that the men could not get the fire under, called with a loud voice upon the god Apollo, and prayed him, if he had ever received at his hands any acceptable gift, to come to his aid, and deliver him from his present danger. As thus with tears he besought the god, suddenly, though up to that time the sky had been clear and the day without a breath of wind, dark clouds gathered, and the storm burst over their heads with rain of such violence, that the flames were speedily extinguished. Cyrus, convinced by this that Croesus was a good man and a favorite of heaven, asked him after he was taken off the pile, "Who it was that had persuaded him to lead an army into his country, and so become his foe rather than continue his friend?" to which Croesus made answer as follows: "What I did, oh! king, was to thy advantage and to my own loss. If there be blame, it rests with the god of the Greeks, who encouraged me to begin the war. No one is so foolish as to prefer war to peace, in which, instead of sons burying their fathers, fathers bury their sons. But the gods willed it so."

Thus did Croesus speak. Cyrus then ordered his fetters to be taken off, and made him sit down near himself, and paid him much respect looking upon him, as did also the courtiers, with a sort of wonder.

DISCUSSION QUESTIONS

1. Solon's warning that "oftentimes God gives men a gleam of happiness and then plunges them into ruin" applies perfectly to Croesus. Do you think Croesus' troubles were mostly of his own making, or was he just unfortunate?

2. The story of Croesus contains many examples of situational irony—events working out in ways that are just the opposite of what was intended. What outcomes in Croesus' story are particularly ironic?

3. Herodotus' account shows the reader many sides of Croesus' character. What does the short exchange at the beginning between Croesus and Bias of Priene reveal about him? What does the story of Adrastus reveal about Croesus? What does Croesus' testing of the oracles reveal about him?

4. What two opposing views of happiness are held by Croesus and Solon at the beginning of this account? Why has Croesus changed his views by the end of the account, when he says that Solon is someone who should "converse with every monarch"?

5. In what way does Herodotus' account demonstrate Solon's philosophy that "man is wholly accident"?

6. How is this ancient account of the destruction of Croesus' kingdom different from typical accounts of events and leaders found in modern history books?

SUGGESTIONS FOR WRITING

1. Herodotus' account of Croesus is filled with foreshadowings in the form of dreams, omens, and prophecies. Make a chart showing (1) these foreshadowing devices and (2) how they are fulfilled. (It is not necessary to include the prophecy that Croesus gets when he is just testing the various oracles.)

2. Imagine that you are a character other than Croesus (Solon, Adrastus, or Cyrus, for example). Write a diary entry describing an encounter you just had with the king. Explain the impressions you formed of Croesus during this encounter.

PLATO

(C. 484–C. 424 B.C.)

An enthusiastic disciple of the philosopher Socrates, Plato was strongly influenced by Socrates' view that "the unexamined life is not worth living." Socrates' persistent questioning of accepted values eventually resulted in accusations that he was "corrupting the young" and "introducing new gods." Tried and convicted on these charges, he was condemned to death. After Socrates' death, Plato traveled widely, later returning to Athens to found his school, the Academy, in the olive grove of Academus. Among his students was the young Aristotle. Most of Plato's writings take the form of dialogues in which Socrates and another speaker discuss such subjects as virtue, justice, friendship, knowledge, and government. All of his known works have survived.

The heart of Plato's philosophy is his concept of Ideas (sometime called Forms or Archetypes), which are abstract ideals that have no earthly embodiment but exist only as intellectual states. *The Republic*, from which this selection is taken, examines one such ideal—the perfect society. In the parable of the cave, Plato presents another ideal—perfect knowledge, which is beyond human reach.

from The Republic

THE PARABLE OF THE CAVE

Translated by Benjamin Jowett

And now I1 will describe in a figure the enlightenment or unenlightenment of our nature:—Imagine human beings living in an underground cave which is open towards the light; they have been there from childhood, having their necks and legs chained, and can only see into the cave. At a distance there is a fire, and between the fire and the prisoners a raised way, and a low wall is built along the way, like the screen over which marionette-players show their puppets. Behind the wall appear moving figures, who hold in their hands various works of art, and among them images of men and animals, wood and stone, and some of the passers-by are talking and others silent. "A strange parable," he2 said, "and strange captives." They are ourselves, I replied; and they see only the shadows of the images which the fire throws on the wall of the cave; to these they give names, and if we add an echo which returns from the wall, the voices of the passengers will seem to proceed from the shadows. Suppose now that you suddenly turn them round and make them look, with pain and grief

---

1. I: the speaker is meant to be Socrates.

2. he: the other speaker is Glaucon, one of Socrates' students.

to themselves, at the real images; will they believe them to be real? Will not their eyes be dazzled, and will they not try to get away from the light to something which they are able to behold without blinking? And suppose further, that they are dragged up the steep and rugged ascent into the presence of the sun himself, will not their sight be darkened with the excess of light? Some time will pass before they get the habit of perceiving at all; and at first they will be able to perceive only shadows and reflections in the water; then they will recognize the moon and the stars, and will at length behold the sun in his own proper place as he is. Last of all they will conclude:—This is he who gives us the year and the seasons, and is the author of all that we see. How will they rejoice in passing from darkness to light! How worthless to them will seem the honors and glories of the cave! But now imagine further, that they descend into their old habitations;—in that underground dwelling they will not see as well as their fellows, and will not be able to compete with them in the measurement of the shadows on the wall; there will be many jokes about the man who went on a visit to the sun and lost his eyes, and if they find anybody trying to set free and enlighten one of their number, they will put him to death,[3] if they can catch him. Now the cave is the world of sight, the fire is the sun, the way upwards is the way to knowledge, and in the world of knowledge the Idea of good is last seen and with difficulty, but when seen is inferred to be the author of good and right—parent of the lord of light in this world, and of truth and understanding in the other. He who attains to the beatific vision is always going upwards; he is unwilling to descend into political assemblies and courts of law; for his eyes are apt to blink at the images or shadows of images which they behold in them—he cannot enter into the ideas of those who have never in their lives understood the relation of the shadow to the substance. But blindness is of two kinds, and may be caused either by passing out of darkness into light or out of light into darkness, and a man of sense will distinguish between them, and will not laugh equally at both of them, but the blindness which arises from fullness of light he will deem blessed and pity the other; or if he laugh at the puzzled soul looking at the sun, he will have more reason to laugh than the inhabitants of the cave at those who descend from above. There is a further lesson taught by this parable of ours. Some persons fancy that instruction is like giving eyes to the blind, but we say that the faculty of sight was always there, and that the soul only requires to be turned round towards the light. And this is conversion; other virtues are almost like bodily habits, and may be acquired in the same manner, but intelligence has a diviner life, and is indestructible, turning either to good or evil according to the direction given. Did you never observe how the mind of a clever rogue peers out of his eyes, and the more clearly he sees, the more evil he does? Now if you take such a one, and cut away from him those leaden weights of pleasure and desire which bind his soul to

---

3. **put him to death:** This is probably an allusion to the death of Socrates, though the actual Socrates could not, of course, have made this allusion.

earth, his intelligence will be turned round, and he will behold the truth as clearly as he now discerns his meaner ends. And have we not decided that our rulers must neither be so uneducated as to have no fixed rule of life, nor so over-educated as to be unwilling to leave their paradise for the business of the world? We must choose out therefore the natures who are most likely to ascend to the light and knowledge of the good; but we must not allow them to remain in the region of light; they must be forced down again among the captives in the cave to partake of their labors and honors. "Will they not think this a hardship?" You should remember that our purpose in framing the State was not that our citizens should do what they like, but that they should serve the State for the common good of all. May we not fairly say to our philosopher,—Friend, we do you no wrong; for in other States philosophy grows wild, and a wild plant owes nothing to the gardener, but you have been trained by us to be the rulers and kings of our hive,[4] and therefore we must insist on your descending into the cave. You must, each of you, take your turn, and become able to use your eyes in the dark, and with a little practice you will see far better than those who quarrel about the shadows, whose knowledge is a dream only, whilst yours is a waking reality. It may be that the saint or philosopher who is best fitted, is also the least inclined to rule, but necessity is laid upon him, and he must no longer live in the heaven of Ideas. And this will be the salvation of the State. For those who rule must not be those who are desirous to rule; and, if you can offer to our citizens a better life than that of rulers generally is, there will be a chance that the rich, not only in this world's goods, but in virtue and wisdom, may bear rule. And the only life which is better than the life of political ambition is that of philosophy, which is also the best preparation for the government of a State.

_____

4. **kings of our hive:** The Greeks referred inaccurately to king rather than queen bees.

DISCUSSION QUESTIONS

1. How do you think Plato would react to the idea of elected leaders? Why? How do his assumptions about government differ from those of the typical American?

2. A parable is a story with a double layer—a surface meaning and an underlying meaning. Explain the underlying meaning of each of the following objects: the underground cave, the fire, the shadows, and the "steep and rugged ascent" out of the cave.

3. Socrates asserts that some teachers "fancy that instruction is like giving eyes to the blind." Why does he feel these teachers are mistaken?

4. The parable states that people who are freed from their chains and brought into the sunlight will not be happy, but will respond with "pain and grief." Why?

SUGGESTION FOR WRITING

Write a modern version of Plato's parable, using images from technology to suggest the "virtual reality" that the prisoners mistake for true knowledge. You might consider images drawn from television, movies, or computers to convey Plato's concept of distorted or incomplete knowledge. Feel free to add drawings if they will help clarify the parable.

PLUTARCH

(C. A.D. 46–C. 120)

Plutarch was born at an unfortunate time in the history of Greece. The Golden Age was over, and Greece existed as a desperately poor country that had fallen to the Roman Empire. Although Plutarch was a talented and energetic man who might have made his mark as a public figure in better times, he had few options as a citizen of a conquered nation. In the small, shabby town where he spent most of his life, he occupied himself with such tasks as overseeing the repair of roads and adjusting local taxes.

Plutarch's life may have been limited by unfortunate circumstances, but he found compensation by reading and learning about famous public figures of the past. He studied philosophy briefly in Athens and then traveled through Greece, Italy, and Egypt, gathering facts for a collection of biographies entitled *Parallel Lives.* Plutarch's method was to pair two figures who excelled in similar fields—such as generals or orators—and after presenting their individual lives, to compare and contrast them. A passionate lover of great deeds and generous acts, Plutarch firmly believed that individuals should constantly try "to contemplate the best." As a result, his biographies present figures who are meant to serve as an inspiration to readers. These figures sometimes make mistakes, but they are generally shining examples of virtue and grand purpose. Over 15 centuries after Plutarch's death, his biographies served as the inspiration for many of Shakespeare's plays.

The biography that appears below is that of Lycurgus, founder of the famous state of Sparta. Lycurgus may have been the only human to create an enduring utopia, or ideal state (though modern readers may find it somewhat less than ideal). Unlike most utopias, which barely last a generation, the one built by Lycurgus lasted over 500 years and was admired throughout the Mediterranean world. ■

LYCURGUS

Translated by John Dryden

There is so much uncertainty in the accounts which historians have left us of Lycurgus, the lawgiver of Sparta, that scarcely anything is asserted by one of them which is not called into question or contradicted by the rest. Their sentiments are quite different as to the family he came of, the voyages he undertook, the place and manner of his death, but most of all when they speak of the laws he made and the commonwealth which he founded. They cannot, by any means, be brought to an agreement as to the very age in which he lived. But that he was of great antiquity may be gathered from a passage in Xenophon,[1] where he makes him contempo-

---

1. Xenophon (zen´ ə fən): soldier and historian (c. 430–c. 354 B.C.).

rary with the Heraclidae.[2] By descent, indeed, the very last kings of Sparta were Heraclidae too; but he seems in that place to speak of the first and more immediate successors of Hercules. But notwithstanding this confusion and obscurity, we shall endeavor to compose the history of his life, adhering to those statements which are least contradicted, and depending upon those authors who are most worthy of credit. . . .

Soüs certainly was the most renowned of all his ancestors, under whose conduct the Spartans made slaves of the Helots,[3] and added to their dominions, by conquest, a good part of Arcadia. There goes a story of this King Soüs, that, being besieged by [his enemies] in a dry and stony place so that he could come at no water, he was at last constrained to agree with them upon these terms, that he would restore to them all his conquests, provided that himself and all his men should drink of the nearest spring. After the usual oaths and ratifications, he called his soldiers together, and offered to him that would forbear drinking, his kingdom for a reward; and when not a man of them was able to forbear, in short, when they had all drunk their fill, at last comes King Soüs himself to the spring, and, having sprinkled his face only, without swallowing one drop, marches off in the face of his enemies, refusing to yield up his conquests, because himself and all his men had not, according to the articles, drunk of their water.

Although he was justly had in admiration on this account, yet his family was not surnamed from him, but from his son Eurypon (of whom they were called Eurypontids); the reason of which was that Eurypon relaxed the rigor of the monarchy, seeking favor and popularity with the many. They, after this first step, grew bolder; and the succeeding kings partly incurred hatred with their people by trying to use force, or, for popularity's sake and through weakness, gave way; and anarchy and confusion long prevailed in Sparta, causing, moreover, the death of the father of Lycurgus. For as he was endeavoring to quell a riot, he was stabbed with a butcher's knife, and left the title of king to his eldest son, Polydectes.

He, too, dying soon after, the right of succession (as every one thought) rested in Lycurgus; and reign he did, until it was found that the queen, his sister-in-law, was with child; upon which he immediately declared that the kingdom belonged to her issue, provided it were male, and that he himself exercised the regal jurisdiction only as his guardian. Soon after, an overture was made to him by the queen, that she would herself in some way destroy the infant, upon condition that he would marry her when he came to the crown. Abhorring the woman's wickedness, he nevertheless did not reject her proposal, but, making show of closing with her, dispatched the messenger with thanks and expressions of joy, but dissuaded her earnestly from procuring herself to miscarry, which would impair her

---

2. Heraclidae: the Dorian Greeks, who adopted Hercules as an ancestor.

3. Helots: members of a pre-Dorian people who were subjugated by the Spartans and served as serfs in Spartan society.

health, if not endanger her life; he himself, he said, would see to it, that the child, as soon as born, should be taken out of the way. By such artifices having drawn on the woman to the time of her lying-in, as soon as he heard that she was in labor, he sent persons to be by and observe all that passed, with orders that if it were a girl they should deliver it to the women, but if a boy, should bring it to him wheresoever he were, and whatsoever doing. It so fell out that when he was at supper with the principal magistrates the queen was brought to bed of a boy, who was soon after presented to him as he was at the table; he, taking him into his arms, said to those about him, "Men of Sparta, here is a king born unto us." This said, he laid him down in the king's place, and named him Charilaus, that is, the joy of the people; because that all were transported with joy and with wonder at his noble and just spirit. His reign had lasted only eight months, but he was honored on other accounts by the citizens, and there were more who obeyed him because of his eminent virtues, than because he was regent to the king and had the royal power in his hands. Some, however, envied and sought to impede his growing influence while he was still young; chiefly the kindred and friends of the queen-mother, who pretended to have been dealt with injuriously. Her brother Leonidas, in a warm debate which fell out betwixt him and Lycurgus, went so far as to tell him to his face that he was well assured that ere long he should see him king; suggesting suspicions and preparing the way for an accusation of him, as though he had made away with his nephew, if the child should chance to fail, though by a natural death. Words of the like import were designedly cast abroad by the queen-mother and her adherents.

Troubled at this, and not knowing what it might come to, he thought it his wisest course to avoid their envy by a voluntary exile, and to travel from place to place until his nephew came to marriageable years, and, by having a son, had secured the succession. Setting sail, therefore, with this resolution, he first arrived at Crete, where, having considered their several forms of government, and got an acquaintance with the principal men among them, some of their laws he very much approved of, and resolved to make use of them in his own country; a good part he rejected as useless.

From Crete he sailed to Asia, with design, as is said, to examine the difference betwixt the manners and rules of life of the Cretans, which were very sober and temperate, and those of the Ionians, a people of sumptuous and delicate habits, and so to form a judgment; just as physicians do by comparing healthy and diseased bodies. Here he had the first sight of Homer's works; and, having observed that the few loose expressions and actions of ill example which are to be found in his poems were much outweighed by serious lessons of state and rules of morality, he set himself eagerly to transcribe and digest them into order, as thinking they would be of good use in his own country. They had, indeed, already obtained some slight repute among the Greeks, and scattered portions, as chance conveyed them, were in the hands of individuals; but Lycurgus first made them really known.

The Egyptians say that he took a voyage into Egypt, and that, being much taken with their way of separating the soldiery from the rest of the nation, he transferred it from them to Sparta, a removal from contact with those employed in low and mechanical occupations giving high refinement and beauty to the state. Some Greek writers also record this.

Lycurgus was much missed at Sparta, and often sent for, "for kings indeed we have," they said, "who wear the marks and assume the titles of royalty, but as for the qualities of their minds, they have nothing by which they are to be distinguished from their subjects;" adding, that in him alone was the true foundation of sovereignty to be seen, a nature made to rule, and a genius to gain obedience. Nor were the kings themselves averse to see him back, for they looked upon his presence as a bulwark against the insolencies of the people.

Things being in this posture at his return, he applied himself, without loss of time, to a thorough reformation, and resolved to change the whole face of the commonwealth; for what could a few particular laws and a partial alteration avail? He must act as wise physicians do, in the case of one who labors under a complication of diseases, by force of medicines reduce and exhaust him, change his whole temperament, and then set him upon a totally new regimen of diet. Having thus projected things, away he goes to Delphi[4] to consult Apollo there; which having done, and offered his sacrifice, he returned with that renowned oracle, in which he is called beloved of God, and rather God than man; that his prayers were heard, that his laws should be the best, and the commonwealth which observed them the most famous in the world. Encouraged by these things, he set himself to bring over to his side the leading men of Sparta, exhorting them to give him a helping hand in his great undertaking; he broke it first to his particular friends, and then by degrees gained others, and animated them all to put his design in execution. When things were ripe for action, he gave order to thirty of the principal men of Sparta to be ready armed at the market-place by break of day, to the end that he might strike a terror into the opposite party. Things growing to a tumult, king Charilaus, apprehending that it was a conspiracy against his person, took sanctuary in the temple of Minerva of the Brazen House; but, being soon after undeceived, and having taken an oath of them that they had no designs against him, he quitted his refuge, and himself also entered into the confederacy with them. Of so gentle and flexible a disposition he was, to which Archelaus, his brother-king,[5] alluded, when, hearing him extolled for his goodness, he said, "Who can say he is anything but good? he is so even to the bad."

Among the many changes and alterations which Lycurgus made, the first and of greatest importance was the establishment of the senate, which, having a power equal to the kings' in matters of great consequence, and, as Plato expresses it, allaying and qualifying the fiery genius of the royal

---

4. **Delphi:** an oracular shrine of Apollo. (See article on page xiii.)

5. **brother-king:** The Spartan government was headed by two kings.

office, gave steadiness and safety to the commonwealth. For the state, which before had no firm basis to stand upon, but leaned one while towards an absolute monarchy, when the kings had the upper hand, and another while towards a pure democracy, when the people had the better, found in this establishment of the senate a central weight, like ballast in a ship, which always kept things in a just equilibrium; the twenty-eight[6] always adhering to the kings so far as to resist democracy, and, on the other hand, supporting the people against the establishment of absolute monarchy. They had no council-house or building to meet in. Lycurgus was of opinion that ornaments were so far from advantaging them in their counsels, that they were rather a hindrance, by diverting their attention from the business before them to statues and pictures, and roofs curiously fretted, the usual embellishments of such places among the other Greeks. The people then being thus assembled in the open air, it was not allowed to any one of their order to give his advice, but only either to ratify or reject what should be propounded to them by the king or senate.

Although Lycurgus had, in this manner, used all the qualifications possible in the constitution of his commonwealth, yet those who succeeded him found the oligarchical element still too strong and dominant, and, to check its high temper and its violence, put, as Plato says, a bit in its mouth, which was the power of the ephori,[7] established a hundred and thirty years after the death of Lycurgus. Elatus and his colleagues were the first who had this dignity conferred upon them, in the reign of king Theopompus, who, when his queen upbraided him one day that he would leave the regal power to his children less than he had received it from his ancestors, said, in answer, "No, greater; for it will last longer." For, indeed, their prerogative being thus reduced within reasonable bounds, the Spartan kings were at once freed from all further jealousies and consequent danger, and never experienced the calamities of their neighbors at Messene and Argos, who, by maintaining their prerogative too strictly, for want of yielding a little to the populace, lost it all.

After the creation of the thirty senators, his next task, and, indeed, the most hazardous he ever undertook, was the making a new division of their lands. For there was an extreme inequality among them, and their state was overloaded with a multitude of indigent and necessitous persons, while its whole wealth had centered upon a very few. To the end, therefore, that he might expel from the state arrogance and envy, luxury and crime, and those yet more inveterate diseases of want and superfluity, he obtained of them to renounce their properties, and to consent to a new division of the land, and that they should live all together on an equal footing; merit to be their only road to eminence, and the disgrace of evil, and credit of worthy acts, their one measure of difference between man and man.

---

6. **the twenty-eight:** the Spartan senate, originally composed of the associates of Lycurgus.

7. **the ephori:** five officials elected annually and having combined executive, legislative, and judicial powers. They made decisions when the kings were at variance.

Upon their consent to these proposals, proceeding at once to put them into execution, he divided the country of Laconia[8] in general into thirty thousand equal shares, and the part attached to the city of Sparta into nine thousand; these he distributed among the Spartans, as he did the others to the country citizens. A lot was so much as to yield, one year with another, about seventy bushels of grain for the master of the family, and twelve for his wife, with a suitable proportion of oil and wine. And this he thought sufficient to keep their bodies in good health and strength; superfluities they were better without. It is reported, that, as he returned from a journey shortly after the division of the lands, in harvest time, the ground being newly reaped, seeing the stacks all standing equal and alike, he smiled, and said to those about him, "Methinks all Laconia looks like one family estate just divided among a number of brothers."

Not contented with this, he resolved to make a division of their movables too, that there might be no odious distinction or inequality left among them; but finding that it would be very dangerous to go about it openly, he took another course, and defeated their avarice by the following stratagem: he commanded that all gold and silver coin should be called in, and that only a sort of money made of iron should be current, a great weight and quantity of which was but very little worth; so that to lay up [even moderate savings] required a pretty large closet, and, to remove it, nothing less than a yoke of oxen. With the diffusion of this money, at once a number of vices were banished from Lacedaemon;[9] for who would rob another of such a coin? Who would unjustly detain or take by force, or accept as a bribe, a thing which it was not easy to hide, nor a credit to have, nor indeed of any use to cut in pieces? For when it was just red hot, they quenched it in vinegar, and by that means spoiled it, and made it almost incapable of being worked.

In the next place, he declared an outlawry of all needless and superfluous arts; but here he might almost have spared his proclamation; for they of themselves would have gone after the gold and silver, the money which remained being not so proper payment for curious work; for, being of iron, it was scarcely portable, neither, if they should take the pains to export it, would it pass among the other Greeks, who ridiculed it. So there was now no more means of purchasing foreign goods and small wares; merchants sent no shiploads into Laconian ports; no rhetoric-master, no itinerant fortune-teller, or gold or silversmith, engraver, or jeweler, set foot in a country which had no money; so that luxury, deprived little by little of that which fed and fomented it, wasted to nothing, and died away of itself. For the rich had no advantage here over the poor, as their wealth and abundance had no road to come abroad by, but were shut up at home doing nothing. And in this way they became excellent artists in common, necessary things; bedsteads, chairs, and tables, and such like staple uten-

---

8. **Laconia:** district in southeastern Greece where Sparta is located.

9. **Lacedaemon** (las′ ə dē′ m ən): Sparta.

sils in a family, were admirably well made there. Their cup, particularly, was very much in fashion, and eagerly bought up by soldiers, as Critias reports; for its color was such as to prevent water, drunk upon necessity and disagreeable to look at, from being noticed; and the shape of it was such that the mud stuck to the sides, so that only the purer part came to the drinker's mouth. For this, also, they had to thank their lawgiver, who, by relieving the artisans of the trouble of making useless things, set them to show their skill in giving beauty to those of daily and indispensable use.

The third and most masterly stroke of this great lawgiver, by which he struck a yet more effectual blow against luxury and the desire of riches, was the ordinance he made, that they should all eat in common, of the same bread and same meat, and of kinds that were specified, and should not spend their lives at home, laid on costly couches at splendid tables, delivering themselves up into the hands of their tradesmen and cooks, to fatten them in corners, like greedy brutes, and to ruin not their minds only but their very bodies, which, enfeebled by indulgence and excess, would stand in need of long sleep, warm bathing, freedom from work, and, in a word, of as much care and attendance as if they were continually sick. Nor were they allowed to take food at home first, and then attend the public tables, for every one had an eye upon those who did not eat and drink like the rest, and reproached them with being dainty and effeminate.

This last ordinance in particular exasperated the wealthier men. They collected in a body against Lycurgus, and from ill words came to throwing stones, so that at length he was forced to run out of the market-place, and make to sanctuary to save his life. By good-hap he outran all excepting one Alcander, a young man otherwise not ill accomplished, but hasty and violent, who came up so close to him, that, when he turned to see who was near him, he struck him upon the face with his stick, and put out one of his eyes. Lycurgus, so far from being daunted and discouraged by this accident, stopped short, and showed his disfigured face and eye beat out to his countrymen; they, dismayed and ashamed at the sight, delivered Alcander into his hands to be punished, and escorted him home, with expressions of great concern for his ill usage. Lycurgus, having thanked them for their care of his person, dismissed them all, excepting only Alcander; and, taking him with him into his house, neither did nor said anything severely to him, but, dismissing those whose place it was, bade Alcander to wait upon him at table. The young man, who was of an ingenuous temper, without murmuring did as he was commanded; and, being thus admitted to live with Lycurgus, he had an opportunity to observe in him, besides his gentleness and calmness of temper, an extraordinary sobriety and an indefatigable industry, and so, from an enemy, became one of his most zealous admirers, and told his friends and relations that Lycurgus was not that morose and ill-natured man they had formerly taken him for, but the one mild and gentle character of the world. And thus did Lycurgus, for chastisement of his fault, make of a wild and passionate young man one of the discreetest citizens of Sparta.

After this misadventure, the Lacedaemonians made it a rule never to carry so much as a staff into their public assemblies.

But to return to their public repasts; they met by companies of fifteen, more or less, and each of them stood bound to bring in monthly a bushel of meal, eight gallons of wine, five pounds of cheese, two pounds and a half of figs, and some very small sum of money to buy flesh or fish with. Besides this, when any of them made sacrifice to the gods, they always sent a dole to the common hall; and, likewise, when any of them had been a hunting, he sent thither a part of the venison he had killed; for these two occasions were the only excuses allowed for supping at home.

They used to send their children to these tables as to schools of temperance; here they were instructed in state affairs by listening to experienced statesmen; here they learned to converse with pleasantry, to make jests without scurrility, and take them without ill humor. In this point of good breeding, the Lacedaemonians excelled particularly, but if any man were uneasy under it, upon the least hint given there was no more to be said to him. It was customary also for the eldest man in the company to say to each of them, as they came in, "Through this" (pointing to the door), "no words go out." When any one had a desire to be admitted into any of these little societies; he was to go through the following probation, each man in the company took a little ball of soft bread, which they were to throw into a deep basin, which a waiter carried round upon his head; those that liked the person to be chosen dropped their ball into the basin without altering its figure, and those who disliked him pressed it betwixt their fingers, and made it flat; and this signified as much as a negative voice. And if there were but one of these flattened pieces in the basin, the suitor was rejected, so desirous were they that all the members of the company should be agreeable to each other.

After drinking moderately, every man went to his home without lights, for the use of them was, on all occasions, forbid, to the end that they might accustom themselves to march boldly in the dark. Such was the common fashion of their meals.

Lycurgus would never reduce his laws into writing; nay, there is a Rhetra[10] expressly to forbid it. For he thought that the most material points, and such as most directly tended to the public welfare, being imprinted on the hearts of their youth by a good discipline, would be sure to remain, and would find a stronger security, than any compulsion would be, in the principles of action formed in them by their best lawgiver, education.

One, then, of the Rhetras was, that their laws should not be written; another is particularly leveled against luxury and expensiveness, for by it it was ordained that the ceilings of their houses should only be wrought by the axe, and their gates and doors smoothed only by the saw. Luxury and a house of this kind could not well be companions. For a man must have a less than ordinary share of sense that would furnish

---

10. **Rhetra:** an ordinance.

such plain and common rooms with silver-footed couches and purple coverlets and gold and silver plate. Doubtless he had good reason to think that they would proportion their beds to their houses, and their coverlets to their beds, and the rest of their goods and furniture to these. It is reported that king Leotychides, the first of that name, was so little used to the sight of any other kind of work, that, being entertained at Corinth in a stately room, he was much surprised to see the timber and ceiling so finely carved and paneled, and asked his host whether the trees grew so in his country.

A third ordinance or Rhetra was, that they should not make war often, or long, with the same enemy, lest that they should train and instruct them in war, by habituating them to defend themselves.

In order to ensure the good education of their youth (which, as I said before, he thought the most important and noblest work of a lawgiver), he went so far back as to take into consideration their very conception and birth, by regulating their marriages. For Aristotle is wrong in saying, that, after he had tried all ways to reduce the women to more modesty and sobriety, he was at last forced to leave them as they were, because that, in the absence of their husbands, who spent the best part of their lives in the wars, their wives, whom they were obliged to leave absolute mistresses at home, took great liberties and assumed the superiority; and were treated with overmuch respect and called by the title of lady or queen. The truth is, he took in their case, also, all the care that was possible; he ordered the maidens to exercise themselves with wrestling, running, throwing the quoit, and casting the dart, to the end that the fruit they conceived might, in strong and healthy bodies, take firmer root and find better growth, and withal that they, with this greater vigor, might be the more able to undergo the pains of child-bearing. And to the end he might take away their over-great tenderness and fear of exposure to the air, and all acquired womanishness, he ordered that the young women should go naked in the processions, as well as the young men, and dance, too, in that condition, at certain solemn feasts, singing certain songs, whilst the young men stood around, seeing and hearing them. On these occasions, they now and then made, by jests, a befitting reflection upon those who had misbehaved themselves in the wars; and again sang encomiums upon those who had done any gallant action, and by these means inspired the younger sort with an emulation of their glory. Those that were thus commended went away proud, elated, and gratified with their honor among the maidens; and those who were rallied were as sensibly touched with it as if they had been formally reprimanded; and so much the more, because the kings and the elders, as well as the rest of the city, saw and heard all that passed. Nor was there anything shameful in this nakedness of the young women; modesty attended them, and all wantonness was excluded. It taught them simplicity and a care for good health, and gave them some taste of higher feelings, admitted as they thus were to the field of noble action and glory. Hence it was natural for them to think and speak as Gorgo, for example, the wife of Leonidas,[11] is said to have done, when some foreign lady, as it would seem, told her that the women of Lacedaemon were the only women of the world who could rule men; "With good reason," she said, "for we are the only women who bring forth men."

These public processions of the maidens, and their appearing naked in their exercises and dancings, were incitements to marriage, operating upon the young with the rigor and certainty, as Plato says, of love, if not of mathematics. But besides all this, to promote it yet more effectually, those who continued bachelors were in a degree disfranchised by law; for they were excluded from the sight of those public processions in which the young men and maidens danced naked, and, in winter-time, the officers compelled them to march naked themselves round the market-place, singing as they went a certain song to their own disgrace, that they justly suffered this punishment for disobeying the laws. Moreover, they were denied that respect and observance which the younger men paid their elders; and no man, for example, found fault with what was said to Dercyllidas, though so eminent a commander; upon whose approach one day, a young man, instead of rising, retained his seat, remarking, "No child of yours will make room for me."

In their marriages, the husband carried off his bride by a sort of force. After this, she who superintended the wedding comes and clips the hair of the bride close round her head, and leaves her upon a mattress in the dark; afterwards comes the bridegroom, in his every-day clothes, sober and composed, as having supped at the common table. After staying some time together, he returns composedly to his own apartment, to sleep as usual with the other young men. And so he continues to do, spending his days, and, indeed, his nights with them, visiting his bride in fear and shame, and with circumspection, when he thought he should not be observed; she, also, on her part, using her wit to help and find favorable opportunities for their meeting, when company was out of the way. In this manner they lived a long time, insomuch that they sometimes had children by their wives before ever they saw their faces by daylight. Lycurgus allowed a man who was advanced in years and had a young wife to recommend some virtuous and approved young man, that she might have a child by him, who might inherit the good qualities of the father, and be a son to himself. On the other side, an honest man who had love for a married woman upon account of her modesty and the well-favoredness of her children, might, without formality, beg her company of her husband, that he might raise, as it were, from this plot of good ground, worthy and well-allied children for himself. And, indeed, Lycurgus was of a persuasion that children were not so much the property of their parents as of the whole commonwealth, and, therefore, would not

---

11. **Leonidas:** the king who commanded the Spartans at Thermopylae against the Persians under Xerxes in 408 B.C.

have his citizens begot by the first comers, but by the best men that could be found; the laws of other nations seemed to him very absurd and inconsistent, where people would be so solicitous for their dogs and horses as to exert interest and pay money to procure fine breeding, and yet kept their wives shut up, to be made mothers only by themselves, who might be foolish, infirm, or diseased.

Nor was it in the power of the father to dispose of the child as he thought fit; he was obliged to carry it before the elders of the tribe to which the child belonged; their business it was carefully to view the infant, and, if they found it stout and well made, they gave order for its rearing, and allotted to it one of the nine thousand shares of land above mentioned for its maintenance, but, if they found it puny and ill-shaped, ordered it to be taken to what was called the Apothetae, a sort of chasm under Taygetus; as thinking it neither for the good of the child itself, nor for the public interest, that it should be brought up, if it did not, from the very outset, appear made to be healthy and vigorous. Upon the same account, the women did not bathe the new-born children with water, as is the custom in all other countries, but with wine, to prove the temper and complexion of their bodies; from a notion they had that epileptic and weakly children faint and waste away upon their being thus bathed, while, on the contrary, those of a strong and vigorous habit acquire firmness and get a temper by it, like steel. There was much care and art, too, used by the nurses; they had no swaddling bands; the children grew up free and unconstrained in limb and form, and not dainty and fanciful about their food; not afraid in the dark, or of being left alone; without any peevishness or ill humor or crying. Upon this account, Spartan nurses were often bought up, or hired by people of other countries.

Nor was it lawful, indeed, for the father himself to breed up the children after his own fancy; but as soon as they were seven years old they were to be enrolled in certain companies and classes, where they all lived under the same order and discipline, doing their exercises and taking their play together. Of these, he who showed the most conduct and courage was made captain; they had their eyes always upon him, obeyed his orders, and underwent patiently whatsoever punishment he inflicted; so that the whole course of their education was one continued exercise of a ready and perfect obedience.

The old men, too, were spectators of their performances, and often raised quarrels and disputes among them, to have a good opportunity of finding out their different characters, and of seeing which would be valiant, which a coward, when they should come to more dangerous encounters. Reading and writing they gave them, just enough to serve their turn; their chief care was to make them good subjects, and to teach them to endure pain and conquer in battle. To this end, as they grew in years, their discipline was proportionately increased; their heads were close-clipped, they were accustomed to go bare-foot, and for the most part to play naked.

After they were twelve years old, they were no longer allowed to wear any under-garment; they had one coat to serve them a year; their bodies were hard and dry, with but little acquaintance of baths and unguents; these human indulgences they were allowed only on some few particular days in the year. They lodged together in little bands upon beds made of the rushes which grew by the banks of the river Eurotas, which they were to break off with their hands without a knife; if it were winter, they mingled some thistle-down with their rushes, which it was thought had the property of giving warmth.

There was always one of the best and honestest men in the city appointed to undertake the charge and governance of them; he again arranged them into their several bands, and set over each of them for their captain the most temperate and boldest of those they called Irens, who were usually twenty years old. This young man, therefore, was their captain when they fought, and their master at home, using them for the offices of his house; sending the oldest of them to fetch wood, and the weaker and less able, to gather salads and herbs, and these they must either go without or steal; which they did by creeping into the gardens, or conveying themselves cunningly and closely into the eating-houses. If they were taken in the fact, they were whipped without mercy, for thieving so ill and awkwardly. They stole, too, all other meat they could lay their hands on, looking out and watching all opportunities, when people were asleep or more careless than usual. If they were caught, they were not only punished with whipping, but hunger, too, being reduced to their ordinary allowance, which was but very slender, and so contrived on purpose, that they might set about to help themselves, and be forced to exercise their energy and address. This was the principal design of their hard fare; there was another not inconsiderable, that they might grow taller; for the vital spirits, not being overburdened and oppressed by too great a quantity of nourishment, which necessarily discharges itself into thickness and breadth, do, by their natural lightness, rise; and the body, giving and yielding because it is pliant, grows in height. The same thing seems, also, to conduce to beauty of shape; a dry and lean habit is a better subject for nature's configuration, which the gross and over-fed are too heavy to submit to properly.

To return from whence we have digressed. So seriously did the Lacedaemonian children go about their stealing, that a youth, having stolen a young fox and hid it under his coat, suffered it to tear out his very bowels with its teeth and claws, and died upon the place, rather than let it be seen. What is practiced to this very day in Lacedaemon is enough to gain credit to this story, for I myself have seen several of the youth endure whipping to death at the foot of the altar of Diana.

The Iren, or under-master, used to stay a little with them after supper, and one of them he bade to sing a song, to another he put a question which required an advised and deliberate answer; for example, Who was the best man in the city? What he thought of such an action of such a man? They used them thus early to pass a right judgment upon persons and things, and to inform themselves of the abilities or defects of their countrymen. If they had not an answer ready to the question Who was a good or who an ill-reputed citizen, they were looked upon as of a dull and careless disposition, and to have little or no sense of virtue and honor; besides this, they were to give a good reason for what they said, and in as few words and as comprehensive as might be; he that failed of this, or answered not to the purpose, had his thumb bit by his master. Sometimes the Iren did this in the presence of the old men and magistrates, that they might see whether he punished them justly and in due measure or not; and when he did amiss, they would not reprove him before the boys, but, when they were gone, he was called to an account and underwent correction, if he had run far into either of the extremes of indulgence or severity.

They taught them, also, to speak with a natural and graceful raillery, and to comprehend much matter of thought in few words. For Lycurgus, who ordered, as we saw, that a great piece of money should be but of an inconsiderable value, on the contrary would allow no discourse to be current which did not contain in few words a great deal of useful and curious sense. King Agis, when some Athenian laughed at their short swords, and said that the jugglers on the stage swallowed them with ease, answered him, "We find them long enough to reach our enemies with"; and as their swords were short and sharp, so, it seems to me, were their sayings. They reach the point and arrest the attention of the hearers better than any. Lycurgus himself seems to have been short and sententious, if we may trust the anecdotes of him; as appears by his answer to one who by all means would set up democracy in Lacedaemon. "Begin, friend," said he, "and set it up in your family." Another asked him why he allowed of such mean and trivial sacrifices to the gods. He replied, "That we may always have something to offer to them." Being asked what sort of martial exercises or combats he approved of, he answered, "All sorts, except that in which you stretch out your hands."[12] Similar answers, addressed to his countrymen by letter, are ascribed to him; as, being consulted how they might best oppose an invasion of their enemies, he returned this answer, "By continuing poor, and not coveting each man to be greater than his fellow." Being consulted again whether it were requisite to enclose the city with a wall, he sent them word, "The city is well fortified which has a wall of men instead of brick." But whether these letters are counterfeit or not is not easy to determine.

Of their dislike to talkativeness, the following apothegms are evidence. King Leonidas said to one who held him in discourse upon some useful matter, but not in due time and place, "Much to the purpose, Sir, elsewhere." King Charilaus, the nephew of Lycurgus, being asked why his uncle had made so few laws, answered, "Men of few words require but few laws." When one blamed Hecateus the sophist[13] because, being invited to the public table, he had not spoken one word all supper-time, Archidamidas answered in his vindication, "He who knows how to speak, knows also when."

---

12. **stretch out your hands:** the gesture of surrender among ancient peoples.

13. **Hecateus the sophist:** historian and geographer (6th–5th centuries B.C.).

Nor was their instruction in music and verse less carefully attended to than their habits of grace and good breeding in conversation. And their very songs had a life and spirit in them that inflamed and possessed men's minds with an enthusiasm and ardor for action; the style of them was plain and without affectation; the subject always serious and moral; most usually, it was in praise of such men as had died in defense of their country, or in derision of those that had been cowards; the former they declared happy and glorified; the life of the latter they described as most miserable and abject. There were also vaunts of what they would do, and boasts of what they had done, varying with the various ages, as, for example, they had three choirs in their solemn festivals, the first of the old men, the second of the young men, and the last of the children; the old men began thus:

> We once were young, and brave and strong;

the young men answered them, singing,

> And we're so now, come on and try;

the children came last and said,

> But we'll be strongest by and by.

Indeed, if we will take the pains to consider their compositions, some of which were still extant in our days, and the airs on the flute to which they marched when going to battle, we shall find that Terpander and Pindar[14] had reason to say that music and valor were allied. For, indeed, before they engaged in battle, the king first did sacrifice to the Muses, in all likelihood to put them in mind of the manner of their education, and of the judgment that would be passed upon their actions, and thereby to animate them to the performance of exploits that should deserve a record. At such times, too, the Lacedaemonians abated a little the severity of their manners in favor of their young men, suffering them to curl and adorn their hair, and to have costly arms, and fine clothes; and were well pleased to see them, like proud horses, neighing and pressing to the course. And therefore, as soon as they came to be well-grown, they took a great deal of care of their hair, to have it parted and trimmed, especially against a day of battle, pursuant to a saying recorded of their lawgiver, that a large head of hair added beauty to a good face, and terror to an ugly one.

When they were in the field, their exercises were generally more moderate, their fare not so hard, nor so strict a hand held over them by their officers, so that they were the only people in the world to whom war gave repose. When their army was drawn up in battle array and the enemy near, the king sacrificed a goat, commanded the soldiers to set their garlands upon their heads, and the pipers to play the tune of the hymn to Castor,[15]

---

14. **Terpander and Pindar:** Terpander (7th century B.C.) was a musician and poet. Pindar (518–438 B.C.) was a lyric poet famous for his odes.

15. **Castor:** one of the twin sons of Zeus and Leda, the other being Polydeuces or Pollux.

and himself began the paean of advance. It was at once a magnificent and a terrible sight to see them march on to the tune of their flutes, without any disorder in their ranks, any discomposure in their minds or change in their countenance, calmly and cheerfully moving with the music to the deadly fight. Men, in this temper, were not likely to be possessed with fear or any transport of fury, but with the deliberate valor of hope and assurance, as if some divinity were attending and conducting them. The king had always about his person some one who had been crowned in the Olympic games; and upon this account a Lacedaemonian is said to have refused a considerable present, which was offered to him upon condition that he would not come into the lists; and when he had with much to-do thrown his antagonist, some of the spectators saying to him, "And now, Sir Lacedaemonian, what are you the better for your victory?" he answered smiling, "I shall fight next the king." After they had routed an enemy, they pursued him till they were well assured of the victory, and then they sounded a retreat, thinking it base and unworthy of a Grecian people to cut men in pieces, who had given up and abandoned all resistance. This manner of dealing with their enemies did not only show magnanimity, but was politic too; for, knowing that they killed only those who made resistance, and gave quarter to the rest, men generally thought it their best way to consult their safety by flight.

Their discipline continued still after they were full-grown men. No one was allowed to live after his own fancy; but the city was a sort of camp, in which every man had his share of provisions and business set out, and looked upon himself not so much born to serve his own ends as the interest of his country. Therefore, if they were commanded nothing else, they went to see the boys perform their exercises, to teach them something useful, or to learn it themselves of those who knew better. And, indeed, one of the greatest and highest blessings Lycurgus procured his people was the abundance of leisure, which proceeded from his forbidding to them the exercise of any mean and mechanical trade. Of the money-making that depends on troublesome going about and seeing people and doing business, they had no need at all in a state where wealth obtained no honor or respect. The Helots tilled their ground for them, and paid them yearly in kind the appointed quantity, without any trouble of theirs. To this purpose there goes a story of a Lacedaemonian who, happening to be at Athens when the courts were sitting, was told of a citizen that had been fined for living an idle life, and was being escorted home in much distress of mind by his condoling friends; the Lacedaemonian was much surprised at it, and desired his friend to show him the man who was condemned for living like a freeman. So much beneath them did they esteem the frivolous devotion of time and attention to the mechanical arts and to money-making.

It need not be said, that, upon the prohibition of gold and silver, all lawsuits immediately ceased, for there was now neither avarice nor poverty among them, but equality, where everyone's wants were supplied, and independence, because those wants were so small. All their time, except when they were in the field, was taken up by the choral dances and the festivals, in hunting, and in attendance on the exercise-grounds and the places of public conversation. Those who were under thirty years of age were not allowed to go into the market-place, but had the necessaries of their family supplied by the care of their relations. Nor was it for the credit of elderly men to be seen too often in the market-place; it was esteemed more suitable for them to frequent the exercise-grounds and places of conversation, where they spent their leisure rationally in conversation, not on money-making and market-prices, but for the most part in passing judgment on some action worth considering; extolling the good, and censuring those who were otherwise, and that in a light and sportive manner, conveying, without too much gravity, lessons of advice and improvement. Nor was Lycurgus himself unduly austere; it was he who dedicated the little statue of Laughter. Mirth, introduced seasonably at their suppers and places of common entertainment, was to serve as a sort of sweetmeat to accompany their strict and hard life. To conclude, he bred up his citizens in such a way that they neither would nor could live by themselves; they were to make themselves one with the public good, and, clustering like bees around their commander, be by their zeal and public spirit carried all but out of themselves, and devoted wholly to their country. What their sentiments were will better appear by a few of their sayings. Paedaretus, not being admitted into the list of the three hundred, returned home with a joyful face, well pleased to find that there were in Sparta three hundred better men than himself.

The senate, as I said before, consisted of those who were Lycurgus's chief aiders and assistants in his plans. The vacancies he ordered to be supplied out of the best and most deserving men past sixty years old; and we need not wonder if there was much striving for it; for what more glorious competition could there be among men, than one in which it was not contested who was swiftest among the swift or strongest of the strong, but who of many wise and good was wisest and best, and fittest to be entrusted for ever after, as the reward of his merits, with the supreme authority of the commonwealth, and with power over the lives, franchises, and highest interests of all his countrymen? The manner of their election was as follows: the people being called together, some selected persons were locked up in a room near the place of election, so contrived that they could neither see nor be seen, but could only hear the noise of the assembly without; for they decided this, as most other affairs of moment, by the shouts of the people. This done, the competitors were not brought in and presented all together, but one after another by lot, and passed in order through the assembly without speaking a word. Those who were locked up had writing-tables with them, in which they recorded and marked each shout by its loudness, without knowing in favor of which candidate each of them was made, but merely that they came first, second, third, and so forth. He who was found to have the most and loudest acclamations was declared senator duly elected. Upon this he had a garland set upon his head, and went in procession to all the temples to give thanks to the gods; a great number of young men followed him with applause, and women, also, singing verses in his honor, and extolling the virtue and happiness of his life. As he went round the city in this manner, each of his relations and friends set a table before him, saying, "The city honors you with this banquet;" but he, instead of accepting, passed round to the common table where he formerly used to eat, and was served as before, excepting that now he had a second allowance, which he took and put by. By the time supper was ended, the women who were of kin to him had come about the door; and he, beckoning to her whom he most esteemed, presented to her the portion he had saved, saying, that it had been a mark of esteem to him, and was so now to her; upon which she was triumphantly waited upon home by the women.

Touching burials, Lycurgus made very wise regulations; for, first of all, to cut off all superstition, he allowed them to bury their dead within the city, and even round about their temples, to the end that their youth might be accustomed to such spectacles, and not be afraid to see a dead body, or imagine that to touch a corpse or to tread upon a grave would defile a man. In the next place, he commanded them to put nothing into the ground with them, except, if they pleased, a few olive leaves, and the scarlet cloth that they were wrapped in. He would not suffer the names to be inscribed, except only of men who fell in the wars, or women who died in a sacred office. The time, too, appointed for mourning, was very short, eleven days; on the twelfth, they were to do sacrifice to Ceres,[16] and leave it off; so that we may see, that as he cut off all superfluity, so in things necessary there was nothing so small and trivial which did not express some homage of virtue or scorn of vice. He filled Lacedaemon all through with proofs and examples of good conduct; with the constant sight of which from their youth up, the people would hardly fail to be gradually formed and advanced in virtue.

And this was the reason why he forbade them to travel abroad, and go about acquainting themselves with foreign rules of morality, the habits of ill-educated people, and different views of government. Withal he banished from Lacedaemon all strangers who could not give a very good reason for their coming thither; not because he was afraid lest they should inform themselves of and imitate his manner of government (as Thucydides[17] says), or learn anything to their good; but rather lest they should introduce something contrary to good manners. With strange people, strange words must be admitted; these novelties produce novelties in thought; and on these follow views and feelings whose discordant character destroys the harmony of the state. He was as careful to save his city from the infection of foreign bad habits, as men usually are to prevent the introduction of a pestilence.

---

16. **Ceres:** goddess of agriculture.

17. **Thucydides:** Athenian historian (c. 471–c. 400 B.C.).

Hitherto I, for my part, see no sign of injustice or want of equity in the laws of Lycurgus, though some who admit them to be well contrived to make good soldiers, pronounce them defective in point of justice. The Cryptia, perhaps (if it were one of Lycurgus's ordinances, as Aristotle says it was), gave both him and Plato, too, this opinion alike of the lawgiver and his government. By this ordinance, the magistrates dispatched privately some of the ablest of the young men into the country, from time to time, armed only with their daggers, and taking a little necessary provision with them; in the daytime, they hid themselves in out-of-the-way places, and there lay close, but, in the night, issued out into the highways, and killed all the Helots they could light upon; sometimes they set upon them by day, as they were at work in the fields, and murdered them. As, also, Thucydides, in his history of the Peloponnesian war, tells us, that a good number of [the Helots], after being singled out for their bravery by the Spartans, garlanded, as enfranchised persons, and led about to all the temples in token of honors, shortly after disappeared all of a sudden, being about the number of two thousand; and no man either then or since could give an account how they came by their deaths. And Aristotle, in particular, adds, that the ephori, so soon as they were entered into their office, used to declare war against [the Helots], that they might be massacred without a breach of religion. It is confessed, on all hands, that the Spartans dealt with them very hardly; for it was a common thing to force them to drink to excess, and to lead them in that condition into their public halls, that the children might see what a sight a drunken man is; they made them to dance low dances, and sing ridiculous songs, forbidding them expressly to meddle with any of a better kind. And, accordingly, when the Thebans made their invasion into Laconia, and took a great number of the Helots, they could by no means persuade them to sing the verses of Terpander, Alcmaon, or Spendon, "For," said they, "the masters do not like it." So that it was truly observed by one, that in Sparta he who was free was most so, and he that was a slave there, the greatest slave in the world. For my part, I am of opinion that these outrages and cruelties began to be exercised in Sparta at a later time, especially after the great earthquake, when the Helots made a general insurrection, and, joining with the Messenians, laid the country waste, and brought the greatest danger upon the city. For I cannot persuade myself to ascribe to Lycurgus so wicked and barbarous a course, judging of him from the gentleness of his disposition and justice upon all other occasions; to which the oracle also testified.

When he perceived that his more important institutions had taken root in the minds of his countrymen, that custom had rendered them familiar and easy, that his commonwealth was now grown up and able to go alone, then, as Plato somewhere tells us, the Maker of the world, when first he saw it existing and beginning its motion, felt joy, even so Lycurgus, viewing with joy and satisfaction the greatness and beauty of his political structure, now fairly at work and in motion, conceived the thought to make it immortal too, and, as far as human forecast could reach, to deliver it down unchangeable to posterity. He called an extraordinary assembly of all the people, and told them that he now thought everything reasonably well established, both for the happiness and the virtue of the state; but that there was one thing still behind, of the greatest importance, which he thought not fit to impart until he had consulted the oracle; in the mean time, his desire was that they would observe the laws without any the least alteration until his return, and then he would do as the god should direct him. They all consented readily, and bade him hasten his journey; but, before he departed, he administered an oath to the two kings, the senate, and the whole commons, to abide by and maintain the established form of polity until Lycurgus should come back. This done, he set out for Delphi, and, having sacrificed to Apollo, asked him whether the laws he had established were good, and sufficient for a people's happiness and virtue. The oracle answered that the laws were excellent, and that the people, while it observed them, should live in the height of renown. Lycurgus took the oracle in writing, and sent it over to Sparta; and, having sacrificed the second time to Apollo, and taken leave of his friends and his son, he resolved that the Spartans should not be released from the oath they had taken, and that he would, of his own act, close his life where he was. He was now about that age in which life was still tolerable, and yet might be quitted without regret. Everything, moreover, about him was in a sufficiently prosperous condition. He, therefore, made an end of himself by a total abstinence from food; thinking it a statesman's duty to make his very death, if possible, an act of service to the state, and even in the end of his life to give some example of virtue and effect some useful purpose. He would, on the one hand, crown and consummate his own happiness by a death suitable to so honorable a life, and, on the other, would secure to his countrymen the enjoyment of the advantages he had spent his life in obtaining for them, since they had solemnly sworn the maintenance of his institutions until his return. Nor was he deceived in his expectations, for the city of Lacedaemon continued the chief city of all Greece for the space of five hundred years, in strict observance of Lycurgus's laws; in all which time there was no manner of alteration made, during the reign of fourteen kings, down to the time of Agis, the son of Archidamus. For the new creation of the ephori, though thought to be in favor of the people, was so far from diminishing, that it very much heightened, the aristocratic character of the government.

In the time of Agis, gold and silver first flowed into Sparta, and with them all those mischiefs which attend the immoderate desire of riches. Lysander promoted this disorder; for, by bringing in rich spoils from the wars, although himself incorrupt, he yet by this means filled his country with avarice and luxury, and subverted the laws and ordinances of Lycurgus; so long as which were in force, the aspect presented by Sparta was rather that of a rule of life followed by one wise and temperate man, than of the political government of a nation. And as the poets feign of Hercules, that, with his lion's skin and his club, he went over the world, punishing lawless and cruel tyrants, so may it be said of the Lacedaemonians, that, with a common staff[18] and a coarse coat, they gained the willing and joyful obedience of Greece, through whose whole extent they suppressed unjust usurpation and despotism, arbitrated in war, and composed civil dissension; and this often without so much as taking down one buckler, but barely by sending some one single deputy, to whose direction all at once submitted, like bees swarming and taking their places around their prince. Such a fund of order and equality, enough and to spare for others, existed in their state.

And therefore I cannot but wonder at those who say that the Spartans were good subjects, but bad governors, and for proof of it allege a saying of King Theopompus, who, when one said that Sparta held up so long because their kings could command so well, replied, "Nay, rather because the people know so well how to obey." For people do not obey, unless rulers know how to command; obedience is a lesson taught by commanders. A true leader himself creates the obedience of his own followers; as it is the last attainment in the art of riding to make a horse gentle and tractable, so is it of the science of government, to inspire men with a willingness to obey. The Lacedaemonians inspired men not with a mere willingness, but with an absolute desire, to be their subjects. For they did not send petitions to them for ships or money, or a supply of armed men, but only for a Spartan commander; and, having obtained one, used him with honor and reverence.

However, it was not the design of Lycurgus that his city should govern a great many others; he thought rather that the happiness of a state, as of a private man, consisted chiefly in the exercise of virtue, and in the concord of the inhabitants; his aim, therefore, in all his arrangements, was to make and keep them free-minded, self-dependent, and temperate. And therefore all those who have written well on politics, as Plato, Diogenes,[19] and Zeno,[20] have taken Lycurgus for their model, leaving behind them, however, mere projects and words; whereas Lycurgus was the author, not in writing but in reality, of a government which none else could so much as copy; and while men in general have treated the individual philosophic character as unattainable, he, by the example of a complete philosophic state, raised himself high above all other lawgivers of Greece. And so Aristotle says they did him less honor at Lacedaemon after his death than he deserved, although he has a temple there, and they offer sacrifices yearly to him as to a god.

---

18. **staff:** the stick around which the Spartans rolled their military dispatches.

19. **Diogenes:** philosopher and founder of the Cynic sect (c . 400–c. 325 B.C.).

20. **Zeno:** philosopher and founder of the Stoic school (325–263 B.C.).

DISCUSSION QUESTIONS

1. How would you describe the Spartan state that Lycurgus founded? Which practices in Sparta do you consider admirable? Which ones do you find **not** particularly admirable?

2. Plutarch begins his biography with a description of some of Lycurgus' ancestors. What does the story of King Soüs (great-grandfather of Lycurgus) contribute to this account?

3. What personal qualities of Lycurgus account for his enormous popularity? Which incidents best demonstrate these qualities?

4. What strategy did Lycurgus devise for discouraging the use of money? What benefits resulted from the elimination of money?

5. One unusual policy of the Spartan warriors was the practice of retreating from an enemy that had taken flight, rather than pursuing and killing the enemy warriors. What was the reasoning behind this retreat? What was the reasoning behind the Spartan law against making "war often, or long, with the same enemy"?

6. What strategy did Lycurgus use to keep Sparta on the path he had set, even after his death? How well did his strategy work?

SUGGESTIONS FOR WRITING

1. Imagine that you are a journalist living in Sparta during Lycurgus' reforms and that you are concerned about some of the changes taking place. Choose one new practice or aspect of life that you find particularly disturbing. Write an editorial explaining your objections and seeking to persuade other Spartans to share your concerns.

2. If Lycurgus were alive today and became principal of your school, he would probably want to make some changes. Imagine that he has given you the assignment of writing a student handbook to explain the new policies of the school. Feel free to use charts, drawings, lists, or anything else that will help make Lycurgus' expectations clear to students. Describe the academic and social climate that will now prevail in the school. Then explain to students how the new values and practices of the school will benefit them in the years to come. (You might also want to rename the school to reflect Lycurgus' philosophy of education.)

SAPPHO

(C. 620–C. 556 B.C.)

One of the earliest and greatest lyric poets, Sappho lived most of her life on the island of Lesbos in the Aegean Sea. During her childhood, political conflicts forced her family into exile, but she later returned to Lesbos, where she married and raised her children. During these years she also gathered a following of young women dedicated to the study of poetry and music. Many of her poems are addressed to these women.

Most of Sappho's work is now lost, and what survives is mainly fragmentary. But even her poetic fragments have had an immense influence on lyric poetry throughout the ages. Her poems are intensely personal, passionate, vivid, and simple. She had a genius for seeing beauty in ordinary objects and for capturing human feeling in a single phrase. ■

POEMS

Translated by Willis Barnstone

CEREMONY

Now the earth with many flowers
puts on her spring embroidery.

FULL MOON

The glow and beauty of the stars
are nothing near the splendid moon
when in her roundness she burns silver
about the world.

WORLD

I could not hope
to touch the sky
with my two arms.

TO APHRODITE AND THE NEREIDS

Kyprian[1] and Nereids,[2] I beg you
to bring my brother home safely,
and let him accomplish whatever
is in his heart.

5   Let him amend his former errors
and be a joy to his friends but
a terror to enemies—though never
again to us.

Let him do honor to his sister,
10   and be free of the black torment
which in other days of sorrow
ravaged his soul.

KLEÏS

I have a small daughter who is beautiful
like a gold flower. I would not trade
my darling Kleïs[3] for all Lydia[4] or even
for lovely Lesbos.

ANDROMEDA, WHAT NOW?

Can this farm girl
in farm-girl finery burn your heart?
She is even ignorant of the way
to lift her gown over her ankles.

A LANKY GROOM

Raise the ceiling and sing
Hymen![5]
Have carpenters raise the roof.
Hymen!
5   The groom who will come in
is tall like towering Ares.[6]

---

1. **Kyprian:** a name for Aphrodite, goddess of love, who was born from the sea and hence a patroness of sailors. The name *Kyprian* comes from the island of Cyprus, which was sacred to her.

2. **Nereids:** sea nymphs, the fifty daughters of Nereus, the Old Man of the Sea.

3. **Kleïs** (klē´is).

4. **Lydia:** a country in Asia Minor, famous for its great wealth.

5. **Hymen:** the god of marriage, invoked in wedding songs.

6. **Ares:** the god of war.

WEDDING SONG

Groom, we virgins at your door
will pass the night singing of the love
between you and your bride. Her limbs
are like violets.

5 Wake and call out the young men
your friends, and you can walk the streets
and we shall sleep less tonight than
the bright nightingale.

WEDDING OF ANDROMACHE

Kypros![7]
A herald came.
Idaos.[8] Racing powerfully.

Of the rest of Asia. Imperishable glory! (He said:)
5 "From holy Thebes and the waters of Plakia,[9]
graceful Andromache[10] coming with the navy
over the salt sea. They come with armbands of gold
and purple gowns and odd trinkets of rare design
and countless silver jars and ivory pins."
10 So he spoke. And Priam sprang to his feet

and the glowing news went from friend to friend
through the wide city. Instantly the sons of Ilios[11]
hitched the mules to their finely-wheeled chariots,
and a throng of wives and slender-ankled girls
15 climbed inside. Priam's daughters rode alone,
while young men led their horses under the cars.[12]
Greatly.
Charioteers.

                         Like gods.
20   Holy.
       They all set out for Ilium

---

7. Kypros: Aphrodite, goddess of love.

8. Idaos: a name meaning "from Ida," a mountain near Troy.

9. Plakia: mountain near Thebes.

10. Andromache (an drom′ə kē): daughter of the king of Thebes, an important city in Greece. Andromache married the Trojan hero, Hector, son of King Priam.

11. the sons of Ilios: the Trojans. Ilios was the founder of Troy, also called *Ilium*.

12. cars: chariots.

in the confusion of sweet flutes and crashing cymbals,
and girls sang a loud heavenly song
whose wonderful echo
25   touched the sky.
Everywhere in the streets.
Bowls and chalices.

Myrrh and cassia and incense rode on the wind.
Old women sang happily
30   and all the men sang out with thrilling force,
calling on Paean,[13] great archer, lord of the lyre,
and sang of Hektor and Andromache like gods.

TO DIKA, NOT TO GO BAREHEADED

Dika, take some shoots of dill, and loop
them skillfully about your lovely hair.
The happy Graces[14] love her who wears flowers
but turn their back on one who goes plain.

TO AN UNEDUCATED WOMAN

When dead you will lie forever forgotten,
for you have no claim to the Pierian[15] roses.
Dim here, you will move more dimly in Hell,
flitting among the undistinguished dead.

HER WEALTH

The golden Muses[16] gave me
true riches: when dead
I shall not be forgotten.

---

13. Paean (pē′ ən): the god Apollo. A paean was also a hymn of praise addressed to Apollo.

14. Graces: the three goddesses, daughters of Zeus, who were personifications of joy and beauty.

15. Pierian: referring to the Muses, from Pieria, the district in northern Greece that was their
birthplace.

16. Muses: the nine goddesses, daughters of Zeus and Mnemosyne (Memory), who presided over
music and poetry and inspired writers.

MONEY AND VIRTUE

If you are rich but not good
you court calamity,
yet being both
                    you stand
5   at the happy top of the world.

SOMEONE, I TELL YOU

Someone, I tell you,
will remember us.

We are oppressed by
Fears of oblivion

5   Yet are always saved
By judgment of good men.

THEN

In gold sandals
dawn like a thief
fell upon me.

DISCUSSION QUESTIONS

1. What are some of the recurring themes in the collection of poems
shown here? What impression do you get of Sappho as a person from
her choice of themes and from the way she handles these themes?

2. What does Sappho reveal about her relationship with her brother in
the poem titled "To Aphrodite and the Nereids"?

3. What do "To an Uneducated Woman," "Her Wealth," and
"Someone, I Tell You" have in common?

4. Sappho makes frequent use of personification in her nature poems.
Point out the ways in which natural forces are personified in
"Ceremony," "Full Moon," and "Then."

5. In "Wedding of Andromache" there is a sense of swift and joyful
movement. Which details contribute to the sense of rapid motion?
Consider the way the lines are laid out as well as the choice of words.

SUGGESTION FOR WRITING

Many of Sappho's writings are only fragments of lost poems, and so the reader can only speculate about the design of the original, full-length poems. Select one of the short fragments given here, such as "Ceremony," "World," or "Then." Think about the image that is given in the fragment and try to imagine what the longer poem might have been like. Then write a longer poem in the style of Sappho, using the fragment either at the beginning, in the middle, or at the end of your poem.

SOPHOCLES

(c. 496–c. 406 B.C.)

During his long life Sophocles wrote over 120 plays, of which only seven survive. Among those seven tragedies is *Oedipus the King,* considered by many people to be the greatest drama of all time. Of almost equal importance is his *Antigone,* a tragedy about a young woman in conflict with the state. Sophocles' works were widely admired by the Greeks, who awarded him the prize for tragedy over and over. Aristotle's famous definition of tragedy and his description of the tragic hero were derived from his knowledge of *Oedipus,* which he considered to be the perfect tragedy.

Sophocles' tragedies are clear, beautifully crafted, and extremely compressed. He tended to write single plays rather than trilogies, focusing on depth rather than breadth. Most of his plays involve a crisis of discovery, and Sophocles often shapes these plays around a special kind of irony that builds on the fact that the audience has complete knowledge of what is happening while the characters have only a limited awareness. He creates dramatic dialogues in which almost every statement means something different to the audience than it does to the characters. The double meaning that is created by such situations has been widely imitated by other dramatists but is still referred to as Sophoclean irony. This type of irony not only carries tremendous dramatic force but also emphasizes the difference between the illusions of human beings and the reality that tends to lie hidden from them. ■

OEDIPUS THE KING

Translated by H. D. F. Kitto

CHARACTERS

OEDIPUS, *King of Thebes*

PRIEST OF ZEUS

CREON, brother of *Iocasta*

TEIRESIAS, *a Seer*

IOCASTA, *Queen of Thebes*

A CORINTHIAN SHEPHERD

A THEBAN SHEPHERD

A MESSENGER

CHORUS OF THEBAN CITIZENS

PRIESTS, ATTENDANTS, ETC.

Scene: *Thebes,*[1] *before the royal palace*

OEDIPUS. My children, latest brood of ancient Cadmus,[2]
What purpose brings you here, a multitude
Bearing the boughs that mark the suppliant?
Why is our air so full of frankincense,
5   So full of hymns and prayers and lamentations?
This, children, was no matter to entrust
To others: therefore I myself am come
Whose fame is known to all—I, Oedipus.
—You, Sir, are pointed out by length of years
10   To be the spokesman: tell me, what is in
Your hearts? What fear? What sorrow? Count on all
That I can do, for I am not so hard
As not to pity such a supplication.

PRIEST. Great King of Thebes, and sovereign Oedipus,
15   Look on us, who now stand before the altars—
Some young, still weak of wing; some bowed with age—
The priests, as I, of Zeus; and these, the best
Of our young men; and in the market-place,
And by Athena's temples and the shrine
20   Of fiery divination, there is kneeling,
Each with his suppliant branch, the rest of Thebes.
The city, as you see yourself, is now
Storm-tossed, and can no longer raise its head
Above the waves and angry surge of death.
25   The fruitful blossoms of the land are barren,
The herds upon our pastures, and our wives
In childbirth, barren. Last, and worst of all,
The withering god of fever swoops on us
To empty Cadmus' city and enrich
30   Dark Hades with our groans and lamentations.
No god we count you, that we bring our prayers,
I and these children, to your palace-door,
But wise above all other men to read
Life's riddles, and the hidden ways of Heaven;
35   For it was you who came and set us free
From the blood-tribute that the cruel Sphinx[3]
Had laid upon our city; without our aid
Or our instruction, but, as we believe,
With god as ally, you gave us back our life.

---

1. **Thebes:** a city in central Greece.

2. **Cadmus:** founder of Thebes.

3. **Sphinx:** a monster, half-lion and half-woman. She sat on a hill near Thebes and devoured all
travelers who could not answer her riddle. None could until Oedipus succeeded, upon which
she killed herself.

40 So now, most dear, most mighty Oedipus,
We all entreat you on our bended knees,
Come to our rescue, whether from the gods
Or from some man you can find means to save.
For I have noted, *that* man's counsel is

45 Of best effect, who has been tried in action.
Come, noble Oedipus! Come, save our city.
Be well advised; for that past service given
This city calls you Savior; of your kingship
Let not the record be that first we rose

50 From ruin, then to ruin fell again.
No, save our city, let it stand secure.
You brought us gladness and deliverance
Before; now do no less. You rule this land;
Better to rule it full of living men

55 Than rule a desert; citadel or ship
Without its company of men is nothing.

OEDIPUS. My children, what you long for, that I know
Indeed, and pity you. I know how cruelly
You suffer; yet, though sick, not one of you

60 Suffers a sickness half as great as mine.
Yours is a single pain; each man of you
Feels but his own. My heart is heavy with
The city's pain, my own, and yours together.
You come to me not as to one asleep

65 And needing to be wakened; many a tear
I have been shedding, every path of thought
Have I been pacing; and what remedy,
What single hope my anxious thought has found
That I have tried. Creon, Menoeceus' son,

70 My own wife's brother, I have sent to Delphi
To ask in Phoebus' house[4] what act of mine,
What word of mine, may bring deliverance.
Now, as I count the days, it troubles me
What he is doing; his absence is prolonged

75 Beyond the proper time. But when he comes
Then write me down a villain, if I do
Not each particular that the god discloses.

PRIEST. You give us hope.—And here is more, for they
Are signaling that Creon has returned.

80 OEDIPUS. O Lord Apollo, even as Creon smiles,
Smile now on us, and let it be deliverance!

---

4. Delphi . . . Phoebus' house: Delphi was the site of a shrine to Apollo, who was called
Phoebus in his aspect as a sun-god. (See article on page xiii.)

PRIEST. The news is good; or he would not be wearing
That ample wreath of richly-berried laurel.[5]

OEDIPUS. We soon shall know; my voice will reach so far:
85   Creon my lord, my kinsman, what response
Do you bring with you from the god of Delphi?

Enter CREON.

CREON. Good news! Our sufferings, if they are guided right,
Can even yet turn to a happy issue.

OEDIPUS. This only leaves my fear and confidence
90   In equal balance: what did Phoebus say?

CREON. Is it your wish to hear it now, in public,
Or in the palace? I am at your service.

OEDIPUS. Let them all hear! Their sufferings distress
Me more than if my own life were at stake.

95   CREON. Then I will tell you what Apollo said—
And it was very clear. There is pollution
Here in our midst, long-standing. This must we
Expel, nor let it grow past remedy.

OEDIPUS. What has defiled us? and how are we to purge it?

100   CREON. By banishing or killing one who murdered,
And so called down this pestilence upon us.

OEDIPUS. Who is the man whose death the god denounces?

CREON. Before the city passed into your care,
My lord, we had a king called Laius.

105   OEDIPUS. So have I often heard.—I never saw him.

CREON. His death, Apollo clearly charges us,
We must avenge upon his murderers.

OEDIPUS. Where are they now? And where shall we disclose
The unseen traces of that ancient crime?

110   CREON. The god said, Here.—A man who hunts with care
May often find what other men will miss.

OEDIPUS. Where was he murdered? In the palace here?
Or in the country? Or was he abroad?

CREON. He made a journey to consult the god,
115   He said—and never came back home again.

---

5. **laurel:** a tree sacred to Apollo and symbolic of victory.

OEDIPUS. But was there no report? no fellow traveler
    Whose knowledge might have helped you in your search?

CREON. All died, except one terror-stricken man,
    And he could tell us nothing—next to nothing.

120   OEDIPUS. And what was that? One thing might lead to much,
    If only we could find one ray of light.

CREON. He said they met with brigands—not with one,
    But a whole company; they killed Laius.

OEDIPUS. A brigand would not *dare*—unless perhaps
125   Conspirators in Thebes had bribed the man.

CREON. There *was* conjecture; but disaster came
    And we were leaderless, without our king.

OEDIPUS. Disaster? With a king cut down like that
    You did not seek the cause? Where was the hindrance?

130   CREON. The Sphinx. *Her* riddle[6] pressed us harder still;
    For Laius—out of sight was out of mind.

OEDIPUS. I will begin again; *I'll* find the truth.
    The dead man's cause has found a true defender
    In Phoebus, and in you. And I will join you
135   In seeking vengeance on behalf of Thebes
    And Phoebus too; indeed, I must: if I
    Remove this taint, it is not for a stranger,
    But for myself: the man who murdered him
    Might make the same attempt on me; and so,
140   Avenging him, I shall protect myself.—
      Now you, my sons, without delay, arise,
    Take up your suppliant branches.—Someone, go
    And call the people here, for I will do
    What can be done; and either, by the grace
145   Of God we shall be saved—or we shall fall.

PRIEST. My children, we will go; the King has promised
    All that we came to ask.—O Phoebus, thou
    Hast given us an answer: give us too
    Protection! grant remission of the plague!

           Exeunt CREON, PRIESTS, *etc.* OEDIPUS *remains.*

---

6. riddle: the riddle of the Sphinx was "What creature walks on four legs in the morning, two
  legs in the afternoon, and three legs in the evening?" The correct answer, which Oedipus
  provided, was "Man, who crawls as a baby, walks upright in his prime, and walks with a staff in
  his declining years."

Enter the CHORUS[7] *representing the citizens of Thebes.*

STROPHE 1

150 CHORUS (*mainly dactyls*). Sweet is the voice of the god, that sounds
    in the
   Golden shrine of Delphi.
   What message has it sent to Thebes? My trembling
   Heart is torn with anguish.
   Thou god of Healing, Phoebus Apollo,
155 How do I fear! What hast thou in mind
   To bring upon us now? what is to be fulfilled
   From days of old?
   Tell me this, O Voice divine,
   Thou child of golden Hope.

ANTISTROPHE 1

160 First on the Daughter of Zeus I call for
   Help, divine Athene;[8]
   And Artemis,[9] whose throne is all the earth, whose
   Shrine is in our city;
   Apollo too, who shoots from afar:
165 Trinity of Powers, come to our defense!
   If ever in the past, when ruin threatened us,
   You stayed its course
   And turned aside the flood of Death,
   O then, protect us now!

STROPHE 2

170 (*agitated*) Past counting are the woes we suffer;
   Affliction bears on all the city, and
   Nowhere is any defense against destruction.
   The holy soil can bring no increase,
   Our women suffer and cry in childbirth
175 But do not bring forth living children.
   The souls of those who perish, one by one,
   Unceasingly, swift as raging fire,
   Rise and take their flight to the dark realms of the dead.

---

7. **Chorus:** In Sophocles' plays the chorus is not as central as it is in Aeschylus. Its voice is that of moderation, and it does not tend to be directly confrontational, as it does in the plays of Aeschylus. The choral odes are *strophic*, meaning that metrical systems are repeated in pairs. The first ode of a pair is called a *strophe*, the second, an *antistrophe*. The words *strophe* and *antistrophe* mean "turn" and "counter-turn." The chorus would recite the strophe marching across the stage in one direction and would then turn and recross the stage in the other direction reciting the antistrophe. The specific kind of metrical system used in each choral ode (dactyls, iambic, choriambic) is shown in parentheses by the translator.

8. **Athene:** goddess of wisdom.

9. **Artemis:** goddess of the hunt and of the moon.

Past counting, those of us who perish:
180 They lie upon the ground, unpitied,
Unburied, infecting the air with deadly pollution.
Young wives, and grey-haired mothers with them,
From every quarter approach the altars
And cry aloud in supplication.
185 The prayer for healing, the loud wail of lament,
Together are heard in dissonance:
O thou golden Daughter of Zeus, grant thy aid!

STROPHE 3

(*mainly iambic*) The fierce god of War has laid aside
His spear; but yet his terrible cry
190 Rings in our ears; he spreads death and destruction.
Ye gods, drive him back to his distant home!
For what the light of day has spared,
That the darkness of night destroys.
Zeus our father! All power is thine:
195 The lightning-flash is thine: hurl upon him
Thy thunderbolt, and quell this god of War!

ANTISTROPHE 3

We pray, Lord Apollo: draw thy bow
In our defense. Thy quiver is full of
Arrows unerring: shoot! slay the destroyer!
200 And thou, radiant Artemis, lend thy aid!
Thou whose hair is bound in gold,
Bacchus,[10] lord of the sacred dance,
Theban Bacchus! Come, show thyself!
Display thy blazing torch; drive from our midst
205 The savage god, abhorred by other gods!

OEDIPUS. Would you have answer to these prayers? Then hear
My words; give heed; your help may bring
Deliverance, and the end of all our troubles.
Here do I stand before you all, a stranger
210 Both to the deed and to the story.—What
Could I have done alone, without a clue?
But I was yet a foreigner; it was later
That I became a Theban among Thebans.
So now do I proclaim to all the city:
215 If any Theban knows by what man's hand
He perished, Laius, son of Labdacus,
Him I command to tell me all he can;
And if he is afraid, let him annul

---

10. **Bacchus:** god of wine.

Himself the charge he fears; no punishment
220   Shall fall on him, save only to depart
Unharmed from Thebes. Further, if any knows
The slayer to be a stranger from abroad,
Let him speak out; I will reward him, and
Besides, he will have all my gratitude.
225   But if you still keep silent, if any man
Fearing for self or friend shall disobey me,
This I will do—and listen to my words:
Whoever he may be, I do forbid
All in this realm, of which I am the King
230   And high authority, to shelter in their houses
Or speak to him, or let him be their partner
In prayers or sacrifices to the gods, or give
Him lustral water;[11] I command you all
To drive him from your doors; for he it is
235   That brings this plague upon us, as the god
Of Delphi has but now declared to me.—
So stern an ally do I make myself
Both of the god and of our murdered king.—
And for the man that slew him, whether he
240   Slew him alone, or with a band of helpers,
I lay this curse upon him, that the wretch
In wretchedness and misery may live.
And more: if with my knowledge he be found
To share my hearth and home, then upon me
245   Descend that doom that I invoke on him.
This charge I lay upon you, to observe
All my commands: to aid myself, the god,
And this our land, so spurned of Heaven, so ravaged.
For such a taint we should not leave unpurged—
250   The death of such a man, and he your king—
Even if Heaven had not commanded us,
But we should search it out. Now, since 'tis I
That wear the crown that he had worn before me,
And have his Queen to wife, and common children
255   Were born to us, but that his own did perish,
And sudden death has carried him away—
Because of this, I will defend his cause
As if it were my father's; nothing I
Will leave undone to find the man who killed
260   The son of Labdacus, and offspring of
Polydorus, Cadmus, and of old Agênor.[12]

---

11. **lustral water:** water used in the lustrum, the rite of purification.

12. **Agênor:** the king of Phoenicia and father of Cadmus, who founded Thebes and became its king. Polydorus, Labdacus, and Laius, the father of Oedipus, followed him on the throne.

On those that disobey, this is my curse:
May never field of theirs give increase, nor
Their wives have children; may our present plagues,
265 And worse, be ever theirs, for their destruction.
But for the others, all with whom my words
Find favor, this I pray: Justice and all
The gods be ever at your side to help you,

CHORUS-LEADER. Your curse constrains me; therefore will I speak.
270 I did not kill him, neither can I tell
Who did. It is for Phoebus, since he laid
The task upon us, to declare the man.

OEDIPUS. True; but to force the gods against their will—
That is a thing beyond all human power.

275 CHORUS-LEADER. All I could say is but a second best.

OEDIPUS. Though it were third best, do not hold it back.

CHORUS-LEADER. I know of none that reads Apollo's mind
So surely as the lord Teiresias;[13]
Consulting him you best might learn the truth.

280 OEDIPUS. Not even this have I neglected: Creon
Advised me, and already I have sent
Two messengers.—Strange he has not come.

CHORUS-LEADER. There's nothing else but old and idle gossip.

OEDIPUS. And what was that? I clutch at any straw.

285 CHORUS-LEADER. They said that he was killed by travelers.

OEDIPUS. So I have heard; but no one knows a witness.

CHORUS-LEADER. But if he is not proof against *all* fear
He'll not keep silent when he hears your curse.

OEDIPUS. And will they fear a curse, who dared to kill?

290 CHORUS-LEADER. Here is the one to find him, for at last
They bring the prophet here. He is inspired,
The only man whose heart is filled with truth.

Enter TEIRESIAS, *led by a boy.*

OEDIPUS. Teiresias, by your art you read the signs
And secrets of the earth and of the sky;
295 Therefore you know, although you cannot see,
The plague that is besetting us; from this

---

13. **Teiresias:** a blind seer, famous throughout Greece.

No other man but you, my lord, can save us.
Phoebus has said—you may have heard already—
In answer to our question, that this plague
300   Will never cease unless we can discover
What men they were who murdered Laius,
And punish them with death or banishment.
Therefore give freely all that you have learned
From birds or other form of divination;
305   Save us; save me, the city, and yourself,
From the pollution that his bloodshed causes.
No finer task, than to give all one has
In helping others; we are in your hands.

TEIRESIAS. Ah, what a burden knowledge is, when knowledge
310   Can be of no avail! I knew this well,
And yet forgot, or I should not have come.

OEDIPUS. Why, what is this? Why are you so despondent?

TEIRESIAS. Let me go home! It will be best for you,
And best for me, if you will let me go.

315   OEDIPUS. But to withhold your knowledge! This is wrong,
Disloyal to the city of your birth.

TEIRESIAS. I know that what you say will lead you on
To ruin; therefore, lest the same befall me too . . .

OEDIPUS. No, by the gods! Say all you know, for we
320   Go down upon our knees, your suppliants.

TEIRESIAS. Because *you* do *not* know! I never shall
Reveal my burden—I will not say *yours.*

OEDIPUS. You know, and will not tell us? Do you wish
To ruin Thebes and to destroy us all?

325   TEIRESIAS. *My* pain, and yours, will not be caused by me.
Why these vain questions?—for I will not speak.

OEDIPUS. You villain!—for you would provoke a stone
To anger: you'll not speak, but show yourself
So hard of heart and so inflexible?

330   TEIRESIAS. You heap the blame on me; but what is yours
You do not know—therefore *I* am the villain!

OEDIPUS. And who would not be angry, finding that
You treat our people with such cold disdain?

TEIRESIAS. The truth will come to light, without *my* help.

335   OEDIPUS. If it is bound to come, you ought to speak it.

TEIRESIAS. I'll say no more, and you, if so you choose,
　　May rage and bluster on without restraint.

OEDIPUS. Restraint? Then I'll show none! I'll tell you all
　　That I can see in you: I do believe
340　　This crime was planned and carried out by you,
　　All but the killing; and were you not blind
　　I'd say your hand alone had done the murder.

TEIRESIAS. So? Then I tell you this: submit yourself
　　To that decree that you have made; from now
345　　Address no word to these men nor to me:
　　You are the man whose crimes pollute our city.

OEDIPUS. What, does your impudence extend thus far?
　　And do you hope that it will go scot-free?

TEIRESIAS. It will. I have a champion—the truth.

350　OEDIPUS. Who taught you that? For it was not your art.

TEIRESIAS. No; you! You made me speak, against my will.

OEDIPUS. Speak what? Say it again, and say it clearly.

TEIRESIAS. Was I not clear? Or are you tempting me?

OEDIPUS. Not clear enough for me. Say it again.

355　TEIRESIAS. You are yourself the murderer you seek.

OEDIPUS. You'll not affront me twice and go unpunished!

TEIRESIAS. Then shall I give you still more cause for rage?

OEDIPUS. Say what you will; you'll say it to no purpose.

TEIRESIAS. *I* know, *you* do not know, the hideous life
360　　Of shame you lead with those most near to you.

OEDIPUS. You'll pay most dearly for this insolence!

TEIRESIAS. No, not if Truth is strong, and can prevail.

OEDIPUS. It is—except in you; for you are blind
　　In eyes and ears and brains and everything.

365　TEIRESIAS. You'll not forget these insults that you throw
　　At me, when all men throw the same at you.

OEDIPUS. You live in darkness; you can do no harm
　　To me or any man who has his eyes.

TEIRESIAS. No; *I* am not to bring you down, because
370　　Apollo is enough; he'll see to it.

OEDIPUS. Creon, or you? Which of you made this plot?

TEIRESIAS. Creon's no enemy of yours; you are your own.

OEDIPUS. O Wealth! O Royalty! Whose commanding art
    Outstrips all other arts in life's contentions!
375   How great a store of envy lies upon you,
    If for this scepter, that the city gave
    Freely to me, unasked—if now my friend,
    The trusty Creon, burns to drive me hence
    And steal it from me! So he has suborned
380   This crafty schemer here, this mountebank,
    Whose purse alone has eyes, whose art is blind.—
    Come, prophet, show your title! When the Sphinx
    Chanted her music here, why did not *you*
    Speak out and save the city? Yet such a question
385   Was one for augury, not for mother wit.
    You were no prophet then; your birds, your voice
    From Heaven, were dumb. But I, who came by chance,
    I, knowing nothing, put the Sphinx to flight,
    Thanks to my wit—no thanks to divination!
390   And now you try to drive me out; you hope
    When Creon's king to bask in Creon's favor.
    You'll expiate the curse? Ay, and repent it,
    Both you and your accomplice. But that you
    Seem old, I'd teach you what you gain by treason!

395 CHORUS-LEADER. My lord, he spoke in anger; so, I think,
    Did you. What help in angry speeches? Come,
    This is the task, how we can best discharge
    The duty that the god has laid on us.

TEIRESIAS. King though you are, I claim the privilege
400   Of equal answer. No, I have the right;
    I am no slave of yours—I serve Apollo,
    And therefore am not listed *Creon's* man.
    Listen—since you have taunted me with blindness!
    You have your sight, and yet you cannot see
405   Where, nor with whom, you live, nor in what horror.
    Your parents—do you know them? Or that you
    Are enemy to your kin, alive or dead?
    And that a father's and a mother's curse
    Shall join to drive you headlong out of Thebes
410   And change the light that now you see to darkness?
    Your cries of agony, where will they not reach?
    Where on Cithaeron[14] will they not re-echo?

---

14. Cithaeron: a mountain near Thebes.

When you have learned what meant the marriage-song
Which bore you to an evil haven here
415   After so fair a voyage? And you are blind
To other horrors, which shall make you one
With your own children. Therefore, heap your scorn
On Creon and on me, for no man living
Will meet a doom more terrible than yours.

420   OEDIPUS. What? Am I to suffer words like this from him?
Ruin, damnation seize you! Off at once
Out of our sight! Go! Get you whence you came!

TEIRESIAS. Had you not called me, I should not be here.

OEDIPUS. And had I known that you would talk such folly,
425   I'd not have called you to a house of mine.

TEIRESIAS. To you I seem a fool, but to your parents,
To those who did beget you, I was wise.

OEDIPUS. Stop! Who were they? Who *were* my parents? Tell me!

TEIRESIAS. This day will show your birth and your destruction.

430   OEDIPUS. You are too fond of dark obscurities.

TEIRESIAS. But do you not excel in reading riddles?

OEDIPUS. I scorn your taunts; my skill has brought me glory.

TEIRESIAS. And this success brought you to ruin too.

OEDIPUS. I am content, if so I saved this city.

435   TEIRESIAS. Then I will leave you. Come, boy, take my hand.

OEDIPUS. Yes, let him take it. You are nothing but
Vexation here. Begone, and give me peace!

TEIRESIAS. When I have had my say. No frown of yours
Shall frighten *me*; you cannot injure me.
440   Here is my message: that man whom you seek
With threats and proclamations for the death
Of Laius, he is living here; he's thought
To be a foreigner, but shall be found
Theban by birth—and little joy will this
445   Bring *him;* when, with his eyesight turned to blindness,
His wealth to beggary, on foreign soil
With staff in hand he'll tap his way along,
His children with him; and he will be known
Himself to be their father and their brother,
450   The husband of the mother who gave him birth,
Supplanter of his father, and his slayer.
—There! Go, and think on this; and if you find

That I'm deceived, say then—and not before—
That I am ignorant in divination.

Exeunt severally TEIRESIAS *and* OEDIPUS.

STROPHE 1

455   CHORUS. The voice of god rang out in the holy cavern,
       Denouncing one who has killed a King—the crime of crimes.
          Who is the man? Let him begone in
       Headlong flight, swift as a horse!
       (*anapests*) For the terrible god, like a warrior armed,
460   Stands ready to strike with a lightning-flash:
          The Furies who punish crime, and never fail,
          Are hot in their pursuit.

ANTISTROPHE 1

       The snow is white on the cliffs of high Parnassus.[15]
       It has flashed a message: Let every Theban join the hunt!
465   Lurking in caves among the mountains,
          Deep in the woods—where is the man?
       (*anapests*) In wearisome flight, unresting, alone,
          An outlaw, he shuns Apollo's shrine;
          But ever the living menace of the god
470   Hovers around his head.

STROPHE 2

       (*choriambics*) Strange, disturbing, what the wise
          Prophet has said. What can he mean?
          Neither can I believe, nor can I disbelieve;
          I do not know what to say.
475   I look here, and there; nothing can I find—
          No strife, either now or in the past,
          Between the kings of Thebes and Corinth.[16]
          A hand unknown struck down the King;
          Though I would learn who it was dealt the blow,
480   That *he* is guilty whom all revere—
          How can I believe this with no proof?

ANTISTROPHE 2

       Zeus, Apollo—they have knowledge;
          They understand the ways of life.
          Prophets are men, like me; that they can understand
485   More than is revealed to me—
          Of that, I can find nowhere certain proof,
          Though one man is wise, another foolish.

---

15. **Parnassus:** a mountain near Thebes, the location of Delphi.

16. **kings . . . Corinth:** The reputed father of Oedipus was Polybus, king of Corinth, who had raised him as if he were his own son.

Until the charge is manifest
I will not credit his accusers.
490 I saw myself how the Sphinx challenged him:
He proved his wisdom; he saved our city;
Therefore how can I now condemn him?

Enter CREON.

CREON. They tell me, Sirs, that Oedipus the King
Has made against me such an accusation
495 That I will not endure. For if he thinks
That in this present trouble I have done
Or said a single thing to do him harm,
Then let me die, and not drag out my days
With such a name as that. For it is not
500 One injury this accusation does me;
It touches my whole life, if you, my friends,
And all the city are to call me traitor.

CHORUS-LEADER. The accusation may perhaps have come
From heat of temper, not from sober judgment.

505 CREON. What was it made him think contrivances
Of mine suborned the seer to tell his lies?

CHORUS-LEADER. Those were his words; I do not know his reasons.

CREON. Was he in earnest, master of himself,
When he attacked me with this accusation?

510 CHORUS-LEADER. I do not closely scan what kings are doing.—
But here he comes in person from the palace.

Enter OEDIPUS.

OEDIPUS. What, *you?* You dare come here? How can you find
The impudence to show yourself before
My house, when you are clearly proven
515 To have sought my life and tried to steal my crown?
Why, do you think me then a coward, or
A fool, that you should try to lay this plot?
Or that I should not see what you were scheming,
And so fall unresisting, blindly, to you?
520 But you were mad, to attempt the throne,
Poor and unaided; this is not encompassed
Without the strong support of friends and money!

CREON. This you must do: now you have had your say
Hear my reply; then yourself shall judge.

525 OEDIPUS. A ready tongue! But I am bad at listening—
To you. For I have found how much you hate me.

CREON. One thing: first listen to what I have to say.

OEDIPUS. One thing: do not pretend you're not a villain.

CREON. If you believe it is a thing worth having,
530   Insensate stubbornness, then you are wrong.

OEDIPUS. If you believe that one can harm a kinsman
    Without retaliation, you are wrong.

CREON. With this I have no quarrel; but explain
    What injury you say that I have done you.

535 OEDIPUS. Did you advise, or did you not, that I
    Should send a man for that most reverend prophet?

CREON. I did, and I am still of that advice.

OEDIPUS. How long a time is it since Laius . . .

CREON. Since Laius did *what?* How can I say?

540 OEDIPUS. Was seen no more, but met a violent death?

CREON. It would be many years now past and gone.

OEDIPUS. And had this prophet learned his art already?

CREON. Yes; his repute was great—as it is now.

OEDIPUS. Did he make any mention then of me?

545 CREON. He never spoke of you within my hearing.

OEDIPUS. Touching the murder: did you make no search?

CREON. No search? Of course we did; but we found nothing.

OEDIPUS. And why did this wise prophet not speak *then?*

CREON. Who knows? Where I know nothing I say nothing.

550 OEDIPUS. This much you know—and you'd do well to answer!

CREON. What is it? If I know, I'll tell you freely.

OEDIPUS. That if he had not joined with you, he'd not
    Have said that I was Laius' murderer.

CREON. If he said this, I did not know.—But I
555   May rightly question you, as you have me.

OEDIPUS. Ask what you will. You'll never prove *I* killed him.

CREON. Why then: are you not married to my sister?

OEDIPUS. I am indeed; it cannot be denied.

CREON. You share with her the sovereignty of Thebes?

560 OEDIPUS. She need but ask, and anything is hers.

CREON. And am I not myself conjoined with you?

OEDIPUS. You are; not rebel therefore, but a traitor!

CREON. Not so, if you will reason with yourself,
  As I with you. This first: would any man,
565 To gain no increase of authority,
  Choose kingship, with its fears and sleepless nights?
  Not I. What I desire, what every man
  Desires, if he has wisdom, is to take
  The substance, not the show, of royalty.
570 For now, through you, I have both power and ease,
  But were I king, I'd be oppressed with cares.
  Not so: while I have ample sovereignty
  And rule in peace, why should I want the crown?
  I am not yet so mad as to give up
575 All that which brings me honor and advantage.
  Now, every man greets me, and I greet him;
  Those who have need of you make much of me,
  Since I can make or mar them. Why should I
  Surrender this to load myself with that?
580 A man of sense was never yet a traitor;
  I have no taste for that, nor could I force
  Myself to aid another's treachery.
    But you can test me: go to Delphi; ask
  If I reported rightly what was said.
585 And further: if you find that I had dealings
  With that diviner, you may take and kill me
  Not with your single vote, but yours and mine,
  But not on bare suspicion, unsupported.
  How wrong it is, to use a random judgment
590 And think the false man true, the true man false!
  To spurn a loyal friend, that is no better
  Than to destroy the life to which we cling.
  This you will learn in time, for Time alone
  Reveals the upright man; a single day
595 Suffices to unmask the treacherous.

CHORUS-LEADER. My lord, he speaks with caution, to avoid
  Grave error. Hasty judgment is not sure.

OEDIPUS. But when an enemy is quick to plot
  And strike, I must be quick in answer too.
600 If I am slow, and wait, then I shall find
  That he has gained his end, and I am lost.

CREON. What do you wish? To drive me into exile?

OEDIPUS. No, more than exile: I will have your life.

CREON. [When will it cease, this monstrous rage of yours?]

605   OEDIPUS. When your example shows what comes of envy.

CREON. Must you be stubborn? Cannot you believe me?

OEDIPUS. [You speak to me as if I were a fool!¹⁷]

CREON. Because I know you're wrong.

OEDIPUS.   Right, for myself!

CREON. It is not right for me!

OEDIPUS. But you're a traitor.

CREON. What if your charge is false?

610   OEDIPUS.   I have to govern.

CREON. Not govern badly!

OEDIPUS.   Listen to him, Thebes!

CREON. You're not the city! I am Theban too.

CHORUS-LEADER. My lords, no more! Here comes the Queen, and not
    Too soon, to join you. With her help, you must
615   Compose the bitter strife that now divides you.

Enter IOCASTA.

IOCASTA. You frantic men! What has aroused this wild
    Dispute? Have you no shame, when such a plague
    Afflicts us, to indulge in private quarrels?
    Creon, go home, I pray. You, Oedipus,
620   Come in; do not make much of what is nothing.

CREON. My sister: Oedipus, your husband here,
    Has thought it right to punish me with one
    Of two most awful dooms: exile, or death.

OEDIPUS. I have: I have convicted him, Iocasta,
625   Of plotting secretly against my life.

CREON. If I am guilty in a single point
    Of such a crime, then may I die accursed.

IOCASTA. O, by the gods, believe him, Oedipus!
    Respect the oath that he has sworn, and have
630   Regard for me, and for these citizens.

---

17. **When will it cease . . . if I were a fool:** The two lines in brackets (604 and 607) have been
    added by the translator in the belief that the originals were lost from the manuscript, causing
    the intervening lines to be wrongly attributed, the first to Creon, the second to Oedipus.

(In what follows, the parts given to the chorus are sung, the rest, presumably, spoken. The rhythm of the music and dance is either dochmiac, 5-time, or a combination of 3- and 5-time.)

STROPHE

CHORUS. My lord, I pray, give consent.
    Yield to us; ponder well.

OEDIPUS. What is it you would have me yield?

CHORUS. Respect a man ripe in years,
635   Bound by this mighty oath he has sworn.

OEDIPUS. Your wish is clear?

CHORUS.   It is.

OEDIPUS.   Then tell it me.

CHORUS. Not to repel, and drive out of our midst a friend,
    Scorning a solemn curse, for uncertain cause.

OEDIPUS. I tell you this: your prayer will mean for me
640   My banishment from Thebes, or else my death.

CHORUS. No, no! by the Sun, the chief of gods,
      Ruin and desolation and all evil come upon me
    If I harbor thoughts such as these!
    No; our land racked with plague breaks my heart.
645   Do not now deal a new wound on Thebes to crown the old!

OEDIPUS. Then let him be, though I must die twice over,
    Or be dishonored, spurned and driven out.
    It's your entreaty, and not his, that moves
    My pity; he shall have my lasting hatred.

650 CREON. You yield ungenerously; but when your wrath
    Has cooled, how it will prick you! Natures such
    As yours give most vexation to themselves.

OEDIPUS. O, let me be! Get from my sight.

CREON.   I go,
    Misjudged by you—but these will judge me better (*indicating*
    CHORUS).

                                Exit CREON.

ANTISTROPHE

655 CHORUS. My lady, why now delay?
    Let the King go in with you.

IOCASTA. When you have told me what has passed.

CHORUS. Suspicion came.—Random words, undeserved,
    Will provoke men to wrath.

IOCASTA. It was from both?

CHORUS.   It was.

660 IOCASTA.   And what was said?

CHORUS. It is enough for me, more than enough, when I
    Think of our ills, that this should rest where it lies.

OEDIPUS. You and your wise advice, blunting my wrath,
    Frustrated me—and it has come to this!

665 CHORUS. This, O my King, I said, and say again:
    I should be mad, distraught,
    I should be a fool, and worse,
    If I sought to drive you away.
    Thebes was near sinking; you brought her safe
670   Through the storm. Now again we pray that you may save us.

IOCASTA. In Heaven's name, my lord, I too must know
    What was the reason for this blazing anger.

OEDIPUS. There's none to whom I more defer; and so,
    I'll tell you: Creon and his vile plot against me.

675 IOCASTA. What has he done, that you are so incensed?

OEDIPUS. He says that I am Laius' murderer.

IOCASTA. From his own knowledge? Or has someone told him?

OEDIPUS. No; that suspicion should not fall upon
    Himself, he used a tool—a crafty prophet.

680 IOCASTA. Why, have no fear of *that*. Listen to me,
    And you will learn that the prophetic art
    Touches our human fortunes not at all.
    I soon can give you proof.—An oracle
    Once came to Laius—from the god himself
685   I do not say, but from his ministers:
    His fate it was, that should he have a son
    By me, that son would take his father's life.
    But he was killed—or so they said—by strangers,
    By brigands, at a place where three ways meet.
690   As for the child, it was not three days old
    When Laius fastened both its feet together
    And had it cast over a precipice.
    Therefore Apollo failed; for neither did
    His son kill Laius, nor did Laius meet
695   The awful end he feared, killed by his son.
      So much for what prophetic voices uttered.
    Have no regard for them. The god will bring
    To light himself whatever thing he chooses.

OEDIPUS. Iocasta, terror seizes me, and shakes
700   My very soul, at one thing you have said.

IOCASTA. Why so? What have I said to frighten you?

OEDIPUS. I think I heard you say that Laius
    Was murdered at a place where three ways meet?

IOCASTA. So it was said—indeed, they say it still.

705   OEDIPUS. Where is the place where this encounter happened?

IOCASTA. They call the country Phokis, and a road
    From Delphi joins a road from Daulia.[18]

OEDIPUS. Since that was done, how many years have passed?

IOCASTA. It was proclaimed in Thebes a little time
710   Before the city offered you the crown.

OEDIPUS. O Zeus, what fate hast thou ordained for me?

IOCASTA. What is the fear that so oppresses you?

OEDIPUS. One moment yet: tell me of Laius.
    What age was he? and what was his appearance?

715   IOCASTA. A tall man, and his hair was touched with white;
    In figure he was not unlike yourself.

OEDIPUS. O God! Did I, then, in my ignorance,
    Proclaim that awful curse against myself?

IOCASTA. What are you saying? How you frighten me!

720   OEDIPUS. I greatly fear that prophet was not blind.
    But yet one question; that will show me more.

IOCASTA. For all my fear, I'll tell you what I can.

OEDIPUS. Was he alone, or did he have with him
    A royal bodyguard of men-at-arms?

725   IOCASTA. The company in all were five; the King
    Rode in a carriage, and there was a Herald.

OEDIPUS. Ah God! How clear the picture is! . . . But who,
    Iocasta, brought report of this to Thebes?

IOCASTA. A slave, the only man that was not killed.

730   OEDIPUS. And is he round about the palace now?

---

18. Phokis . . . Daulia: Phokis was a district in central Greece north of the Gulf of Corinth. Daulia was a city in Phokis, about twelve miles east of Delphi.

IOCASTA. No, he is not. When he returned, and saw
    You ruling in the place of the dead King,
    He begged me, on his bended knees, to send him
    Into the hills as shepherd, out of sight,
735   As far as could be from the city here.
    I sent him, for he was a loyal slave;
    He well deserved this favor—and much more.

OEDIPUS. Could he be brought back here—at once—to see me?

IOCASTA. He could; but why do you desire his coming?

740 OEDIPUS. I fear I have already said, Iocasta,
    More than enough; and therefore I will see him.

IOCASTA. Then he shall come. But, as your wife, I ask you,
    What is the terror that possesses you?

OEDIPUS. And you shall know it, since my fears have grown
745   So great; for who is more to me than you,
    That I should speak to *him* at such a moment?
    My father, then, was Polybus of Corinth;
    My mother, Merope. My station there
    Was high as any man's—until a thing
750   Befell me that was strange indeed, though not
    Deserving of the thought I gave to it.
    A man said at a banquet—he was full
    Of wine—that I was not my father's son.
    It angered me; but I restrained myself
755   That day. The next I went and questioned both
    My parents. They were much incensed with him
    Who had let fall the insult. So, from them,
    I had assurance. Yet the slander spread
    And always chafed me. Therefore secretly,
760   My mother and my father unaware,
    I went to Delphi. Phoebus would return
    No answer to my question, but declared
    A thing most horrible: he foretold that I
    Should mate with my own mother, and beget
765   A brood that men would shudder to behold,
    And that I was to be the murderer
    Of my own father.
       Therefore, back to Corinth
    I never went—the stars alone have told me
    Where Corinth lies—that I might never see
770   Cruel fulfilment of that oracle.
    So journeying, I came to that same spot
    Where, as you say, this King was killed. And now,
    This is the truth, Iocasta: when I reached
    The place where three ways meet, I met a herald,

775 And in a carriage drawn by colts was such
A man as you describe. By violence
The herald and the older man attempted
To push me off the road. I, in my rage,
Struck at the driver, who was hustling me.
780 The old man, when he saw me level with him,
Taking a double-goad, aimed at my head
A murderous blow. He paid for that, full measure.
Swiftly I hit him with my staff; he rolled
Out of his carriage, flat upon his back.
785 I killed them all.—But if, between this stranger
And Laius there was any bond of kinship,
Who could be in more desperate plight than I?
Who more accursed in the eyes of Heaven?
For neither citizen nor stranger may
790 Receive me in his house, nor speak to me,
But he must bar the door. And it was none
But I invoked this curse on my own head!
And I pollute the bed of him I slew
With my own hands! Say, am I vile! Am I
795 Not all impure? Seeing I must be exiled,
And even in my exile must not go
And see my parents, nor set foot upon
My native land; or, if I do, I must
Marry my mother, and kill Polybus
800 My father, who engendered me and reared me.
If one should say it was a cruel god
Brought this upon me, would he not speak right?
    No, no, you holy powers above! Let me
Not see that day! but rather let me pass
805 Beyond the sight of men, before I see
The stain of such pollution come upon me!

CHORUS-LEADER. My lord, this frightens me.
    But you must hope,
    Until we hear the tale from him that saw it.

OEDIPUS. That is the only hope that's left to me;
810 We must await the coming of the shepherd.

IOCASTA. What do you hope from him, when he is here?

OEDIPUS. I'll tell you: if his story shall be found
    The same as yours, then I am free of guilt.

IOCASTA. But what have *I* said of especial note?

815 OEDIPUS. You said that he reported it was brigands
    Who killed the King. If he still speaks of 'men,'
    It was not I; a single man, and 'men,'

Are not the same. But if he says it was
A traveler journeying alone, why then,
820   The burden of the guilt must fall on me.

IOCASTA. But that *is* what he said, I do assure you!
He cannot take it back again! Not I
Alone, but the whole city heard him say it!
But even if he should revoke the tale
825   He told before, not even so, my lord,
Will he establish that the King was slain
According to the prophecy. For that was clear:
His son, and mine, should slay him.—He, poor thing,
Was killed himself, and never killed his father.
830   Therefore, so far as divination goes,
Or prophecy, I'll take no notice of it.

OEDIPUS. And that is wise.—But send a man to bring
The shepherd; I would not have that neglected.

IOCASTA. I'll send at once.—But come with me; for I
835   Would not do anything that could displease you.

Exeunt OEDIPUS *and* IOCASTA.

STROPHE 1

CHORUS (*in a steady rhythm*). I pray that I may pass my life
In reverent holiness of word and deed.
For there are laws enthroned above;
Heaven created them,
840   Olympus was their father,
And mortal men had no part in their birth;
Nor ever shall their power pass from sight
In dull forgetfulness;
A god moves in them; he grows not old.

ANTISTROPHE 1

845   Pride makes the tyrant—pride of wealth
And power, too great for wisdom and restraint;
For Pride will climb the topmost height;
Then is the man cast down
To uttermost destruction.
850   There he finds no escape, no resource.
But high contention for the city's good
May the gods preserve.
For me—may the gods be my defense!

STROPHE 2

If there is one who walks in pride
855   Of word or deed, and has no fear of Justice,
No reverence for holy shrines—
May utter ruin fall on him!

So may his ill-starred pride be given its reward.
Those who seek dishonorable advantage
860 And lay violent hands on holy things
And do not shun impiety—
Who among these will secure himself from the wrath of God?
If deeds like these are honored,
Why should I join in the sacred dance?

ANTISTROPHE 2

865 No longer shall Apollo's shrine,
The holy center of the Earth,[19] receive my worship;
No, nor his seat at Abae,[20] nor
The temple of Olympian Zeus,[21]
If what the god foretold does not come to pass.
870 Mighty Zeus—if so I should address Thee—
O great Ruler of all things, look on this!
Now are thy oracles falling into contempt, and men
Deny Apollo's power.
Worship of the gods is passing away.

Enter IOCASTA, *attended by a girl carrying a wreath and incense.*

875 IOCASTA. My lords of Thebes, I have bethought myself
To approach the altars of the gods, and lay
These wreaths on them, and burn this frankincense.
For every kind of terror has laid hold
On Oedipus; his judgment is distracted.
880 He will not read the future by the past
But yields himself to any who speaks fear.
Since then no words of mine suffice to calm him
I turn to Thee, Apollo—Thou art nearest—
Thy suppliant, with these votive offerings.
885 Grant us deliverance and peace, for now
Fear is on all, when we see Oedipus,
The helmsman of the ship, so terrified.

(*A reverent silence, while* IOCASTA *lays the wreath at the altar and sets
fire to the incense. The wreath will remain and the incense
smoke during the rest of the play.*)

Enter a SHEPHERD FROM CORINTH.

---

19. **The holy center of the Earth:** The *omphalos* ("navel"), a round stone in the shrine at Delphi, was believed to mark the center of the earth.

20. **Abae:** a city in Phokis, site of a shrine to Apollo.

21. **The temple of Olympian Zeus:** Olympia, a site in the western Peloponnesus, was the main sanctuary of Zeus in Greece.

CORINTHIAN. Might I inquire of you where I may find
The royal palace of King Oedipus?
890   Or, better, where himself is to be found?

CHORUS-LEADER. There is the palace; himself, Sir, is within,
But here his wife and mother of his children.

CORINTHIAN. Ever may happiness attend on her,
And hers, the wedded wife of such a man.

895 IOCASTA. May you enjoy the same; your gentle words
Deserve no less.—Now, Sir, declare your purpose;
With what request, what message have you come?

CORINTHIAN. With good news for your husband and his house.

IOCASTA. What news is this? And who has sent you here?

900 CORINTHIAN. I come from Corinth, and the news I bring
Will give you joy, though joy be crossed with grief.

IOCASTA. What is this, with its two-fold influence?

CORINTHIAN. The common talk in Corinth is that they
Will call on Oedipus to be their king.

905 IOCASTA. What? Does old Polybus no longer reign?

CORINTHIAN. Not now, for Death has laid him in his grave.

IOCASTA. Go quickly to your master, girl; give him
The news.—You oracles, where are you now?
This is the man whom Oedipus so long
910   Has shunned, fearing to kill him; now he's dead,
And killed by Fortune, not by Oedipus.

Enter OEDIPUS, *very nervous.*

OEDIPUS. My dear Iocasta, tell me, my dear wife,
Why have you sent to fetch me from the palace?

IOCASTA. Listen to *him,* and as you hear, reflect
915   What has become of all those oracles.

OEDIPUS. Who is this man?—What has he to tell me?

IOCASTA. He is from Corinth, and he brings you news
About your father. Polybus is dead.

OEDIPUS. What say you, sir? Tell me the news yourself.

920 CORINTHIAN. If you would have me first report on this,
I tell you; death has carried him away.

OEDIPUS. By treachery? Or did sickness come to him?

CORINTHIAN. A small mischance will lay an old man low.

OEDIPUS. Poor Polybus! He died, then, of a sickness?

925 CORINTHIAN. That, and the measure of his many years.

OEDIPUS. Ah me! Why then, Iocasta, should a man
Regard the Pythian house of oracles,[22]
Or screaming birds, on whose authority
I was to slay my father? But he is dead;
930 The earth has covered him; and here am I,
My sword undrawn—unless perchance *my* loss
Has killed him; so might I be called his slayer.
But for those oracles about my father,
Those he has taken with him to the grave
935 Wherein he lies, and they are come to nothing.

IOCASTA. Did I not say long since it would be so?

OEDIPUS. You did; but I was led astray by fear.

IOCASTA. So none of this deserves another thought.

OEDIPUS. Yet how can I not fear my mother's bed?

940 IOCASTA. Why should we fear, seeing that man is ruled
By chance, and there is room for no clear forethought?
No; live at random, live as best one can.
So do not fear this marriage with your mother;
Many a man has suffered this before—
945 But only in his dreams. Whoever thinks
The least of this, he lives most comfortably.

OEDIPUS. Your every word I do accept, if she
That bore me did not live; but as she does—
Despite your wisdom, how can I but tremble?

950 IOCASTA. Yet there is comfort in your father's death.

OEDIPUS. Great comfort, but still fear of her who lives.

CORINTHIAN. And who is this who makes you so afraid?

OEDIPUS. Merope, my man, the wife of Polybus.

CORINTHIAN. And what in *her* gives cause of fear in *you?*

955 OEDIPUS. There was an awful warning from the gods.

CORINTHIAN. Can it be told, or must it be kept secret?

OEDIPUS. No secret. Once Apollo said that I
Was doomed to lie with own mother, and
Defile my own hands with my father's blood.

---

22. **Pythian house of oracles:** the shrine of Apollo at Delphi.

960   Wherefore has Corinth been, these many years,
My home no more. My fortunes have been fair.—
But it is good to see a parent's face.

CORINTHIAN. It was for fear of *this* you fled the city?

OEDIPUS. This, and the shedding of my father's blood.

965 CORINTHIAN. Why then, my lord, since I am come in friendship,
I'll rid you here and now of that misgiving.

OEDIPUS. Be sure, your recompense would be in keeping.

CORINTHIAN. It was the chief cause of my coming here
That your return might bring me some advantage.

970 OEDIPUS. Back to my parents I will never go.

CORINTHIAN. My son, it is clear, you know not what you do. . . .

OEDIPUS. Not know? What is this? Tell me what you mean.

CORINTHIAN. If for this reason you avoid your home.

OEDIPUS. Fearing Apollo's oracle may come true.

975 CORINTHIAN. And you incur pollution from your parents?

OEDIPUS. That is the thought that makes me live in terror.

CORINTHIAN. I tell you then, this fear of yours is idle.

OEDIPUS. How? Am I not their child, and they my parents?

CORINTHIAN. Because there's none of Polybus in you.

980 OEDIPUS. How can you say so? Was he not my father?

CORINTHIAN. I am your father just as much as he!

OEDIPUS. A stranger equal to the father? How?

CORINTHIAN. Neither did he beget you, nor did I.

OEDIPUS. Then for what reason did he call me son?

985 CORINTHIAN. He had you as a gift—from my own hands.

OEDIPUS. And showed such love to me? Me, not his own?

CORINTHIAN. Yes; his own childlessness so worked on him.

OEDIPUS. You, when you gave me: had you bought, or found me?

CORINTHIAN. I found you in the woods upon Cithaeron.

990 OEDIPUS. Why were you traveling in that neighborhood?

CORINTHIAN. I tended flocks of sheep upon the mountain.

OEDIPUS. You were a shepherd, then, wandering for hire?

CORINTHIAN. I was, my son; but that day, your preserver.

OEDIPUS. How so? What ailed me when you took me up?

995 CORINTHIAN. For that, your ankles might give evidence.

OEDIPUS. Alas! why speak of this, my life-long trouble?

CORINTHIAN. I loosed the fetters clamped upon your feet.

OEDIPUS. A pretty gift to carry from the cradle!

CORINTHIAN. It was for this they named you Oedipus.[23]

1000 OEDIPUS. Who did, my father or my mother? Tell me.

CORINTHIAN. I cannot; he knows more, from whom I had you.

OEDIPUS. It was another, not yourself, that found me?

CORINTHIAN. Yes, you were given me by another shepherd.

OEDIPUS. Who? Do you know him? Can you name the man?

1005 CORINTHIAN. They said that he belonged to Laius.

OEDIPUS. What—him who once was ruler here in Thebes?

CORINTHIAN. Yes, he it was for whom this man was shepherd.

OEDIPUS. And is he still alive, that I can see him?

CORINTHIAN (*turning to the* CHORUS).
   You that are native here would know that best.

1010 OEDIPUS. Has any man of you now present here
   Acquaintance with this shepherd, him he speaks of?
   Has any seen him, here, or in the fields?
   Speak; on this moment hangs discovery.

CHORUS-LEADER. It is, I think, the man that you have sent for,
1015   The slave now in the country. But who should know
   The truth of this more than Iocasta here?

OEDIPUS. The man he speaks of: do you think, Iocasta,
   He is the one I have already summoned?

IOCASTA. What matters who he is? Pay no regard.—
1020   The tale is idle; it is best forgotten.

OEDIPUS. It cannot be that I should have this clue
   And then not find the secret of my birth.

IOCASTA. In God's name stop, if you have any thought
   For your own life! My ruin is enough.

---

23. **Oedipus:** The Greek word *oedipus* means "swollen foot."

1025 OEDIPUS. Be not dismayed; nothing can prove you base.
  Not though I find my mother thrice a slave.

IOCASTA. O, I beseech you, do not! Seek no more!

OEDIPUS. You cannot move me. I *will* know the truth.

IOCASTA. I know that what I say is for the best.

1030 OEDIPUS. This 'best' of yours! I have no patience with it.

IOCASTA. O may you never learn what man you are!

OEDIPUS. Go, someone, bring the herdsman here to me,
  And leave her to enjoy her pride of birth.

IOCASTA. O man of doom! For by no other name
1035   Can I address you now or evermore.

Exit IOCASTA.

CHORUS-LEADER. The Queen has fled, my lord, as if before
  Some driving storm of grief. I fear that from
  Her silence may break forth some great disaster.

OEDIPUS. Break forth what will! My birth, however humble,
1040   I am resolved to find. But she, perhaps,
  Is proud, as women will be; is ashamed
  Of my low birth. But I do rate myself
  The child of Fortune, giver of all good,
  And I shall not be put to shame, for I
1045   Am born of Her; the Years who are my kinsmen
  Distinguished my estate, now high, now low;
  So born, I could not make me someone else,
  And not do all to find my parentage.

STROPHE 1

CHORUS (*animated rhythm*). If I have power of prophecy,
1050   If I have judgment wise and sure, Cithaeron
  (I swear by Olympus),
  Thou shalt be honored when the moon
  Next is full, as mother and foster-nurse
  And birth-place of Oedipus, with festival and dancing,
1055   For thou hast given great blessings to our King.
  To Thee, Apollo, now we raise our cry:
  O grant our prayer find favor in thy sight!

ANTISTROPHE 1

  Who is thy mother, O my son?
  Is she an ageless nymph among the mountains,
1060   That bore thee to Pan?[24]

---

24. **Pan:** god of woods and fields, patron of shepherds.

Or did Apollo father thee?
For dear to him are the pastures in the hills.
Or Hermes,[25] who ruleth from the summit of Kyllene?[26]
Or Dionysus[27] on the mountain-tops,
1065   Did he receive thee from thy mother's arms,
A nymph who follows him on Helicon?[28]

OEDIPUS. If I, who never yet have met the man,
May risk conjecture, I think I see the herdsman
Whom we have long been seeking. In his age
1070   He well accords; and more, I recognize
Those who are with him as of my own household.
But as for knowing, you will have advantage
Of me, if you have seen the man before.

CHORUS-LEADER. 'Tis he, for certain—one of Laius' men,
1075   One of the shepherds whom he trusted most.

Enter the THEBAN SHEPHERD.

OEDIPUS. You first I ask, you who have come from Corinth:
Is that the man you mean?

CORINTHIAN.   That very man.

OEDIPUS. Come here, my man; look at me; answer me
My questions. Were you ever Laius' man?

1080 THEBAN. I was his slave—born in the house, not bought.

OEDIPUS. What was your charge, or what your way of life?

THEBAN. Tending the sheep, the most part of my life.

OEDIPUS. And to what regions did you most resort?

THEBAN. Now it was Cithaeron, now the country round.

1085 OEDIPUS. And was this man of your acquaintance there?

THEBAN. In what employment? Which is the man you mean?

OEDIPUS. Him yonder. Had you any dealings with him?

THEBAN. Not such that I can quickly call to mind.

CORINTHIAN. No wonder, Sir, but though he has forgotten
1090   I can remind him. I am very sure,

---

25. Hermes: the messenger of Zeus.

26. Kyllene: a mountain near Corinth.

27. Dionysus: another name for the god of wine.

28. Helicon: a mountain in central Greece.

He knows the time when, round about Cithaeron,
He with a double flock, and I with one,
We spent together three whole summer seasons,
From spring until the rising of Arcturus.[29]

1095 Then, with the coming on of winter, I
Drove my flocks home, he his, to Laius' folds.
Is this the truth? or am I telling lies?

THEBAN. It is true, although it happened long ago.

CORINTHIAN. Then tell me: do you recollect a baby
1100 You gave me once to bring up for my own?

THEBAN. Why this? Why are you asking me this question?

CORINTHIAN. My friend, *here* is the man who was that baby!

THEBAN. O, devil take you! Cannot you keep silent?

OEDIPUS. Here, Sir! This man needs no reproof from you.
1105 Your tongue needs chastisement much more than his.

THEBAN. O best of masters, how am I offending?

OEDIPUS. Not telling of the child of whom he speaks.

THEBAN. He? He knows nothing. He is wasting time.

OEDIPUS (*threatening*). If you'll not speak from pleasure, speak
from pain.

1110 THEBAN. No, no, I pray! Not torture an old man!

OEDIPUS. Here, someone, quickly! Twist this fellow's arms!

THEBAN. Why, wretched man? What would you know besides?

OEDIPUS. That child: you gave it him, the one he speaks of?

THEBAN. I did. Ah God, would I had died instead!

1115 OEDIPUS. And die you shall, unless you speak the truth.

THEBAN. And if I do, then death is still more certain.

OEDIPUS. This man, I think, is trying to delay me.

THEBAN. Not I! I said I gave the child—just now.

OEDIPUS. And got it—where? Your own? or someone else's?

1120 THEBAN. No, not my own. Someone had given it me.

OEDIPUS. Who? Which of these our citizens? From what house?

THEBAN. No, I implore you, master! Do not ask!

---

29. **Arcturus:** a bright star that appears in September, serving as a sign to the ancient Greeks that
summer was ending and that it was time to prepare for winter.

OEDIPUS. You die if I must question you again.

THEBAN. Then, 'twas a child of one in Laius' house.

1125 OEDIPUS. You mean a slave? Or someone of his kin?

THEBAN. God! I am on the verge of saying it.

OEDIPUS. And I of hearing it, but hear I must.

THEBAN. His own, or so they said. But she within
Could tell you best—your wife—the truth of it.

OEDIPUS. What, did she give you it?

1130 THEBAN.   She did, my lord.

OEDIPUS. With what intention?

THEBAN.   That I should destroy it.

OEDIPUS. Her own?—How could she?

THEBAN.   Frightened by oracles.

OEDIPUS. What oracles?

THEBAN. That it would kill its parents.

OEDIPUS. Why did you let it go to this man here?

1135 THEBAN. I pitied it, my lord. I thought to send
The child abroad, whence this man came. And he
Saved it, for utter doom. For if you are
The man he says, then you were born for ruin.

OEDIPUS. Ah God! Ah God! This is the truth, at last!
1140 O Sun, let me behold thee this once more,
I who am proved accursed in my conception,
And in my marriage, and in him I slew.

Exeunt severally OEDIPUS, CORINTHIAN, THEBAN.

STROPHE 1

CHORUS (*glyconics*). Alas! you generations of men!
Even while you live you are next to nothing!
1145 Has any man won for himself
More than the shadow of happiness,
A shadow that swiftly fades away?
Oedipus, now as I look on you,
See your ruin, how can I say that
1150 Mortal man can be happy?

ANTISTROPHE 1

For who won greater prosperity?
Sovereignty and wealth beyond all desiring?
The crooked-clawed, riddling Sphinx,

Maiden and bird, you overcame;
1155 You stood like a tower of strength to Thebes.
So you received our crown, received the
Highest honors that we could give—
King in our mighty city.

STROPHE 2

Who more wretched, more afflicted now,
1160 With cruel misery, with fell disaster,
Your life in dust and ashes?
O noble Oedipus!
How could it be? to come again
A bridegroom of her who gave you birth!
1165 How could such a monstrous thing
Endure so long, unknown?

ANTISTROPHE 2

Time sees all, and Time, in your despite,
Disclosed and punished your unnatural marriage—
A child, and then a husband.
1170 O son of Laius,
Would I had never looked on you!
I mourn you as one who mourns the dead.
First you gave me back my life,
And now, that life is death.

Enter, from the palace, a MESSENGER.

1175 MESSENGER. My lords, most honored citizens of Thebes,
What deeds am I to tell of, you to see!
What heavy grief to bear, if still remains
Your native loyalty to our line of kings.
For not the Ister, no, nor Phasis'[30] flood
1180 Could purify this house, such things it hides,
Such others will it soon display to all,
Evils self-sought. Of all our sufferings
Those hurt the most that we ourselves inflict.

CHORUS-LEADER. Sorrow enough—too much—in what was known
1185 Already. What new sorrow do you bring?

MESSENGER. Quickest for me to say and you to hear:
It is the Queen, Iocasta—she is dead.

CHORUS-LEADER. Iocasta, dead? But how! What was the cause?

MESSENGER. By her own hand. Of what has passed, the worst
1190 Cannot be yours: that was, to see it.
But you shall hear, so far as memory serves,

---

30. Ister . . . Phasis. Ister was the Greek name for the lower Danube River. The Phasis, now called
the Rion, is a river of Asia Minor that empties into the Black Sea.

The cruel story.—In her agony
She ran across the courtyard, snatching at
Her hair with both her hands. She made her way
1195   Straight to her chamber; she barred fast the doors
And called on Laius, these long years dead,
Remembering their by-gone procreation.
"Through this did you meet death yourself, and leave
To me, the mother, child-bearing accursed
1200   To my own child." She cried aloud upon
The bed where she had borne a double brood,
Husband from husband, children from a child.
And thereupon she died, I know not how;
For, groaning, Oedipus burst in, and we,
1205   For watching him, saw not *her* agony
And how it ended. He, ranging through the palace,
Came up to each man calling for a sword,
Calling for her whom he had called his wife,
Asking where was she who had borne them all,
1210   Himself and his own children. So he raved.
And then some deity showed him the way,
For it was none of us that stood around;
He cried aloud, as if to someone who
Was leading him; he leapt upon the doors,
1215   Burst from their sockets the yielding bars, and fell
Into the room; and there, hanged by the neck,
We saw his wife, held in a swinging cord.
He, when he saw it, groaned in misery
And loosed her body from the rope. When now
1220   She lay upon the ground, awful to see
Was that which followed: from her dress he tore
The golden brooches that she had been wearing,
Raised them, and with their points struck his own eyes,
Crying aloud that they should never see
1225   What he had suffered and what he had done,
But in the dark henceforth they should behold
Those whom they ought not; nor should recognize
Those whom he longed to see. To such refrain
He smote his eyeballs with the pins, not once,
1230   Nor twice; and as he smote them, blood ran down
His face, not dripping slowly, but there fell
Showers of black rain and blood-red hail together.
    Not on his head alone, but on them both,
Husband and wife, this common storm has broken.
1235   Their ancient happiness of early days
Was happiness indeed; but now, today,
Death, ruin, lamentation, shame—of all
The ills there are, not one is wanting here.

CHORUS-LEADER. Now is there intermission in his agony?

1240 MESSENGER. He shouts for someone to unbar the gates,
And to display to Thebes the parricide,
His mother's—no, I cannot speak the words;
For, by the doom he uttered, he will cast
Himself beyond our borders, nor remain
1245 To be a curse at home. But he needs strength,
And one to guide him; for these wounds are greater
Than he can bear—as you shall see; for look!
They draw the bolts. A sight you will behold
To move the pity even of an enemy.

The doors open. OEDIPUS *slowly advances.*

CHORUS. O horrible, dreadful sight. More dreadful far
(*These verses sung or chanted in a slow march-time.*) Than any I
1250   have yet seen. What cruel frenzy
Came over you? What spirit with superhuman leap
Came to assist your grim destiny?
Ah, most unhappy man!
But no! I cannot bear even to look at you,
1255 Though there is much that I would ask and see and hear.
But I shudder at the very sight of you.

OEDIPUS (*sings in the dochmiac rhythm*). Alas! alas! and woe for my
    misery!
Where are my steps taking me?
My random voice is lost in the air.
1260 O God! how hast thou crushed me!

CHORUS-LEADER (*spoken*). Too terribly for us to hear or see.

OEDIPUS (*sings*). O cloud of darkness abominable,
My enemy unspeakable,
In cruel onset insuperable.
1265 Alas! alas! Assailed at once by pain
Of pin-points and of memory of crimes.

CHORUS-LEADER. In such tormenting pains you well may cry
A double grief and feel a double woe.

OEDIPUS (*sings*). Ah, my friend!
1270 Still at my side? Still steadfast?
Still can you endure me?
Still care for me, a blind man?
(*speaks*) For it is you, my friend; I know 'tis you;
Though all is darkness, yet I know your voice.

1275 CHORUS-LEADER. O, to destroy your sight! How could you bring
Yourself to do it? What god incited you?

OEDIPUS (*sings*). It was Apollo, friends, Apollo.
    He decreed that I should suffer what I suffer;
    But the hand that struck, alas! was my own,
1280   And not another's.
    For why should I have sight.
    When sight of nothing could give me pleasure?

CHORUS. It was even as you say.

OEDIPUS. What have I left, my friends, to see,
1285   To cherish, whom to speak with, or
    To listen to, with joy?
    Lead me away at once, far from Thebes;
    Lead me away, my friends!
    I have destroyed; I am accursed, and, what is more,
1290   Hateful to Heaven, as no other.

CHORUS-LEADER (*speaks*). Unhappy your intention, and unhappy
    Your fate. O would that I had never known you!

OEDIPUS (*sings*). Curses on him, whoever he was,
    Who took the savage fetters from my feet,
1295   Snatched me from death, and saved me.
    No thanks I owe him,
    For had I died that day
    Less ruin had I brought on me and mine.

CHORUS. That wish is my wish too.

1300 OEDIPUS. I had not then come and slain my father.
    Nor then would men have called me
    Husband of her that bore me.
    Now am I God's enemy, child of the guilty,
    And she that bore me has borne too my children;
1305   And if there is evil surpassing evil,
        That has come to Oedipus.

CHORUS-LEADER. How can I say that you have counseled well?
    Far better to be dead than to be blind.

OEDIPUS. That what is done was not done for the best
1310   Seek not to teach me: counsel me no more.
    I know not how I could have gone to Hades
    And with these eyes have looked upon my father
    Or on my mother; such things have I done
    To them, death is no worthy punishment.
1315   Or could I look for pleasure in the sight
    Of my own children, born as they were born?
    Never! No pleasure there, for eyes of mine,
    Nor in this city, nor its battlements
    Nor sacred images. From these—ah, miserable!—

1320   I, the most nobly born of any Theban
Am banned for ever by my own decree
That the defiler should be driven forth,
The man accursed of Heaven and Laius' house.
Was I to find such taint in me, and then
1325   With level eyes to look *them* in the face?
Nay more: if for my ears I could have built
Some dam to stay the flood of sound, that I
Might lose both sight and hearing, and seal up
My wretched body—that I would have done.
1330   How good to dwell beyond the reach of pain!
    Cithaeron! Why did you accept me? Why
Did you not take and kill me? Never then
Should I have come to dwell among the Thebans.
    O Polybus! Corinth! and that ancient home
1335   I thought my father's—what a thing you nurtured!
How fair, how foul beneath! For I am found
Foul in myself and in my parentage.
    O you three ways, that in a hidden glen
Do meet: you narrow branching roads within
1340   The forest—you, through my own hands, did drink
My father's blood, that was my own.—Ah! do you
Remember what you saw me do? And what
I did again in Thebes? You marriages!
You did beget me: then, having begotten,
1345   Bore the same crop again, and brought to light
Commingled blood of fathers, brothers, sons,
Brides, mothers, wives; all that there can be
Among the human kind most horrible!
    But that which it is foul to do, it is
1350   Not fair to speak of. Quick as you can, I beg,
Banish me, hide me, slay me! Throw me forth
Into the sea, where I may sink from view.
I pray you, deign to touch one so afflicted,
And do not fear: there is no man alive
1355   Can bear this load of evil but myself.

CHORUS-LEADER. To listen to your prayers, Creon is here,
  For act or guidance opportune; for he,
  In your defection, is our champion.

Enter CREON.

OEDIPUS. Alas! alas! How can I speak to him?
1360   What word of credit find? In all my commerce
  With him aforetime I am proven false.

CREON. No exultation, Oedipus, and no reproach
  Of injuries inflicted brings me here;
  But if the face of men moves not your shame,

1365 Then reverence show to that all-nurturing fire,
 The holy Sun, that he be not polluted
 By such accursed sight, which neither Earth
 Nor rain from Heaven nor sunlight can endure.
  Take him within, and quickly: it is right
1370 His kinsmen only should behold and hear
 Evils that chiefly on his kinsmen fall.

 OEDIPUS. In Heaven's name—since you cheat my expectation,
 So noble towards my baseness—grant me this:
 It is for you I ask it, not myself.

1375 CREON. What is this supplication that you make?

 OEDIPUS. Drive me at once beyond your bounds, where I
 Shall be alone, and no one speak to me.

 CREON. I would have done it; but I first desired
 To ask the God what he would have me do.

1380 OEDIPUS. No, his command was given in full, to slay
 Me, the polluter and the parricide.

 CREON. Those were his words; but in our present need
 It would be wise to ask what we should do.

 OEDIPUS. You will inquire for such a wretch as I?

1385 CREON. I will; for now *you* may believe the god.

 OEDIPUS. Yes; and on you I lay this charge and duty:
 Give burial, as you will, to her who lies
 Within—for she is yours, and this is proper;
 And, while I live, let not my father's city
1390 Endure to have me as a citizen.
 My home must be the mountains—on Cithaeron,
 Which, while they lived, my parents chose to be
 My tomb: they wished to slay me; now they shall.
 For this I know: sickness can never kill me,
1395 Nor any other evil; I was not saved
 That day from death, except for some strange doom.
 My fate must take the course it will.—Now, for my sons,
 Be not concerned for them: they can, being men,
 Fend for themselves, wherever they may be:
1400 But my unhappy daughters, my two girls,
 Whose chairs were always set beside my own
 At table—they who shared in every dish
 That was prepared for me—oh Creon! these
 Do I commend to you. And grant me this:
1405 To take them in my arms, and weep for them.
 My lord! most noble Creon! could I now
 But hold them in my arms, then I should think

I had them as I had when I could see them.
Ah! what is this?

1410 Ah Heaven! do I not hear my dear ones, sobbing?
Has Creon, in his pity, sent to me
My darling children? Has he? Is it true?

CREON. It is; they have been always your delight;
So, knowing this, I had them brought to you.

1415 OEDIPUS. Then Heaven reward you, and for this kind service
Protect you better than it protected me!
Where are you, children? Where? O come to me!
Come, let me clasp you with a brother's arms,
These hands, which helped your father's eyes, once bright,
1420 To look upon you as they see you now—
Your father who, not seeing, nor inquiring,
Gave you for mother her who bore himself.
See you I cannot; but I weep for you,
For the unhappiness that must be yours,
1425 And for the bitter life that you must lead.
What gathering of the citizens, what festivals,
Will you have part in? Your high celebrations
Will be to go back home, and sit in tears.
And when the time for marriage comes, what man
1430 Will stake upon the ruin and the shame
That *I* am to my parents and to you?
Nothing is wanting there: your father slew
His father, married her who gave him birth,
And then, from that same source whence he himself
1435 Had sprung, got you.—With these things they will taunt you;
And who will take you then in marriage?—Nobody;
But you must waste, unwedded and unfruitful.
Ah, Creon! Since they have no parent now
But you—for both of us who gave them life
1440 Have perished—suffer them not to be cast out
Homeless and beggars; for they are your kin.
Have pity on them, for they are so young,
So desolate, except for you alone.
Say "Yes," good Creon! Let your hand confirm it.
1445 And now, my children, for my exhortation
You are too young; but you can pray that I
May live henceforward—where I should; and you
More happily than the father who begot you.

CREON. Now make an end of tears, and go within.

1450 OEDIPUS. Then I must go—against my will.

CREON. There is a time for everything.

OEDIPUS. You know what I would have you do?

CREON. If you will tell me, I shall know.

OEDIPUS. Send me away, away from Thebes.

1455 CREON. The God, not I, must grant you this.

OEDIPUS. The gods hate no man more than me!

CREON. Then what you ask they soon will give.

OEDIPUS. You promise this?

CREON.   Ah no! When I
    Am ignorant, I do not speak.

1460 OEDIPUS. Then lead me in; I say no more.

CREON. Release the children then, and come.

OEDIPUS. What? Take these children from me? No!

CREON. Seek not to have your way in all things:
    Where you had your way before,
1465   Your mastery broke before the end.

(*There was no doubt a short concluding utterance from the* CHORUS.
What stands in the manuscript appears to be spurious.)

DISCUSSION QUESTIONS

1. On several occasions Oedipus is warned to cease asking questions,
but he persists until the horrible truth is known. Iocasta, for example,
asks him to "Seek no more!" but his response is "I *will* know the
truth." Do you admire his persistence, or do you regard it as foolish?

2. *Oedipus the King* contains frequent references to blindness and
lameness. How does Sophocles make use of these afflictions to
reinforce his theme? What is the particular significance of Teiresias'
blindness and of Oedipus' eventual loss of his eyesight? What might
be the significance of Oedipus' injured ankles?

3. Sophocles' heroes are usually complex and must be seen from more
than one point of view to be judged properly. What impression do
we receive of Oedipus from (a) the way he deals with his subjects at
the beginning of the play, (b) his reaction to the words of Teiresias,
(c) his treatment of Creon, (d) his relationship with Iocasta and his
daughters, and (e) his behavior at the end of the play?

4. Oedipus completely misunderstands the motivation behind Iocasta's
request that he stop asking about his parentage. What does he *think*
her motive is? What is her *actual* motive?

5. One of the larger ironies in this play is that Oedipus, a man so insightful that he can unravel the Sphinx's riddle, does not even know who he is. What other dramatic ironies does Sophocles make use of in *Oedipus the King*?

6. On a number of occasions, the Chorus indicates that Oedipus' fate is typical of human life rather than a special case. (See, for example, the choral ode that begins "Alas! You generations of men!" in lines 1143-1150.) In what way can these bizarre happenings be considered typical?

SUGGESTION FOR WRITING

Oedipus the King is constructed on a series of revelations, each one leading closer to the inevitable truth. Make a poster that visually presents the various stages leading from ignorance to knowledge. (You might consider using a staircase, for example, with steps representing each stage. Or the various stages might be shown as a peeling away of layers that finally reveals the hidden "core." There are numerous other possibilities.) Whatever visual effects you use, be sure to demonstrate what Oedipus learns from each of the following characters:

- Creon, his brother-in-law

- Teiresias, the blind prophet

- Iocasta, his wife

- the Corinthian shepherd

- the Theban shepherd

Do not simply summarize these scenes, but briefly indicate what Oedipus learns or suspects about his past from each successive encounter.

Literature of Rome

CATULLUS

(84–54 B.C.)

Catullus came to Rome from Verona as a young man, sent by his father to gain cultivation. He spent his time enjoying the pleasures of the moment and began writing poetry on such subjects as drinking, loving, and quarreling. His poems are extremely direct, passionate, and centered on personal feelings. Although their pagan themes caused the poems to be ignored during the early Christian era, they were revived during the Middle Ages and have been influential ever since. The personal, emotional voice that speaks in these poems has become a standard for lyric poets.

The poems that follow are all addressed to Lesbia, a wealthy Roman woman whose real name was Clodia. She was a clever and elegant person who entertained regularly, surrounding herself with politically influential people. Catullus' poems to Lesbia, taken together, present an outline of an ultimately frustrating love affair. ■

HAPPINESS

Translated by E. A. Havelock

> To sit where I can see your face
> And hear your laughter come and go
> Is greater bliss than all the gods
>   Can ever know.
>
> 5 The bright dream carries me away:
> Watching your lips, your hair, your cheek,
> I have so many things to say,
>   Yet cannot speak.
>
> I look, I listen, and my soul
> 10 Flames with a fire unfelt before;
> Till sense swims, and I feel and see
>   And hear no more.

KISSES

Translated by George Lamb

> Love, my Lesbia, while we live;
>   Value all the cross advice
> That the surly greybeards give
>   At a single farthing's price.[1]

---

1. farthing's price: A farthing was a coin of very small value.

5   Suns that set again may rise;
       We, when once our fleeting light,
    Once our day in darkness dies,
       Sleep in one eternal night.

    Give me kisses thousand-fold,
10   Add to them a hundred more;
    Other thousands still be told,
       Other hundreds o'er and o'er.

    But, with thousands when we burn,
       Mix, confuse the sum at last,
15   That we may not blushing learn
       All that have between us passed.

    None shall know to what amount
       Envy's due for so much bliss;
    None—for none shall ever count
20   All the kisses we will kiss.

ON LESBIA'S INCONSTANCY

Translated by Theodore Martin

    My mistress says, there's not a man
       Of all the many that she knows,
    She'd rather wed than me, not one,
       Though Jove[2] himself were to propose.

5   She says so;—but what woman says
       To him who fancies he has caught her,
    'Tis only fit it should be writ
       In air or in the running water.

INFERENCE

Translated by Jonathan Swift

    Lesbia forever on me rails
    To talk of me she never fails.
    Now, hang me, but for all her art,
    I find that I have gained her heart.
5   My proof is this: I plainly see
    The case is just the same with me;
    I curse her every hour sincerely,
    Yet, hang me, but I love her dearly.

---

2. Jove: the god Jupiter.

LOVE'S UNREASON

Translated by Theodore Martin

> I hate and love—the why I cannot tell,
> But by my tortures know the fact too well.

DISCUSSION QUESTIONS

1. How would you describe Catullus' love for Lesbia? Do you think it is possible to love and hate someone at the same time?

2. By reading these five poems in order, we can infer a great deal about the history of Catullus' relationship with Lesbia. How do the poet's feelings change over time?

3. In the second stanza of "Kisses," human beings are contrasted with the sun. What is the point of this comparison?

4. In the poem "On Lesbia's Inconstancy," what is implied when Catullus says that Lesbia's promises are written "in air or in the running water"?

5. Explain the "Inference" that is made by Catullus in the poem of that title.

SUGGESTION FOR WRITING

Select a subject about which you have mixed or contradictory feelings. Write a short poem in the direct and simple style of Catullus, expressing your thoughts and feelings on the subject.

HORACE

(65–8 B.C.)

The son of a freed slave, Horace received a good education in Rome and Athens and witnessed the civil wars that resulted in the unification of the Roman Empire under Caesar Augustus. He eventually got a job as a government clerk and began writing poetry. In a stroke of good fortune, Augustus' wealthy and powerful minister, Maecenas, read some of his poetry and offered to be his patron. With Maecenas as a patron and friend, Horace received a country retreat, the Sabine Farm, where he could live and write as he pleased, completely free from financial worries for the rest of his life.

Unlike the burning intensity of Catullus' poetry, Horace's poems are models of moderation, common sense, and serenity. He is famous for his cool and steady head and for his polished and precise style, which is difficult to translate. Horace enjoyed the small pleasures of everyday life and wrote on a wide variety of subjects, from cooking to Greek philosophy. He took delight in country living, his Sabine Farm often serving as a symbol of the simple pastoral life in his poetry. Sociable, witty, and fun-loving by nature, Horace frequently entertained friends there and engaged them in lively conversations. After Virgil's death in 19 B.C., he became the preeminent poet of the Roman Empire. ■

from *The Odes*

BOOK 1, ODE 15

Translated by James Michie

> When Paris, the perfidious shepherd boy,[1]
> Kidnapped his host's wife and set sail for Troy,
> Nereus[2] imposed a calm upon the seas
> And checked the eager winds, to utter these
> 5 Grim words of prophecy: "Ill fare you now
> That take her homewards whom all Greece shall vow
> To get again with armies pledged to undo
> Your love-knot—Priam's ancient kingdom too.
> Ah, what a terrible sweat of death is brewing
> 10 For war-horses and warriors! What huge ruin
> You bring your people! I see Pallas[3] getting
> Helmet and shield and chariot ready, whetting

---

1. **shepherd boy:** As a young man, Paris, the son of Priam, king of Troy, had been a herdsman on Mt. Ida. Later he kidnapped Helen, wife of Menelaus, King of Sparta, precipitating the Greek expedition to Troy.

2. **Nereus:** a sea god, sometimes called the Old Man of the Sea.

3. **Pallas:** the goddess Athena.

Her fury. Serenade admiring girls
On the unwarlike lyre, comb your long curls,
15 Or, confident of Aphrodite's aid,[4]
Loll in your lover's bedroom and evade
The ponderous spears, the darts of Cretan reed,
Yet death, though late may come the sorry time,
Shall drag your adulterous tresses in the grime.
20 Have you no visions of the Ithacan,[5]
Troy's executioner, or the old man,
Nestor of Pylos? Fast and furious,
Teucer comes after you, and Sthenelus,
A skilled foot-soldier and, when called to steer,
25 By no means a slow-driving charioteer.
You shall meet Meriones, and also know
That son more famous than his father—lo,
Fierce Diomedes raging on your track;
Whom you shall run from, gasping, head thrown back
30 (Was this the scene you promised her in bed?)
As the poor timid deer, gone from its head
All thoughts of grazing, bolts when it has seen
A wolf at the other end of the ravine.
Achilles' angry faction[6] may delay
35 Troy's and the Trojan mothers' mourning day,
Yet the predestined count of years must come:
Greek fire shall burn the roofs of Ilium."[7]

BOOK 1, ODE 37

Translated by Helen Rowe Henze

*This ode was written in celebration of the victory of Octavian over Antony and Cleopatra
at Actium in 31 B.C.*

Now is the time for drinking, now is the time
With foot set free to stamp on the ground, and now,
  Oh, now the time with Salian feasts[8] to
    Honor the couch of the gods, my comrades!

---

4. **Aphrodite's aid:** Paris, forced to judge a beauty contest involving Hera, Athena, and
Aphrodite, gained the support of Aphrodite by favoring her in the contest.

5. **the Ithacan:** Odysseus, who devised the stratagem of the wooden horse by which Troy was
eventually taken. All the following names (lines 22–28) are those of Greek heroes.

6. **Achilles' angry faction:** Achilles' refusal to fight because of Agamemnon's treatment of him
temporarily gave the Trojans the advantage.

7. **Ilium:** Troy.

8. **Salian feasts:** the magnificent banquets held by the Salii, the priests of Mars.

Before this moment, it had been sin to draw
The Caecuban[9] from ancestral vaults below,
    The while the maddened queen was planning
        Ruin for Rome and a grave for empire.

With her polluted crew of base, shameful men
10 She planned; and she was frenzied enough to hope
    For anything, for she was then so
        Drunk with sweet fortune. But fury faded

When only one ship barely escaped the flames;
Her mind, already crazed by Egyptian wine,
15   Did Caesar drive to true fear as she
        Fled forth from Italy, and he followed

With urgent oars as hawk does the gentle doves,
Or hunter follows hare on the snowy fields
    Of Thessaly; pressed close that he might
20   Put her in chains, this portentous monster.

But seeking for the means to a nobler death,
She did not fear the sword, as is woman's way,
    Nor tried by her swift fleet to find some
        Place of concealment on hidden coast lines.

25 She even dared to visit her fallen court
With tranquil brow, and bravely she dared lay hold
    Of scaly serpents, that she might drink
        Into her body their deadly venom.

Determined still more boldly on death, she grudged
30 The fierce Liburnian galleys,[10] and scorned to be
    A discrowned queen led forth in triumph—
        She was no humble or tame-souled woman!

BOOK 2, ODE 15

Translated by James Michie

> *Eager to help Augustus in his efforts to return Rome to a simpler life that was less corrupted by wealth and power, Horace often wrote poetry that praised the virtues of plain living and insisted that the past was more moral than the present. This poem was written in that spirit.*

---

9. Caecuban: a vintage wine.

10. Liburnian galleys: light, shallow warships of a pattern adopted by the Romans from the Liburnians, a people living on the east coast of the Adriatic Sea.

Soon I foresee few acres for harrowing
Left once the rich men's villas have seized the land;
    Fishponds that outdo Lake Lucrinus[11]
        Everywhere; bachelor plane-trees ousting

5   Vine-loving elms; thick myrtle-woods, violet-beds,
All kinds of rare blooms tickling the sense of smell,
    Perfumes to drown those olive orchards
        Nursed in the past for a farmer's profit;

Quaint garden-screens, too, woven of laurel-boughs
10   To parry sunstroke. Romulus[12] never urged
    This style of life; rough-bearded Cato[13]
        Would have detested the modern fashions.

Small private wealth, large communal property—
So ran the rule then. No one had porticoes
15   Laid out with ten-foot builder's measures,
        Trapping the cool of the northern shadow.

BOOK 3, ODE 30

Translated by Helen Rowe Henze

More enduring than bronze I've built my monument
Overtopping the royal pile of the pyramids,
Which no ravenous rain, neither Aquilo's[14] rage
Shall suffice to destroy, nor the unnumbered years
5   As they pass one by one, nor shall the flight of time.
I shall not wholly die; no, a great part of me
Shall escape from death's Queen;[15] still shall my fame rise fresh
In posterity's praise, while to the Capitol
Still the high priest and mute maiden ascend the Hill.
10   From where Aufidus[16] brawls and from that thirsty land
In which Daunus[17] once ruled over his rustic tribes,
I, grown great though born low,[18] I shall be named as first

---

11. **Lake Lucrinus:** a small salt-water lake near Naples.

12. **Romulus:** the legendary founder of Rome.

13. **Cato:** a Roman politician (234 B.C.–149 B.C.) renowned for his patriotism, called Cato the Elder to distinguish him from his grandson, Cato the Younger.

14. **Aquilo:** the Roman name for the North Wind.

15. **death's Queen:** Persephone, goddess of the Underworld.

16. **Aufidus:** a river in Apulia, a district southwest of Rome.

17. **Daunus:** a legendary king of Apulia.

18. **born low:** Horace's father was a freed slave who owned a small farm.

To have spun Grecian song into Italian strands
With their lyrical modes.[19] Take this proud eminence
15 Won by your just deserts; and with the Delphic bay,[20]
O Melpomene,[21] now graciously bind my hair.

TRUE GREATNESS

Translated by Jonathan Swift

Virtue concealed within our breast
Is inactivity at best;
But never shall the Muse endure
To let your virtues lie obscure,
5 Or suffer Envy to conceal
Your labors for the public weal.[22]
  Within your breast all wisdom lies,
Either to govern or advise;
Your steady soul preserves her frame
10 In good and evil times the same.
Pale Avarice and lurking Fraud
Stand in your sacred presence awed;
Your hand alone from gold abstains,
Which drags the slavish world in chains.
15 Him for a happy man I own
Whose fortune is not overgrown;
And happy he who wisely knows
To use the gifts that heaven bestows;
Or if it please the powers divine,
20 Can suffer want and not repine.
The man who, infamy to shun,
Into the arms of death would run,
That man is ready to defend
With life his country or his friend.

THE ORIGIN OF SATIRE

Translated by Alexander Pope

Our rural ancestors, with little blessed,
Patient of labor when the end was rest,
Indulged the day that housed their annual grain

---

19. first . . . lyrical modes: Horace introduced the use of Greek meters into Latin poetry.

20. Delphic bay: the laurel, sacred to Apollo, was used to crown the winners of literary competitions. Delphi was Apollo's main shrine.

21. Melpomene: the Muse of tragedy.

22. weal: welfare, the public good.

With feasts, and offerings, and a thankful strain:
5   The joy their wives, their sons, and servants share,
Ease of their toil, and partners of their care:
The laugh, the jest, attendants on the bowl,
Smoothed every brow, and opened every soul:
With growing years the pleasing license grew,
10   And taunts alternate innocently flew.
But times corrupt, and nature ill-inclined,
Produced the point that left a sting behind;
Till, friend with friend and families at strife,
Triumphant malice raged through private life.
15   Who felt the wrong, or feared it, took the alarm,
Appealed to law, and justice lent her arm.
At length, by wholesome dread of statutes bound,
The poets learned to please, and not to wound:
Most warped to flattery's side; but some, more nice,
20   Preserved the freedom, and forbore the vice.
Hence satire rose, that just the medium hit,
And heals with morals what it hurts with wit.

THE ART OF POETRY AGAIN

Translated by Lord Byron

Poets and painters, as all artists know,
May shoot a little with a lengthened bow;[23]
We claim this mutual mercy for our task,
And grant in turn the pardon which we ask;
5   But make not monsters spring from gentle dams—
Birds breed not vipers, tigers nurse not lambs.

    In fine, to whatsoever you aspire,
Let it at least be simple and entire.

    The greater portion of the rhyming tribe
10   (Give ear, my friends, for thou hast been a scribe)
Are led astray by some peculiar lure.
I labor to be brief—become obscure;
One falls while following elegance too fast;
Another soars, inflated with bombast;
15   Too low a third crawls on, afraid to fly:
He spins his subject to satiety;
Absurdly varying, he at last engraves
Fish in the woods, and boars beneath the waves!

---

23. **shoot . . . bow:** the expression "to draw the long bow" means to exaggerate.

Unless your care's exact, your judgment nice,
20   The flight from folly leads but into vice.

Dear authors! suit your topics to your strength,
And ponder well your subject and its length;
Nor lift your load before you're quite aware
What weight your shoulders will, or will not, bear.
25   But lucid Order, and Wit's siren voice,
Await the poet, skillful in his choice;
With native eloquence he soars along,
Grace in his thoughts, and music in his song.

Let judgment teach them wisely to combine
30   With future parts the now omitted line:
This shall the author choose, or that reject,
Precise in style, and cautious to select;
Nor slight applause will candid pens afford
To him who furnishes a wanting word.
35   Then fear not, if 'tis needful, to produce
Some term unknown, or obsolete in use.

As forests shed their foliage by degrees,
So fade expressions which in season please;
And we and ours, alas! are due to fate,
40   And works and words but dwindle to a date.
Though as a monarch nods, and commerce calls,
Impetuous rivers stagnate in canals;
Though swamps subdued and marshes drained sustain
The heavy plowshare and the yellow grain,
45   And rising ports along the busy shore
Protect the vessel from old Ocean's roar,
All, all, must perish; but, surviving last,
The love of letters half preserves the past.
True, some decay, yet not a few revive;
50   Though those shall sink which now appear to thrive,
As custom arbitrates, whose shifting sway
Our life and language must alike obey.

'Tis hard to venture where our betters fail,
Or lend fresh interest to a twice-told tale;
55   And yet, perchance, 'tis wiser to prefer
A hackneyed plot, than choose a new, and err;
Yet copy not too closely, but record,
More justly, thought for thought than word for word;
Nor trace your prototype through narrow ways,
60   But only follow where he merits praise.

But many a skillful judge abhors to see
What few admire—irregularity.
This some vouchsafe to pardon; but 'tis hard
When such a word contents a British bard.
65 And must the bard his glowing thoughts confine,
Lest censure hover o'er some faulty line?
Remove whate'er a critic may suspect,
To gain the paltry suffrage of '*correct*'?
Or prune the spirit of each daring phrase,
70 To fly from error, not to merit praise?

Ye, who seek finished models, never cease,
By day and night, to read the works of Greece.

Sometimes a sprightly wit, and tale well told,
Without much grace, or weight, or art, will hold
75 A longer empire o'er the public mind
Than sounding trifles, empty, though refined.

Two objects always should the poet move,
Or one or both—to please or to improve.
Whate'er you teach, be brief, if you design
80 For our remembrance your didactic line;
Redundance places memory on the rack,
For brains may be o'erloaded, like the back.

Young men with aught but elegance dispense;
Maturer years require a little sense.
85 To end at once:—that bard for all is fit
Who mingles well instruction with his wit.

But everything has faults, nor is't unknown
That harps and fiddles often lose their tone,
And wayward voices, at their owner's call,
90 With all his best endeavors, only squall.
Where frequent beauties strike the reader's view,
We must not quarrel for a blot or two;
But pardon equally to books or men,
The slips of human nature, and the pen.

95 Yet if an author, spite of foe or friend,
Despises all advice too much to mend,
But ever twangs the same discordant string,
Give him no quarter, howsoe'er he sing.

As pictures, so shall poems be; some stand
100 The critic eye, and please when near at hand;

But others at a distance strike the sight;
This seeks the shade, but that demands the light,
Nor dreads the connoisseur's fastidious view,
But, ten times scrutinized, is ten times new.

THE TOWN MOUSE AND THE COUNTRY MOUSE

Translated by Smith Palmer Bovie

This was what I had prayed for: a small piece of land
With a garden, a fresh-flowing spring of water at hand
Near the house, and, above and behind, a small forest stand.
But the gods have done much better for me, and more—
5   It's perfect. I ask nothing else, except to implore,
O Son of Maia,[24] that you make these blessings my own
For the rest of my life. If my property has not grown
By my making a series of deals, neither will it shrink
By my mismanagement. If I'm not one of those who think:
10   "If only that corner were mine, that lies adjacent
To my strip, cutting in in a manner that's really indecent!"
Or, "If only some luck came my way, like the find which,
Leading the plowman to buried treasure, made him rich
Enough to buy the land he formerly plowed for hire,
15   Thanks to Hercules!" If what I have is all I desire
And makes me content, then to this one last wish I aspire:
Make my herd grow fat, and everything else I lay claim to,
Except my brains. And, Mercury, still be the same to
Horace as you have been, his great good guardian. To complete
20   My removal from city streets to mountain retreat,
What else should I do but celebrate it now satirically,
Dwelling, far from town (and far from lyrically),
In my pedestrian style, on how far from that bit of hell
Known as big city life is life in my citadel.
25   Social-climbing can't get me down here, or the lead-weight blows
Of siroccos,[25] or for once and for all plague-laden falls
Lay me out, and enrich the layout in funeral halls.
    Instead, I begin this morning by addressing you, Monarch
Of Morning, or more openly, Janus,[26] if you prefer it:
30   In allegiance to whom men begin all the work of their days—
For so heaven wills it. Be the principal source of my praise.

---

24. **Son of Maia:** the god Mercury, who was a patron of literature.

25. **siroccos:** hot dry winds, blowing from North Africa across southern Europe.

26. **Janus:** the god of doors and gates. By extension Janus became the god of beginnings and hence the god of morning.

At Rome the mornings are different: you rush me right off
To court to vouch for a friend. "Hey there! Get going!
Or someone else will answer this call before you!"
35 And I *have* to, whether the north wind is raking the land
Or winter drags snow-laden days through diminishing curves.
　　　After saying in court, good and loud, things that may some day
Incriminate me, I fight my way back through the crowd
In the streets, tripping over some slowpoke's toes. "What's up,
40 You blockhead? What gives?" some stupid assails me. "Oh, Horace,
It's you, is it, racing back home to Maecenas,[27] so full of
The fact that you knock over everything blocking your path!"
Well . . . the name of Maecenas *is* honey to me, I admit it.
　　　But as soon as I reach the depressing Esquiline Quarter,[28]
45 A hundred conflicting concerns pour down on my head
And stream around me. "Roscius wants you to meet him tomorrow
Before seven in the morning, at Libo's Wall." "Oh, Quintus,
The clerks request you to remember to return to the Forum
Today for a big new matter of mutual interest."
50 "Do have Maecenas affix his seal to these papers."
If I say, "Well, I'll try," he insists, "You can *do* it if you *want* to."
　　　It is now seven years—actually, nearer the eighth—
Since Maecenas began to admit me into his company
Of friends, insofar as a friend is just good company
55 On a trip, someone to talk to about such subjects as:
"What time is it?" . . . "Oh, about the fight: is the Thracian Bantam
A match for the Sheik?" . . . "These frosty mornings can nip you
If you don't wrap up." And small-change talk like this,
Which it's perfectly safe to deposit in leaky ears.
60 And the whole time, daily and hourly, our intimate Horace
Was *envied*. He watched the games from the stands with M.
He played some ball on the Campus,[29] *and* with M.
"Fortune's Favorite Son," they thought in unison.
　　　A hair-raising rumor rolls through the streets from the Rostra,[30]
65 And whoever bumps into me seeks my advice. "Dear fellow,
You ought to know, you live so much nearer the gods,
What's up in the Balkans?" "Nothing, as far as I know."
"Oh, you're still making fun of us!" But may the gods undo me
If I've heard a word. "What about the veterans' allotments
70 Of land Caesar promised? Will they be on the three-cornered isle,[31]

---

27. Maecenas: a patron and friend of Horace.

28. Esquiline Quarter: the location of Horace's house in Rome.

29. the Campus: the Campus Martius, or Field of Mars, a large, open space adjoining the Tiber, used by the Romans for military drill and recreation.

30. the Rostra: the speaker's platform in the Forum at Rome.

31. the three-cornered isle: Sicily.

Or Italian soil?" When I swear I know nothing about it,
They marvel at me for being the sole human being
Who knows how to keep an important unfathomable secret.
       Amid such lightweight concerns the light of my day
75   Sputters out, leaving me limp, only able to pray:
              Oh, countryside mine, when will I see you again,
              Read my favorite classical authors, and then
              Get some sleep and get back to my lazy routine of life,
              Of pleasure mercifully free from worry and strife?
80   When shall we dine on beans, Pythagoras' cousins,[32]
       And eat, cooked in bacon, country greens in their dozens?
       Those nights and feasts of the gods! When friends and I sup
       In *my lar's* presence,[33] while the saucy slaves lick up
       What's left untouched on the plates. Each guest drains his cup,
85   Big or small, as it suits him: no Prohibition[34]
       To govern his choice except his free disposition
       To toss off heroic amounts and keep a clear head,
       Or gradually mellow with moderate potions instead.
       And then we start talking, not about other men's lives
90   And property and assets but of things on which wisdom thrives.
       Not whether Lepos is really a good dancer or not
       But whether happiness comes from the money you've got
       Or, rather, derives from virtue. What makes men friends?
       Self-interest, or rectitude? This subject lends
95   Interest to us: the good life, and its ends.
              From time to time, my good old neighbor, Cervius,
       Rattles off an old wives' tale, to make a point:
       If someone praises Arellius' wealth, without knowing
       What worries it brings, Cervius starts off like this:
100 "Once upon a time, a country mouse
       Welcomed a town mouse in his poor little hole of a house
       In the sticks, both host and guest being quite old friends.
       The country mouse roughed it, of course; he kept a close eye
       On his larder, but not so myopic he couldn't enlarge
105 His view, with a view to a friend's entertainment. What else?
       He was not the mouse to begrudge a friend the choice chick-peas
       Set aside in a special place, or the long grains of oats;
       But, eager to conquer the fastidious disdain of a guest
       Who tended to turn up his tooth after sampling each dainty,
110 He brought in by mouth and served, to vary the meal,
       A dried grape seed and some half-nibbled pieces of bacon.

---

32. Pythagoras' cousins: The Pythagoreans abstained from eating beans in the belief that they
    were inhabited by the souls of the dead.

33. *my lar's* presence: The lar was a household god who protected the members of the family.

34. Prohibition: The laws of Rome prohibited individuals from drinking too much (or too little!)
    wine.

The master of the house, stretched out on his couch of chaff
(New chaff), ate spelt and darnel, leaving the best
For his guest to digest. Finally, the town mouse spoke up:

115   'What pleasure can it be for you, my friend,
    Roughing it out here on the edge of a precipitous forest?
    Surely you put *people* and *the city* ahead of this wildwood?
    Take my advice, and my road, with me as your guide.
    All earthly creatures, after all, have drawn as their lot

120   A mortal life: there is no escape from death
    For large or small. Therefore, while you still can,
    Enjoy a happy career, my good man, live well;
    Live mindful of how short life really is.'

                          When these words
Dawned on the yokel, he bounced off gaily from home,
125 And both set out together, according to plan,
Hoping to sneak through the walls of the city by night.
And night was poised, midway across the heavens,
When both set foot in a rich man's house, where crimson
Coverings blazed against ivory couches, and leftovers
130 From last night's feast were stacked up high in the baskets.
Well, the host then made his rural guest stretch out
On the crimson covers and began dashing madly about,
With his clothes tucked up like a waiter's, serving up dish
After dish and taking a taste, as a proper slave does,
135 Of each course before serving it. The other mouse meanwhile
Leaned back at ease, delighted with the change in affairs
And with all this good living, and was playing to perfection
    the part
Of the satisfied guest, when a sudden loud rattling of doors
Shook them both right off of their couches. Frightened, they
    scampered
140 Across the whole length of the room, and, even more frightening,
The big house began to ring, at the very same time,
With the barking of colossal hounds. Says the country mouse:
    'I have no use for this kind of life. And good-bye!
    My woodland and hole, where I'm safe from traps like these,
145   Will be quite good enough, my slim pickings quite food
      enough.'"

DISCUSSION QUESTIONS

1. In Book 2, Ode 15, Horace expresses the view that Roman citizens
need to return to the ways of older generations represented by
Romulus and Cato. In another work he actually claims that "our
parents, worse than our grandparents, gave birth to us who are worse

than they, and we shall in our turn bear offspring still more evil." Do you think this idea is still common? Is there any truth to it? How do you account for this view?

2. In Book 1, Odes 15 and 37, Horace presents two well-known figures of legend and history: Paris, the lover of Helen, and Cleopatra, the lover of Mark Anthony. How does he view these famous lovers? Why?

3. In Book 3, Ode 30, Horace expresses the view that he will "not wholly die." What will keep him alive? How does this poem compare thematically to Sappho's poem entitled "Her Wealth"?

4. In "True Greatness" Horace describes some of the characteristics of a truly virtuous person. What are they?

5. In "The Origin of Satire" Horace presents the historical development of satire. What are the various stages through which satire passed before it reached the stage described in the last line? What, according to Horace, is the goal of satire?

6. What are the two aims of poetry presented in "The Art of Poetry Again"? Throughout this poem, Horace often uses words such as *judgment, caution,* and *sense* to describe good poets, words that emphasize careful planning rather than inspiration. Is there any evidence that he also values daring and creativity?

7. In "The Town Mouse and the Country Mouse," how does the ancient fable of the two mice at the end of this poem relate to the rest of the work? What impression of Horace as a person does the reader receive from reading this selection?

SUGGESTION FOR WRITING

Horace is known as a poet who often sets up an antithesis, or a set of opposing ideas, in his poetry. Select one poem that you think operates as an antithesis. Describe the two opposing ideas that are presented. Then explain which one Horace seems to favor and why.

JUVENAL

(C. A.D. 60–140)

Very little is known about the personal life of Juvenal beyond the fact that he offended the emperor Domitian and was forced to spend several years in exile as a result. When Domitian died in A.D. 96, Juvenal returned to Rome and began composing his sixteen Satires. In contrast to Horace's gentle satires, those of Juvenal are floods of furious rage. Their target is usually the corrupt social and political life of the Rome of his day.

Poor most of his life, Juvenal was often compelled to depend on people he despised for his livelihood, such as the patron he describes in the Fifth Satire. Juvenal's proud nature responded with resentment to the rude treatment he received from many Romans, and he generally saw life as a disgusting and desperate business. Even the Thirteenth Satire, designed to console a friend who has been cheated, abuses everyone concerned, including the friend. To this day, extremely intense, angry satire is often referred to as *Juvenalian* satire, named for one of the most bitter writers of the ancient world. Milder satire is often described as *Horatian* satire (for Horace). ∎

from *The Satires*

THE FIFTH SATIRE: AGAINST MEAN PATRONS AND DESPICABLE CLIENTS

Translated by Rolfe Humphries

> Trebius, if you persist in these ways, so utterly shameless
> That you think it is the highest good to live on another man's table,
> If you can stand for treatment the cheapest satellites never
> Would have endured at the unjust board of an earlier Caesar,
> 5 Then I'd not trust your word under oath. I know, it takes little,
> Little enough, to keep a belly content; if that's lacking,
> Is there no place on the sidewalk, no room on one of the bridges,
> No smaller half of a beggar's mat where you could be standing?
> Is a free meal worth its cost in insult, your hunger
> 10 So demanding? By God, it would be more honest to shiver
> No matter where you are, and gnaw on moldy dog-biscuit.
>
> First, get this into your head: an invitation to dinner
> Means a payment in full for all of your previous service.
> One meal is your share of the profit of this great friendship. Your master
> 15 Puts it on your account, a rare enough entry, sufficient,
> Just the same, to balance his books. Perhaps two months later
> It may please him again to invite his neglected client

Lest the lowest place at the lowest table be empty.
"Join us," he says. The height of good luck! What more could you
  ask for?

20 Trebius has good cause to break off his sleep, to come running,
Shoelaces not yet tied, worried that someone else,
Or everyone else, may arrive before he does with his greetings,
While the stars fade out in the early hours of the morning,
While the planets wheel, sluggish and cold in the heavens.

25 What a dinner it is! Blotting paper would shudder
To sop up wine like this, which turns the guests into madmen.
At first it's only insults.
To the main event, a battle royal, the freedmen
Versus the rest of you, with goblets and crockery flying.

30 You stop a jug with your face, pick up a napkin to wipe it,
Find your bloody nose has turned the damask to crimson,
While your host drinks wine drawn off when the consuls were
  bearded,[1]
Juice of grapes that were trod during wars a hundred years past.
Will he send one thimbleful to his cardiac friend? No. Never.

35 Tomorrow he'll drink again, a vintage from Setian or Alban
Mountains, the jar so black with soot and dust that he cannot
Tell where it came from, what year, such wine as Paetus and
  Priscus,
Chaplet-crowned haters of Tyrants, would drink on republican
  birthdays
Honoring Brutus and Cassius.[2]
                                    Your noble patron, this Virro,

40 Holds cups encrusted with amber, saucers jagged with beryl,
Never letting them go; to you no gold is entrusted,
Or, if it ever is, a watcher leans over your shoulder
Keeping count of each jewel, watching your sharpened nails.
Pardon precautions like these, but his jasper is wonderful, truly.

45 Virro, and many like him, transfer from their rings to their goblets
Stones like these, the kind Aeneas[3] wore on his scabbard.
You will drink from a cup that is cracked and fit for the junk pile,
Tradable, maybe, for sulfur, one of those four-nozzled vessels
Named after Nero's fool, the cobbler Beneventum.

50 If his stomach's inflamed from the food and wine, he is given
Water, sterilized first by boiling, then cooled in the snow.

---

1. **when the consuls were bearded:** In Republican times no one under forty could be elected consul. Under the Empire even children sometimes held the office.

2. **Brutus and Cassius:** leaders of the group of conspirators who assassinated Julius Caesar in 44 B.C.

3. **Aeneas:** hero of Virgil's *Aeneid*, an epic poem dealing with the mythical ancestors of the Romans.

You did not get the same wine, I complained; that's half of the
story,
The water is different, too. You are handed the cup by the fellow
Who runs in front of his car, a Gaetulian[4] out of the stables,
55 Or by the bony hand of some black Moor, not a person
You'd enjoy meeting at night where the tombs[5] line the roads of
the city.
Standing in front of your host is the very flower of Asia,
Bought for a higher price than the whole estates of old kings,
Tullus, the fighter, and Ancus[6] were worth. In fact, you could
throw in
60 All of the goods of all of the kings[7] of the Rome of the legends.
This being so, if you thirst, look for your African server.
His expensive boy cannot mix a drink for a poor man,
But he's so lovely, so young! When do you think he will listen,
Whether it's hot or cold you request? Oh no, it's beneath him
65 To serve an old client; he's irked that you ask, or sit while he's
standing.
Every great house is full of these supercilious slave boys.
Look at this one, who grumbles, handing you the hard bread
Made of the coarsest bran, or the moldy jawbreaking crackers.
But our lord receives the tenderest, snowiest, finest
70 Proof of the kneader's art. Respect the breadbasket, please!
Keep hands off! If you reach—such nerve is hard to imagine—
Some one will cry, "Put it down! You shameless guest, can't you
ever
Learn which kind is yours, and tell your bread by its color?"
Was it for this, you'll think, that you left your wife in the
morning,
75 Ran up hill through the cold, with the hail rattling down in the
springtime,
With your porous cloak distilling water in buckets?

In comes a lobster, immense, in fact, too large for the platter,
Waving its tail in contempt at the crowd, as it rides along, high-
borne,
To the table's head, with asparagus for a garnish.
80 What do you get? One prawn, half an egg—the kind of a supper
People leave at the tombs of the dead by way of a token.

---

4. **Gaetulian:** a member of a North African tribe conquered by the Romans about the time of
Christ.

5. **the tombs:** the haunt of thieves.

6. **Tullus . . . Ancus:** Tullus Hostilius, the third king of Rome (673–642 B.C.), subjugated Alba,
Rome's principal rival; Ancus (640–616 B.C.) was successor to Tullus.

7. **all of the kings:** Traditionally, the reigns of seven kings of Rome, beginning with that of
Romulus (753–716 B.C.) and ending with that of Tarquinius Superbus (534–510 B.C.), preced-
ed the founding of the Republic.

He soaks his fish in the best olive oil; you get some pale coleslaw
Reeking of stuff that would smell very fine if used in a lantern,
Grease that has ridden the Nile in the meanest African lighters.

85 Used as a lotion, it gives you absolute privacy, bathing,
Guaranteed, furthermore, as a preventive of snake bite.
Virro will have a mullet, from Corsica or Taormina,[8]
Since our seas are fished out, so desperate are our gluttons.
Too many nets are spread near home, and our Tuscan fishes

90 Never attain full size, so the provinces have to supply them.
That's where the market is found by the legacy-hunters. Laenas
Makes his purchases there, and Aurelia sells, at a profit.
Virro is given a lamprey, the greatest that Sicily ever
Sent to our coast; when the wind from the south is still in his
  prison,

95 Drying his wings,[9] all craft despise the wrath of Charybdis.[10]
You get an eel, so-called, but it looks much more like a
  blacksnake,
Or you may get a pike from the Tiber, mottled with ice-spots,
A riverbank denizen, fat from the rush of the sewers,
Tough enough to swim uptown as far as Subura.

100 A word in the ear of our host, if he'd be so kind as to listen:
"No one asks for such gifts as Seneca, Piso, or Cotta[11]
Sent to their humble friends, when giving was reckoned an honor
Greater than titles or symbols of power. All we can ask for
Is that you dine with us on decent terms, just another

105 Citizen like ourselves. Do this—all right, all right, we can't stop you
Being rich for yourself and poor to your friends. They all do it."
What comes in now? Goose liver, tremendous, and also a capon
Big as a goose, and a boar, worthy of blond Meleager's[12]
Steel, served piping hot, and truffles, assuming the season

110 Right for their growth, with enough spring thunder to swell their
  production.
What did that gourmet say? Alledius, I think his name was—

---

8. Taormina: a city on the coast of Sicily, north of Mt. Etna, founded by the Carthaginians.

9. drying his wings: Auster, the South Wind, bringer of mists and fog, was very dangerous to mariners. The four winds were imprisoned in a cave by Aeolus, master of the winds, and released at the pleasure of the gods.

10. Charybdis: a dangerous whirlpool traditionally believed to be in the Straits of Messina between Italy and Sicily.

11. Seneca, Piso, or Cotta: Seneca (c. 5 B.C.–A.D. 65), Stoic philosopher and dramatist, Piso (d. A.D. 65), leader of an unsuccessful conspiracy against Nero, and Cotta (consul in 75 B.C.), a distinguished orator, were all renowned for their wealth.

12. Meleager: slayer of the huge Calydonian boar.

"Keep your wheat for yourself, O Libya; unyoke your oxen,
Just so you send us your truffles!"
                                    Meanwhile, to make you more angry,
You will behold the carver, the sleight-of-hand master, performing,
115 Prancing around, and waving his knife like a wand. How important
So his master says, to make the right gestures when carving
Rabbit or fowl! Shut your mouth, don't act like a freeborn Roman,
Don't think those three words of your name have any real meaning.
Do you want to be dragged from the house by the heels, like
    Cacus[13] the monster
120 After the beating he took from Hercules? When will Virro
Pass you the cup? He won't. And he won't risk any pollution
Touching his lips to the rim which a wretch like you has infected.
Which of you has the nerve, is so abandoned or silly
As to say to that prince "Drink up!" When your jacket is shabby
125 There are many remarks it is better to leave unspoken,
But should a god, or some chap who looked like a god, be more kindly
Than your fates ever were, and give you the cool twenty thousand
Suiting the rank of knight, how quickly you'd find yourself
    Someone,
Not a nobody now, but Virro's most intimate crony.
130 "Something for Trebius there! Give Trebius one more helping!
Brother, wouldn't you like a cut from the loin?" Money, money,
You are the one he calls brother, the one he gives homage and honor.
One word of caution, though: if you want to be patron and prince,
Let no little Aeneas go playing about in your hallways,
135 Let no small princess appear as father's small sweetheart.
Nothing will bring you more friends than a wife who is certified barren,
But, the way things are now, should your wife present you with triplets,
Virro'd be utterly charmed with your chattering brood, and to show it,
Order for each a little green shirt, and peanuts, and pennies,
140 When the small parasites come and hang around at his table.

---

13. **Cacus:** a three-headed fire-breathing giant who lived on the Palatine Hill and pillaged the surrounding countryside. Hercules killed him for stealing cattle.

Toadstools the poor will get, but Virro is feasted on mushrooms
Such as Claudius[14] ate, before the one his wife gave him.
(Since then, he ate no more.) To himself and the rest of the
    Virros
Fruit will be served. Such fruit you'd be happy with even a smell
    of,
145   Fruit such as grew in the days when Autumn was never-ending,
Fruit you would think had been robbed from the girls of the
    Golden Orchards.[15]
You get a rotten old apple, the kind that is given a monkey
All rigged out with a helmet and shield, and afraid of a
    whipping
While he is being trained to toss the spear from a goat's back.
150   Maybe you think that Virro is cheap. That's hardly the reason.
He does this to hurt, on purpose. What comedy ever,
What buffoon, is more fun than a gut that rumbles in protest?
So, in case you don't know, all this is done to compel you,
Force you, to tears of rage, and the grinding of squeaky molars.
155   You're a free man (you think) and the guest of a royal good
    fellow.
He knows, too damn well, you're the slave of the smell of his
    kitchen.
Oh, he's perfectly right. Only a slave would endure him
More than once. I don't care how poor you were in your
    childhood,
Whether you wore on your neck amulets golden or leather.
160   You are sucked in, now, by the hope of a dinner. "He'll give us,
Surely," you say, "at least the remains of a rabbit, the scraps
Off a wild-boar's haunch, or a picked-over carcass of capon."
So you sit there dumb, all of you, silent, expectant,
Bread in your hand untouched, ready to spring into action.
165   He's a wise man to treat you like this, for if you can stand it,
You can stand anything else, and, by God, I think that you ought
    to!
Some day you'll offer your shaved-off heads to be slapped, and a
    flogging
Won't seem fearful at all. You have done what you could to deserve
    them,
Trebius. Such a feast! And such a wonderful friendship!

---

14. **Claudius:** The Emperor Claudius (10 B.C.–A.D. 54) was thought to have died from eating a
dish of poisoned mushrooms given him by his wife Agrippina.

15. **the Golden Orchards:** Situated at the edge of the world, guarded by a dragon, and tended by
the three Hesperides, daughters of Atlas, was a tree bearing golden apples. As one of his twelve
labors, Hercules killed the dragon and plucked the apples from the tree.

THE THIRTEENTH SATIRE: FOR A DEFRAUDED FRIEND

Translated by Rolfe Humphries

Any performance that sets an evil example displeases
Even its author himself: to begin with, punishment lies
In the fact that no man, if guilty, is ever acquitted
With himself as judge, though he may have won in the courtroom
5   Bribing the praetor[16] in charge, or stuffing the urn with false ballots.
How do you think all men are feeling, Calvinus, about
Your charge of breach of trust, this latest criminal action?
But you are pretty well off, you'll not be sunk by such losses,
You're not the only one; this kind of case is familiar,
10   Not to say trite, one grain from the piled-up anthill of fortune.
Let's cut out the excessive laments. A man's indignation
Ought not burn out of bounds, nor be bigger than his wound is.
You, on the other hand, can hardly endure an iota,
The littlest least of light loss, and your bowels are all in an uproar
15   Simply because a friend declines to return you a sacred
Trust, committed to him. But does this really surprise you,
A man of your age, sixty years, born when Fonteius was consul?[17]
Has not, in all this time, experience taught you better?

Great, to be sure, is Wisdom, who gives us her holy scripture:
20   Fortune bows down to her, but we also consider as happy
Those whom life has taught to put up with discomforts and
    nuisance
Without tossing the yoke. What day is ever so festal
That it fails to produce a thief, a swindler, a traitor,
Profits made out of crime (all sorts), and money won by the
    dagger,
25   Won by the poisoned cup? There are few good men, not as many
As the gates of Thebes, or the mouths of the Nile.[18] We are living
In the ninth age of the world, more base than the era of iron.[19]
Nature finds no name for this wickedness, having no metal
Fit to call it by, no alloy like its corruption.
30   We invoke the faith of gods and men with a clamor
Loud as free handouts earn Faesidius when he's orating.
Tell me, old boy (I say *boy*, because you ought to be wearing

---

16. **praetor:** magistrate.

17. **when Fonteius was consul:** A.D. 67.

18. **the gates of Thebes, or the mouths of the Nile:** both seven in number.

19. **the ninth age . . . the era of iron:** The Greek poet Hesiod lists five ages—golden, silver, brass, heroic, and iron—in a generally descending order of excellence. The reference to the *ninth age* is hyperbole.

Phylacteries[20] round your neck, the badge of your second
    childhood).
Tell me, don't you know the allurements of other men's money?
35   Don't you know that the mob laughs at your simple behavior
When you insist that a man, any man in the world, should be
    truthful,
Never perjure himself, but believe in divinity's presence
Where the temples rise and the altars are colored with crimson?
Once upon a time men lived this way, in the old days,
40   Long before Saturn took up the sickle instead of the scepter,[21]
With Juno a cute little girl, and Jove, in the caverns of Ida
Sequestered,[22] not even a prince. Not yet did the dwellers in
    Heaven
Banquet above the clouds, with Hebe and Ganymede[23]
Bringing the cups; not yet did Vulcan swig down his nectar,
45   Wipe off his sweaty arms black from Aeolian anvils.[24]
Each god used to dine by himself, no such rabble of idols
As there is today, and the stars were content with a smaller
Roster of heavenly powers, a lesser load for poor Atlas.
No one had drawn by lot the gloomy underworld empire;
50   There was no glowering Dis beside his Sicilian consort,[25]
There was no wheel, no rack, no black and punishing vulture,[26]
There were no Furies[27] at all, but the Shades, without any
    monarchs
In the realms below, were quite contented and happy.
Lack of probity then was something truly surprising,

---

20. **Phylacteries:** amulets to ward off evil.

21. **the sickle . . . the scepter:** Saturn, originally a Roman agricultural deity, became identified
with the Greek god Cronus (also Kronos), whose reign marked the golden age. Cronus was
dethroned by his son Zeus, whose Roman counterpart was Jupiter.

22. **Jove . . . sequestered:** The young Jupiter, or Jove, was hidden on Mt. Ida in Crete from his
father Saturn. Saturn had consumed all of his other children to escape the fate of being overcome by one of them.

23. **Hebe and Ganymede:** the cupbearers of the gods.

24. **Vulcan . . . Aeolian anvils:** Vulcan was the god of fire and smith to the gods. The Aeolian
Islands are a group of volcanic islands near Sicily that were regarded as Vulcan's forges.

25. **Dis . . . Sicilian consort:** Pluto, or Dis, the ruler of the Underworld, abducted Proserpina,
daughter of the agricultural goddess Ceres, from the fields of Sicily and made her his queen.

26. **no wheel . . . punishing vulture:** The reference is to the punishments inflicted in the
Underworld on Ixion, Sisyphus, and Tityus respectively. Ixion was bound to a perpetually turning wheel for attempting to seduce Hera. Sisyphus, for being an informer, was condemned to
roll a huge rock up a slope. When he neared the top, the rock would roll to the bottom again.
Tityus, for attempting to rape Leto, the mother of Artemis and Apollo, was condemned to
have a vulture perpetually tear at his liver.

27. **Furies:** the three avenging deities said to have sprung from the blood of Uranus after his muti-
lation by Cronus.

55   A terrible sin, they thought, and worthy of death, if a young man
     Did not rise and stand to show his regard for his elders.
     Any bearded man, no matter who, was entitled
     To a boy's respect, though the latter's home might be richer,
     With more strawberries there, and huger mountains of acorns.
60   Reverence came to the man who was older, if only by four years.
     Was the first down of youth equal to honored old age?

     But today, if a friend does not deny that you gave him
     Money to keep in trust, if he gives back the old leather wallet
     With the rusty coins, what a portent we call it! Prodigious!
65   Garland and slaughter a lamb! Make it a matter of record!
     If I see a man of integrity, what an occasion!
     Really a freak, I would say, like a boy with a double member,
     Like fishes found under a plow while the wide-eyed yokel marvels,
     Like a pregnant mule, like a rain of stones. This upsets me
70   As would a cluster of bees if it swarmed on the roof of a temple,
     As would a river that poured torrents of milk to the ocean.

     You have been robbed, you complain, of something like five
         hundred dollars—
     A swindle, a sacrilege! But what if another man's losses
     Equal ten thousand? what if still another has lost even more,
75   So much more, in fact, that a strongbox could never contain it?
     It's simple, it's easy enough, if no mortal man knows about it,
     For the thief to scorn or despise the gods who are watching from
         Heaven
     Hear his loud voice as he lies! Look at his brazen expression!
     By the rays of the Sun (he swears), by Jupiter's lightning,
80   By the spear of Mars, the darts of Apollo of Delphi,
     By Diana's quiver, by the trident of Aegean Neptune,
     Then, for good measure, he adds Hercules' bow and Minerva's
     Lance and anything else in the ordnance supply-rooms of Heaven.
     If he's a father, he adds, with tears, "May I eat for my dinner
85   The boiled head of my son with Egyptian vinegar dressing,
     If I'm not telling the truth!"

     Some men think that luck determines everything mortal,
     Nobody governs the world, but Nature revolves in their courses
     The changes of day and of year;[28] and men like these, without
         awe,
90   Touch any altars you please. Another type always is fearful
     Punishment follows crime, he thinks there are gods, but no
         matter,

---

28. **Some men . . . and of year:** The reference is to the Epicureans who followed the materialist
   doctrines of the Greek Atomists.

He perjures himself just the same. "Let Isis[29] decide what she
    pleases
With this body of mine, let her shatter my sight with her
    sistrum,[30]
Just so, in blindness, I keep the coins I deny I have stolen;
95   Ulcers that bleed, or one lung, or half a leg—these are worth it.
If Lados, the champion runner, were poor, but still had his senses,
Needing no hellebore[31] cure, no psychotherapist's counsel,
He should not hesitate to pray for the rich man's ailment
Known as the gout: what good is speed, the renown of a sprinter?
100   Can you make a meal on a branch of Olympian olive?
Maybe the wrath of the gods is great, but it's certainly tardy.
If they take the pains to punish all of the guilty,
When will they get to me? And I might find the god can be
    prayed to,
Pardoning deeds like mine. The fates of criminals differ.
105   One gets the cross, another the crown, for the same
    misdemeanor."

So he consoles his mind for his guilt and trembles in terror.
Call him to purge himself at the shrine, and he'll get there before
    you,
Ready to drag you there, to worry and nag you to test him.
Nothing like nerve and gall to make a bad case look better;
110   Boldness induces belief. He brazens it out, like the comic
Runaway clown in the play composed by the clever Catullus.[32]
All you can do, poor dupe, is to bellow louder than Stentor,
Louder than Homer's Mars:[33] "Do you hear this, Jupiter? Do you
Not so much as move your lips, when you ought to be vocal,
115   Marble though you may be, or bronze? Then why are we placing
On your burning coals the packets of holy incense,
Calves' liver, white hog-caul? As far as I can discover,
There's no choice to be made between your images, graven,
And Vagellius' bust."

---

29. Isis: the chief goddess of Egypt, widely worshipped in Rome. She was reputed to punish iniquity with blindness.

30. sistrum: a rattle-like percussion instrument.

31. hellebore: a medicinal herb used by the ancient Greeks and Romans in the treatment of mental disorders.

32. Catullus: lyric poet (c. 84–54 B.C.). See page 225.

33. Stentor . . . Homer's Mars: According to Homer, the voice of Stentor, a Greek herald, was equal to those of 50 men, and that of the war-god Mars to those of 10,000 men.

And now, for your consolation,
120 Hear what a man can say who is neither a Cynic nor Stoic,
(They don't differ much more than a tunic's thickness would
measure),
A man who holds no brief for Epicurean contentment
With the growing slips in one diminutive garden.[34]
Puzzling cases should be referred to the best of physicians,
125 But yours could be diagnosed by a chiropractor's apprentice.
If you can show me no deed in the whole wide world as disgusting
As what happened to you, I'll have nothing to say, I'll not tell you
To leave off thumping your chest with your fists, or pounding
your cheeks
With the flat of your palm. Since ruin has been accepted,
130 The doors of the house must be closed, and the weeping and
wailing be louder
Than they would be for a death. The loss of money is awful,
Such a terrible thing that no one can counterfeit mourning,
No one be content with merely rending his garments,
Rubbing his eyes to produce crocodile tears. If your money
135 Is gone, you will really cry with genuine lamentation.

But if you see all the courts filled up with complaints like your
own,
If the tablets are read, inspected, turned over and over,
Then are pronounced a fraud, mere wood and wax, or waste
paper,
In spite of the handwriting there, or the print of the sardonyx seal-
ring,
140 Kept in its ivory case, alas! my dear fellow, Calvinus,
Do you think this makes you unique, some kind of a white hen's
chicken,
The rest of us all common fowl, hatched out of eggs ill-omened?
You have not lost very much, you could bear this with moderate
choler
If you would turn your eyes toward greater crimes. Take, for
instance,
145 The hired hoodlum, the fire lit by the arsonist's sulfur
Burning the gates of your house; or think of those robbers of
temples
Taking off great cups whose very rust should be worshipped,
The gifts of the people, or crowns, the oblations of ancient
monarchs.

---

34. **Cynic . . . Stoic . . . Epicurean . . . one diminutive garden:** Cynicism, Stoicism, and
Epicureanism were three schools of Hellenistic philosophy. Epicureanism was called the
Philosophy of the Garden because its founder, Epicurus, taught in a garden in Athens.

If these are not there, a lesser profaner arises

150 To shave the gilded face of Neptune, or Hercules' thigh,
To strip the gold leaf off Castor.[35] Why not? But the thief prefers
   bigger
Game, the melting down of Jupiter, Lord of the Thunder.
Or consider, again, the makers and merchants of poison,
The parricide thrown to the sea in the hide of an ox, and beside
   him,

155 Since the fates are adverse, an entirely innocent monkey.[36]
This is only a part of the criminal calendar, running,
Daily, from dawn to dark: if you're eager to learn the behavior
Of the human race, this courthouse should more than suffice you.
Spend a few days there, and when you come out, you will hardly

160 Dare call yourself out of luck. Would a goiter surprise anybody
If it appeared in the Alps? Would a tourist in upper Egypt
Marvel that bubbies[37] there were bigger than big fat babies?
Who is stunned at the sight of a blond-haired, blue-eyed German
Making horns of his hair, with ringlets moistened and twisted?

165 This is the way things are, and all share a common nature.
A pygmy runs to the wars in his diminutive armor,
Facing the Thracian cranes, their resonant clouds and their
   swooping,
Soon to be caught, overmatched, by his enemy, and swept upward,
Borne in crooked claws through the curving air.[38] If you saw this

170 Here in Rome, you would laugh yourself sick; but there, where the
   cohorts
Tower twelve inches high, at these continuous battles
Nobody ever guffaws.

                              "Shall he go scot free, then, this traitor,
Swindler, perjurer, crook?" Well, now, suppose he is hustled
Off in the heaviest chains, or—what more could your anger be
   asking?—

175 Put to death at our whim. You still don't recover your money,
You don't get any refund. "But the least drop of blood from the
   headless
Body will give me some comfort, a solace to mix with my hatred.

---

35. Castor: one of the twin sons of Jupiter and Leda worshiped by the Romans. The other twin was Pollux.

36. parricide . . . monkey: The traditional punishment for parricide was to put the condemned man into a sack with a cock, a dog, and a monkey and throw them all into the sea.

37. bubbies: breasts.

38. a pygmy runs . . . the curving air: Homer refers in the *Iliad* to the battles between the pygmies of Egypt and migrating cranes.

Vengeance is sweeter than life!" That's how the ignorant babble,
Those whose hearts you see on fire for the slightest of reasons
180 Or for no reason at all. But you will not hear a Chrysippus[39]
Talking like this, you won't hear the gentle genius of Thales[40]
Making any such sounds, and the old man who lived near
    Hymettus,[41]
The honeysweet mountain, would not have forced on his cruel
    accuser
So much as one drop of the hemlock he had to drink in his
    dungeon.
185 Wisdom, by slow degrees, strips off our vices and follies,
Teaching us what is right. For Vengeance always is silly,
The proof of a mean little mind, and here is one way you can tell it:
No one enjoys revenge nearly so much as a woman.

But why should you think they have gotten away with their
    crimes, when awareness
190 Of their evil deeds holds their minds in bemusement,
Lashing with strokes unheard, and the soul supplies its own
    torture
Wielding the secret whip? A terrible punishment, truly,
Far more savage than those of Caedicius or Rhadamanthus,[42]
To carry in one's own heart, by night, by day, his accuser.
195 Once upon a time a Spartan was told by the priestess
Of the Pythian shrine[43] that punishment surely awaited
Any man who planned, as he did, to hold on to the money
Placed in his trust, and then compound the offense by false
    witness.
He was asking, it seems, what was the mind of Apollo,
200 Whether the god would approve or sanction any such project.
So he gave it all back, because he was frightened, not honest,
Nevertheless, in the end, he found that the voice from the temple
Told the reverend truth, for, with his sons and his household,
With relations far removed from immediate kinship,
205 He was destroyed. The mere wish to sin brings on retribution.
He who plots a crime, though it never is openly mentioned,
Has the guilt of the deed.
                        Suppose he succeeds in his purpose.

---

39. Chrysippus: a Stoic philosopher (c. 290–208 B.C.).

40. Thales: the first great figure of Greek philosophy (c. 640–546 B.C.).

41. old man who lived near Hymettus: Socrates (c. 469-399 B.C.). Hymettus is a mountain near
    Athens. Socrates was condemned to drink hemlock for supposedly corrupting Athenian youth
    with his philosophy.

42. Caedicius or Rhadamanthus: Caedicius was apparently one of Nero's courtiers.
    Rhadamanthus judged the dead upon their entrance to the Underworld.

43. Pythian shrine: the shrine of Apollo at Delphi. (See article on page xiii.)

He is forever obsessed by anxiety, even at dinner.
His jaws are as dry as if he were sick; his bread he can't swallow,
210 Can't even chew, poor wretch, and he spits out his wine on the floor,
Finding the precious old Alban vintage completely distasteful.
Show him a better wine, and he starts to wrinkle his forehead,
Making a face as wry as if it had come from Falernum,
Vinegar, sourer than swill. In the night, if his worry permits him
215 Even the briefest rest, and his tossing limbs become quiet,
In his dreams he sees, straightway, the temple, the altar
Of the outraged god, and, even more of a burden
On his night-sweating soul, he sees you, looming above him,
Larger than life, a threat, a menace, exacting confession.
220 Such men tremble and pale at every flash of the lightning;
When it thunders, they swoon at the very first rumble from heaven,
Not as if it were chance, or the madness of winds, but that fire
Falls on earth in wrath, vindictive deliberate judgment.
That storm did no harm, but the next is all the more frightful
225 For the illusion of calm, the false postponement of vengeance.
If they begin to ache with pains in the side, and a fever,
They are certain the god has sent this illness upon them,
These are the stones he hurls, these are his lances and arrows.
They dare not vow to his shrine a bleating victim, nor offer
230 The Lares[44] a crested cock; the guilty sick are not granted
Hope: what victim is not more entitled to living than they are?
The nature of evil men is mostly capricious and shifty.
When they commit a crime, they have more than enough resolution,
But the sense of right and wrong—that seems to come to them only
235 After the deed is done. Still, habit becomes second nature—
Back to the scene of the crime. Who ever places a limit
On his own season of evil? When does he ever recover
The blush that has been expelled in disgrace from the hardened forehead?
Whom have you ever seen content with one villainous action?
240 Sooner or later this rascal of ours will get into trouble,
Step in the noose, succumb to the hook of the dungeon in darkness,
Face the Aegean rock,[45] the cliffs and crags that are crowded

---

44. **Lares:** the household gods who protected the Roman family.

45. **Aegean rock:** Exile to various remote spots was a common punishment during the reign of Nero.

With our illustrious exiles. You will rejoice that a bitter
Punishment comes to the name you hate, and you will be happy,

245   At long last, and admit that the gods have all of their senses,
That not one is deaf, or blind like Tiresias[46] the prophet.

---

46. Tiresias: the blind seer who figures in the story of Oedipus.

DISCUSSION QUESTIONS

1. In your opinion, does satire serve a useful purpose? What does it accomplish? What kinds of subjects would you say are appropriate for satire? What kinds are inappropriate?

2. Both of these satires take the form of dramatic monologues—a poem in which a speaker addresses an imaginary person. In the first case the imaginary individual is Trebius, and in the second case he is Calvinus. Who are these two individuals supposed to be? What is the effect of addressing the poems to these specific characters?

3. In the Fifth Satire, how does Virro insult and intimidate his guests? What is his motive for behaving in this manner?

4. How does Juvenal attempt to console Calvinus in the Thirteenth Satire? If you were Calvinus, how would you respond to this kind of consolation?

SUGGESTION FOR WRITING

Imagine that all of Virro's clients have met and have decided that they will present a protest letter to their patron. The first goal of the letter is to explain why they consider their treatment at the last dinner party to be unjust. The second goal is to lay down some guidelines for future dinner engagements. You have been appointed to draft the letter. Try to present the case as clearly and persuasively as you can.

MARTIAL

(C. A.D. 43–C. 104)

Martial was born in Spain but went to Rome as a young man to make his fortune as a writer. Having very little money, he had to spend time ingratiating himself with various patrons in order to make ends meet. Witty and amiable, he succeeded in gaining the friendship of many nobles and literary figures and was on good terms with the emperor Domitian. He is largely responsible for developing the epigram—a sharp, witty poem with a sting at the end—into its modern form. Altogether he produced over 1,500 short poems and epigrams, mostly about the vices of ancient Roman society. ■

from *The Epigrams*

THE COOK

Translated by J. A. Pott

> Because I beat my cook who spoiled the dinner
> You say, "Oh cruel wretch, oh greedy sinner,
> Such penalties for greater faults are fit."
> What greater crime, I ask, can cooks commit?

A TOTAL ABSTAINER

Translated by Paul Nixon

> Though you serve richest wines,
> Paulus, Rumor opines
> That they poisoned your four wives, I think.
> It's of course all a lie;
> 5 None believes less than I—
>   No, I really don't care for a drink.

TO LUPUS

Translated by Paul Nixon

> You gave me a farm—so you called it, at least,
>   In a sort of rhetorical turn—
> But I'm forced to relate that the total estate
>   Doesn't hold as much dirt as an urn.

5 A grove of Diana, you told me, I think,
   Was a notable sight on the place:
  But beyond one poor beet, overcome by the heat,
   Of grove I deny there's a trace.

  The wing of a cricket would cover that farm,
10   And an overfed ant with the gout
  Couldn't find enough crops to tickle his chops
   To last till the sun flickered out.

  Moreover that garden you bragged so about
   Proves a worm-eaten rose with one leaf,
15 And the lawn's yield of grass doesn't greatly surpass
   Its produce of gravy and beef.

  A cucumber hasn't got room to lie straight,
   And a snake's bound to live there in pieces.
  A grasshopper hopped just one day and then stopped—
20   Starved to death, with its stomach in creases.

  A mole is the sole agriculturist there,
   And he's hardly got room to turn around.
  Why, a mushroom can't spread, or a flower wave its head
   Sans trespass on my neighbor's ground.

25 An undergrown mouse when he gets at that farm
   Makes it look as though hit by the plague,
  And my whole crop of hay was carried away
   By a thrush hardly out of the egg.

  A statue of Pan—minus head, legs, and trunk—
30   Casts its shade over all the domain:
  And the shell of a clam, without sign of a jam,
   My harvest complete can contain.

  Now pardon, my friend, if my praise has been faint—
   We can seldom express what we feel:
35 So I merely will add that I'd be mighty glad
   To swap farm for a thirty-cent meal.

A PROMISING YOUTH

Translated by J. A. Pott

  At sixty years of age is he
   A man of promise still:
  Methinks he needs eternity
   That promise to fulfill.

TO LIGURINUS

Translated by F. A. Wright

You never your friends, sir, to dinner invite
Except when you have some bad verse to recite.
We have scarcely sat down when on our weary ears
Comes the sound of "Book One," ere the hors d'oeuvre appears.
5   You read through Book Two while the entree we wait;
Book Three makes dessert and the savory late.
Then comes Number Four and at last Number Five:
Even dainties so frequent a surfeit would give.
If you won't to the waste-paper merchant consign
10   Your poems, in future alone you must dine.

TO POLLA

Translated by Sir Charles Sedley

Leave off thy paint, perfumes, and youthful dress,
And nature's failing honestly confess;
Double we see those faults which art would mend,
Plain downright ugliness would less offend.

A HINTED WISH

Translated by Samuel Johnson

You told me, Maro, whilst you live
You'd not a single penny give,
But that, whene'er you chanced to die,
You'd leave a handsome legacy:
5   You must be mad beyond redress
If my next wish you cannot guess.

OLD AGE

Translated by Alexander Pope

At length my friend (while Time, with still career,
Wafts on his gentle wing his eightieth year)
Sees his past days safe out of Fortune's power,
Nor dreads approaching fate's uncertain hour;
5   Reviews his life, and in the strict survey
Finds not one moment he could wish away,
Pleased with the series of each happy day.

Such, such a man extends his life's short space,
And from the goal again renews the race;
10   For he lives twice, who can at once employ
The present well, and even the past enjoy.

THE POET

Translated by Lord Byron

He unto whom thou art so partial,
Oh, reader! is the well-known Martial,
The Epigrammatist: while living,
Give him the fame thou wouldst be giving:
5   So shall he hear, and feel, and know it—
Post-obits[1] rarely reach a poet.

PROCRASTINATION

Translated by Abraham Cowley

Tomorrow you will live, you always cry;
In what far country does this morrow lie,
That 'tis so mighty long ere it arrive?
Beyond the Indies does this morrow live?
5   'Tis so far fetched, this morrow, that I fear
'Twill be both very old and very dear.
Tomorrow I will live, the fool does say;
Today itself's too late: the wise lived yesterday.

---

1. post-obits: short for *post-obituary;* praise that appears after someone's death.

DISCUSSION QUESTIONS

1. Do you think that modern readers would tend to respond differently to "The Cook" than most ancient Romans did? Why?

2. Discuss the effect of the last line in "A Total Abstainer."

3. "To Lupus" is a series of hyperboles (exaggerations) concerning the farm that Martial has been given as a gift. What is Martial's opinion of the farm? What exaggerated details about this farm does he provide to amuse the reader?

4. What various kinds of human foolishness is Martial poking fun at in "A Promising Youth," "To Ligurinus," and "To Polla"?

5. What is the poet's wish in "A Hinted Wish"? Why?

6. How would you characterize the tone (the author's attitude toward his subject) in "Old Age"? How is this poem different from the other poems by Martial?

SUGGESTION FOR WRITING

Many of Martial's epigrams are addressed directly to individuals. Try your hand at writing an epigram entitled "To Martial," in which you humorously point out one of his weaknesses or character flaws.

OVID

(43 B.C.–A.D. 17)

Ovid received an excellent education, mainly because his father planned for him to have a law career and saw education as the means to that goal. After a short stint as a judge in the Roman courts, however, Ovid realized that he was not suited to the work and began moving in literary circles. At this time he wrote his famous *Art of Love,* a humorous manual in verse on how to find and keep a lover. This work was widely admired by the fashionable people of Rome, but it infuriated the Emperor Augustus, who was trying to bring about moral reform in the Roman Empire. During this time Ovid also wrote his masterpiece, *The Metamorphoses,* a long narrative poem about the adventures of heroes and deities that includes over 200 tales from Greek and Roman myths. All of these tales involve some sort of metamorphosis, a transformation or significant change.

When Ovid was about 50 years of age, his life suddenly took an unfortunate turn. He was exiled by Augustus to a remote fishing village on the Black Sea, where he repeatedly wrote poems and letters begging to be allowed to return to Rome. His pleas, however, were ignored, and he died in exile about ten years later. Ovid's charming and elegant tales continued to exercise a strong influence on writers throughout the Middle Ages and the Renaissance. ■

from *The Metamorphoses*

THE CREATION

Translated by Rolfe Humphries

My intention is to tell of bodies changed
To different forms; the gods, who made the changes,
Will help me—or I hope so—with a poem
That runs from the world's beginning to our own days.

5   Before the ocean was, or earth, or heaven,
Nature was all alike, a shapelessness,
Chaos, so-called, all rude and lumpy matter,
Nothing but bulk, inert, in whose confusion
Discordant atoms warred: there was no sun
10   To light the universe; there was no moon
With slender silver crescents filling slowly;
No earth hung balanced in surrounding air;
No sea reached far along the fringe of shore.
Land, to be sure, there was, and air, and ocean,
15   But land on which no man could stand, and water
No man could swim in, air no man could breathe,

Air without light, substance forever changing,
Forever at war: within a single body
Heat fought with cold, wet fought with dry, the hard
20 Fought with the soft, things having weight contended
With weightless things.
                          Till God, or kindlier Nature,
Settled all argument, and separated
Heaven from earth, water from land, our air
From the high stratosphere, a liberation
25 So things evolved, and out of blind confusion
Found each its place, bound in eternal order.
The force of fire, that weightless element,
Leaped up and claimed the highest place in heaven;
Below it, air; and under them the earth
30 Sank with its grosser portions; and the water,
Lowest of all, held up, held in, the land.

Whatever god it was, who out of chaos
Brought order to the universe, and gave it
Division, subdivision, he molded earth,
35 In the beginning, into a great globe,
Even on every side, and bade the waters
To spread and rise, under the rushing winds
Surrounding earth; he added ponds and marshes,
He banked the river-channels, and the waters
40 Feed earth or run to sea, and that great flood
Washes on shores, not banks. He made the plains
Spread wide, the valleys settle, and the forest
Be dressed in leaves; he made the rocky mountains
Rise to full height, and as the vault of Heaven
45 Has two zones, left and right, and one between them
Hotter than these, the Lord of all Creation
Marked on the earth the same design and pattern.
The torrid zone too hot for men to live in,
The north and south too cold, but in the middle
50 Varying climate, temperature and season.
Above all things the air, lighter than earth,
Lighter than water, heavier than fire,
Towers and spreads; there mist and cloud assemble,
And fearful thunder and lightning and cold winds,
55 But these, by the Creator's order, held
No general dominion; even as it is,
These brothers brawl and quarrel; though each one
Has his own quarter, still, they come near tearing
The universe apart. Eurus[1] is monarch

---

1. **Eurus . . . Auster:** the gods of the East, West, North, and South Winds.

60   Of the lands of dawn, the realms of Araby,
       The Persian ridges under the rays of morning.
       Zephyrus holds the west that glows at sunset,
       Boreas, who makes men shiver, holds the north,
       Warm Auster governs in the misty southland,
65   And over them all presides the weightless ether,
       Pure without taint of earth.
                           These boundaries given,
       Behold, the stars, long hidden under darkness,
       Broke through and shone, all over the spangled heaven,
       Their home forever, and the gods lived there,
70   And shining fish were given the waves for dwelling
       And beasts the earth, and birds the moving air.

       But something else was needed, a finer being,
       More capable of mind, a sage, a ruler,
       So Man was born, it may be, in God's image,
75   Or Earth, perhaps, so newly separated
       From the old fire of Heaven, still retained
       Some seed of the celestial force which fashioned
       Gods out of living clay and running water.
       All other animals look downward; Man,
80   Alone, erect, can raise his face toward Heaven.

THE STORY OF BAUCIS AND PHILEMON

Translated by Rolfe Humphries

                  An oak-tree stands
       Beside a linden, in the Phrygian hills.[2]
       There's a low wall around them. I have seen
       The place myself; a prince once sent me there
5   To land ruled by his father. Not far off
       A great marsh lies, once habitable land,
       But now a playground full of coots and divers.
       Jupiter came here, once upon a time,
       Disguised as mortal man, and Mercury,
10   His son, came with him, having laid aside
       Both wand and wings. They tried a thousand houses,
       Looking for rest; they found a thousand houses
       Shut in their face. But one at last received them,
       A humble cottage, thatched with straw and reeds.
15   A good old woman, Baucis, and her husband,

---

2. **Phrygian hills:** Phrygia was a country of Asia Minor, whose boundaries were variously given by ancient writers.

A good old man, Philemon, used to live there.
They had married young, they had grown old together
In the same cottage; they were very poor,
But faced their poverty with cheerful spirit
20   And made its burden light by not complaining.
It would do you little good to ask for servants
Or masters in that household, for the couple
Were all the house; both gave and followed orders.
So, when the gods came to this little cottage,
25   Ducking their heads to enter, the old man
Pulled out a rustic bench for them to rest on,
As Baucis spread a homespun cover for it.
And then she poked the ashes around a little,
Still warm from last night's fire, and got them going
30   With leaves and bark, and blew at them a little,
Without much breath to spare, and added kindling,
The wood split fine, and the dry twigs, made smaller
By breaking them over the knee, and put them under
A copper kettle, and then she took the cabbage
35   Her man had brought from the well-watered garden,
And stripped the outer leaves off. And Philemon
Reached up, with a forked stick, for the side of bacon,
That hung below the smoky beam, and cut it,
Saved up so long, a fair-sized chunk, and dumped it
40   In the boiling water. They made conversation
To keep the time from being too long, and brought
A couch with willow frame and feet, and on it
They put a sedge-grass mattress, and above it
Such drapery as they had, and did not use
45   Except on great occasions. Even so,
It was pretty worn, it had only cost a little
When purchased new, but it went well enough
With a willow couch. And so the gods reclined.
Baucis, her skirts tucked up, was setting the table
50   With trembling hands. One table leg was wobbly;
A piece of shell fixed that. She scoured the table,
Made level now, with a handful of green mint,
Put on the olives, black or green, and cherries
Preserved in dregs of wine, endive and radish,
55   And cottage cheese, and eggs, turned over lightly
In the warm ash, with shells unbroken. The dishes,
Of course, were earthenware, and the mixing-bowl
For wine was the same silver, and the goblets
Were beech, the inside coated with yellow wax.
60   No time at all, and the warm food was ready,
And wine brought out, of no particular vintage,
And pretty soon they had to clear the table

For the second course: here there were nuts and figs
And dates and plums and apples in wide baskets—
65 Remember how apples smell?—and purple grapes
Fresh from the vines, and a white honeycomb
As centerpiece, and all around the table
Shone kindly faces, nothing mean or poor
Or skimpy in good will.
                                        The mixing-bowl,
70 As often as it was drained, kept filling up
All by itself, and the wine was never lower.
And this was strange, and scared them when they saw it.
They raised their hands and prayed, a little shaky—
"Forgive us, please, our lack of preparation,
75 Our meager fare!" They had one goose, a guardian,
Watchdog, he might be called, of their estate,
And now decided they had better kill him
To make their offering better. But the goose
Was swift of wing, too swift for slow old people
80 To catch, and they were weary from the effort,
And could not catch the bird, who fled for refuge,
Or so it seemed, to the presence of the strangers.
"Don't kill him," said the gods, and then continued:
"We are gods, you know: this wicked neighborhood
85 Will pay as it deserves to; do not worry,
You will not be hurt, but leave the house, come with us,
Both of you, to the mountain-top!" Obeying,
With staff and cane, they made the long climb, slowly
And painfully, and rested, where a bowman
90 Could reach the top with a long shot, looked down,
Saw water everywhere, only their cottage
Standing above the flood. And while they wondered
And wept a little for their neighbors' trouble,
The house they used to live in, the poor quarters
95 Small for the two of them, became a temple:
Forked wooden props turned into marble columns;
The thatch grew brighter yellow; the roof was golden;
The doors were gates, most wonderfully carved;
The floor that used to be of earth was marble.
100 Jupiter, calm and grave, was speaking to them:
"You are good people, worthy of each other,
Good man, good wife—ask us for any favor,
And you shall have it." And they hesitated,
Asked, "Could we talk it over, just a little?"
105 And talked together, apart, and then Philemon
Spoke for them both: "What we would like to be
Is to be priests of yours, and guard the temple,
And since we have spent our happy years together,

May one hour take us both away; let neither
110   Outlive the other, that I may never see
The burial of my wife, nor she perform
That office for me." And the prayer was granted.
As long as life was given, they watched the temple,
And one day, as they stood before the portals,
115   Both very old, talking the old days over,
Each saw the other put forth leaves, Philemon
Watched Baucis changing, Baucis watched Philemon,
And as the foliage spread, they still had time
To say "Farewell, my dear!" and the bark closed over,
120   Sealing their mouths. And even to this day
The peasants in that district show the stranger
The two trees close together, and the union
Of oak and linden in one. The ones who told me
The story, sober ancients, were no liars,
125   Why should they be? And my own eyes have seen
The garlands people bring there; I brought new ones,
Myself, and said a verse: *The gods look after*
Good people still, and cherishers are cherished."

THE STORY OF DAEDALUS AND ICARUS

Translated by Rolfe Humphries

Homesick for homeland, Daedalus[1] hated Crete
And his long exile there, but the sea held him.
"Though Minos blocks escape by land or water,"
Daedalus said, "surely the sky is open,
5   And that's the way we'll go. Minos' dominion
Does not include the air." He turned his thinking
Toward unknown arts, changing the laws of nature.
He laid out feathers in order, first the smallest,
A little larger next it, and so continued,
10   The way that pan-pipes rise in gradual sequence.
He fastened them with twine and wax, at middle,
At bottom, so, and bent them, gently curving,
So that they looked like wings of birds, most surely.
And Icarus, his son, stood by and watched him,
15   Not knowing he was dealing with his downfall,
Stood by and watched, and raised his shiny face
To let a feather, light as down, fall on it,
Or stuck his thumb into the yellow wax,

---

1. Daedalus: an Athenian commissioned by Minos, king of Crete, to construct the Labyrinth as a prison for the Minotaur. Upon its completion, Daedalus himself was confined there.

Fooling around, the way a boy will, always,
20 Whenever a father tries to get some work done.
Still, it was done at last, and the father hovered,
Poised, in the moving air, and taught his son:
"I warn you, Icarus, fly a middle course:
Don't go too low, or water will weigh the wings down;
25 Don't go too high, or the sun's fire will burn them.
Keep to the middle way. And one more thing,
No fancy steering by star or constellation,
Follow my lead!" That was the flying lesson,
And now to fit the wings to the boy's shoulders.
30 Between the work and warning the father found
His cheeks were wet with tears, and his hands trembled.
He kissed his son (*Good-bye,* if he had known it),
Rose on his wings, flew on ahead, as fearful
As any bird launching the little nestlings
35 Out of high nest into thin air. *Keep on,*
Keep on, he signals, *follow me!* He guides him
In flight—O fatal art!—and the wings move
And the father looks back to see the son's wings moving.
Far off, far down, some fisherman is watching
40 As the rod dips and trembles over the water,
Some shepherd rests his weight upon his crook,
Some plowman on the handles of the plowshare,
And all look up, in absolute amazement,
At those air-borne above. They must be gods!
45 They were over Samos, Juno's sacred island,
Delos and Paros toward the left, Lebinthus
Visible to the right, and another island,
Calymne, rich in honey. And the boy
Thought *This is wonderful!* and left his father,
50 Soared higher, higher, drawn to the vast heaven,
Nearer the sun, and the wax that held the wings
Melted in that fierce heat, and the bare arms
Beat up and down in air, and lacking oarage
Took hold of nothing. *Father!* he cried, and *Father!*
55 Until the blue sea hushed him, the dark water
Men call the Icarian now. And Daedalus,
Father no more, called "Icarus, where are you!
Where are you, Icarus? Tell me where to find you!"
And saw the wings on the waves, and cursed his talents,
60 Buried the body in a tomb, and the land
Was named for Icarus.
                                    During the burial
A noisy partridge, from a muddy ditch,
Looked out, drummed with her wings in loud approval.
No other bird, those days, was like the partridge,

65   Newcomer to the ranks of birds; the story
Reflects no credit on Daedalus. His sister,
Ignorant of the fates, had sent her son
To Daedalus as apprentice, only a youngster,
Hardly much more than twelve years old, but clever,

70   With an inventive turn of mind. For instance,
Studying a fish's backbone for a model,
He had notched a row of teeth in a strip of iron,
Thus making the first saw, and he had bound
Two arms of iron together with a joint

75   To keep them both together and apart,
One standing still, the other traversing
In a circle, so men came to have the compass.
And Daedalus, in envy, hurled the boy
Headlong from the high temple of Minerva,

80   And lied about it, saying he had fallen
Through accident, but Minerva, kind protectress
Of all inventive wits, stayed him in air,
Clothed him with plumage; he still retained his aptness
In feet and wings, and kept his old name, Perdix,

85   But in the new bird-form, Perdix, the partridge,
Never flies high, nor nests in trees, but flutters
Close to the ground, and the eggs are laid in hedgerows.
The bird, it seems, remembers, and is fearful
Of all high places.

DISCUSSION QUESTIONS

1. It is sometimes said that Ovid's *Metamorphoses* were the inspiration for the fairy tale format that has come down from the Middle Ages. What features do Ovid's stories have in common with traditional fairy tales?

2. Ovid's account of the creation is an interesting combination of factual knowledge and fanciful explanations. What definite, scientific knowledge of the earth is revealed in this account? What fanciful explanation does Ovid give for the blowing of the winds? (If you are familiar with the Biblical creation story in Genesis Chapter 1, compare the two accounts.)

3. What test do Jupiter and Mercury use to separate the wicked from the good in the story of Baucis and Philemon? How many people do you think would pass this test today? Why was the particular virtue sought by the gods more important in the ancient world than it is today?

4. What favor do Baucis and Philemon ask of the gods? What does this request reveal about the kind of people they are? Why is their metamorphosis into trees appropriate?

5. In the story of Daedalus and Icarus, how does Ovid foreshadow the fate of Icarus?

6. Ovid is known for his extremely graceful transitions (connections) between one story and the next. How does he move from Icarus' story into the story of Perdix?

7. What talent do Daedalus and his nephew Perdix share? Why does Daedalus try to kill Perdix?

8. A myth that explains the origin of a natural phenomenon is sometimes called an etiological myth. In what way is the story of Daedalus and Perdix an etiological myth?

SUGGESTION FOR WRITING

Write an etiological myth explaining the origin of a natural phenomenon. Provide plenty of details to make your account both interesting and clear.

PLINY THE YOUNGER

(C. A.D. 62–113)

Pliny the Younger was a wealthy government official who helped administer the vast and complex Roman Empire. He was the nephew and heir of Pliny the Elder, who wrote a well-known book on natural history. During his career he held positions in the courts, the treasuries, and the army. His most important works are his *Letters*, which were obviously written to be read by the public and which he himself arranged and collected into ten books. Pliny's letters are a rich source of information about Roman life and customs, addressing political and social issues of the day and revealing a man who is shrewd, efficient, and pleased with himself. The most famous of these letters are the two describing the eruption of Vesuvius, which Pliny witnessed first hand. These two letters are included in the collection below. ■

from *The Letters*

BOOK 6, LETTER 16: TO TACITUS

Translated by William Melmoth

Your[1] request that I would send you an account of my uncle's[2] end, so that you may transmit a more exact relation of it to posterity, deserves my acknowledgments; for if his death shall be celebrated by your pen, the glory of it, I am aware, will be rendered for ever deathless. For notwithstanding he perished, as did whole peoples and cities, in the destruction of a most beautiful region, and by a misfortune memorable enough to promise him a kind of immortality; notwithstanding he has himself composed many and lasting works; yet I am persuaded, the mentioning of him in your immortal writings, will greatly contribute to eternize his name. Happy I esteem those, whom Providence has gifted with the ability either to do things worthy of being written, or to write in a manner worthy of being read; but most happy they, who are blessed with both talents: in which latter class my uncle will be placed both by his own writings and by yours. The more willingly do I undertake, nay, solicit, the task you set me.

He was at that time with the fleet under his command at Misenum.[3] On the 24th of August, about one in the afternoon, my mother desired him to observe a cloud of very unusual size and appearance. He had

---

1. **Your:** this letter is addressed to Tacitus (c. A.D. 55–120), a Roman historian. See page 285.

2. **my uncle, Pliny the Elder** (A.D. 23–79): naturalist and encyclopedist.

3. **Misenum:** a cliff forming the north coast of the Bay of Naples, site of a Roman naval station. Pliny the Elder was the admiral in command of the fleet there.

sunned himself, then taken a cold bath, and after a leisurely luncheon was engaged in study. He immediately called for his shoes and went up an eminence from whence he might best view this very uncommon appearance. It was not at that distance discernible from what mountain this cloud issued, but it was found afterwards to be Vesuvius. I cannot give you a more exact description of its figure, than by resembling it to that of a pine-tree, for it shot up a great height in the form of a trunk, which extended itself at the top into several branches; because I imagine, a momentary gust of air blew it aloft, and then failing, forsook it; thus causing the cloud to expand laterally as it dissolved, or possibly the downward pressure of its own weight produced this effect. It was at one moment white, at another dark and spotted, as if it had carried up earth or cinders.

My uncle, true savant that he was, deemed the phenomenon important and worth a nearer view. He ordered a light vessel to be got ready, and gave me the liberty, if I thought proper, to attend him. I replied I would rather study; and, as it happened, he had himself given me a theme for composition. As he was coming out of the house he received a note from Rectina, the wife of Bassus, who was in the utmost alarm at the imminent danger (his villa stood just below us, and there was no way to escape but by sea); she earnestly entreated him to save her from such deadly peril. He changed his first design and what he began with a philosophical, he pursued with an heroical turn of mind. He ordered large galleys to be launched, and went himself on board one, with the intention of assisting not only Rectina, but many others; for the villas stand extremely thick upon that beautiful coast. Hastening to the place from whence others were flying, he steered his direct course to the point of danger, and with such freedom from fear, as to be able to make and dictate his observations upon the successive motions and figures of that terrific object.

And now cinders, which grew thicker and hotter the nearer he approached, fell into the ships, then pumice-stones too, with stones blackened, scorched, and cracked by fire, then the sea ebbed suddenly from under them, while the shore was blocked up by landslips from the mountains. After considering a moment whether he should retreat, he said to the captain who was urging that course, "Fortune befriends the brave; carry me to Pomponianus." Pomponianus was then at Stabiae, distant by half the width of the bay (for, as you know, the shore, insensibly curving in its sweep, forms here a receptacle for the sea). He had already embarked his baggage; for though at Stabiae the danger was not yet near, it was full in view, and certain to be extremely near, as soon as it spread; and he resolved to fly as soon as the contrary wind should cease. It was full favorable, however, for carrying my uncle to Pomponianus. He embraces, comforts, and encourages his alarmed friend, and in order to soothe the other's fears by his own unconcern, desires to be conducted to a bathroom; and after having bathed, he sat down to supper with great cheerfulness, or at least (what is equally heroic) with all the appearance of it.

In the meanwhile Mount Vesuvius was blazing in several places with spreading and towering flames, whose refulgent brightness the darkness of the night set in high relief. But my uncle, in order to soothe apprehensions, kept saying that some fires had been left alight by the terrified country people, and what they saw were only deserted villas on fire in the abandoned district. After this he retired to rest, and it is most certain that his rest was a most genuine slumber; for his breathing, which, as he was pretty fat, was somewhat heavy and sonorous, was heard by those who attended at his chamber-door. But the court which led to his apartment now lay so deep under a mixture of pumice-stones and ashes, that if he had continued longer in his bedroom, egress would have been impossible. On being aroused, he came out, and returned to Pomponianus and the others, who had sat up all night. They consulted together as to whether they should hold out in the house, or wander about in the open. For the house now tottered under repeated and violent concussions, and seemed to rock to and fro as if torn from its foundations. In the open air, on the other hand, they dreaded the falling pumice-stones, light and porous though they were; yet this, by comparison, seemed the lesser danger of the two; a conclusion which my uncle arrived at by balancing reasons, and the others by balancing fears. They tied pillows upon their heads with napkins; and this was their whole defense against the showers that fell round them.

It was now day everywhere else, but there a deeper darkness prevailed than in the most obscure night; relieved, however, by many torches and divers illuminations. They thought proper to go down upon the shore to observe from close at hand if they could possibly put out to sea, but they found the waves still run extremely high and contrary. There my uncle having thrown himself down upon a disused sail, repeatedly called for, and drank, a draught of cold water; soon after, flames, and a strong smell of sulfur, which was the forerunner of them, dispersed the rest of the company in flight; him they only aroused. He raised himself up with the assistance of two of his slaves, but instantly fell; some unusually gross vapor, as I conjecture, having obstructed his breathing and blocked his windpipe, which was not only naturally weak and constricted, but chronically inflamed. When day dawned again (the third from that he last beheld) his body was found entire and uninjured, and still fully clothed as in life; its posture was that of a sleeping, rather than a dead man.

Meanwhile my mother and I were at Misenum. But this has no connection with history, and your inquiry went no farther than concerning my uncle's death. I will therefore put an end to my letter. Suffer me only to add, that I have faithfully related to you what I was either an eyewitness of myself, or heard at the time, when report speaks most truly. You will select what is most suitable to your purpose; for there is a great difference between a letter, and an history; between writing to a friend, and writing for the public. Farewell.

BOOK 6, LETTER 20: TO CORNELIUS TACITUS

Translated by William Melmoth

The letter which, in compliance with your request, I wrote to you concerning the death of my uncle, has raised, you say, your curiosity to know not only what terrors, but what calamities I endured when left behind at Misenum (for there I broke off my narrative).

"Though my shocked soul recoils, my tongue shall tell."[4]

My uncle having set out, I gave the rest of the day to study—the object which had kept me at home. After which I bathed, dined, and retired to short and broken slumbers. There had been for several days before some shocks of earthquake, which the less alarmed us as they are frequent in Campania;[5] but that night they became so violent that one might think that the world was not being merely shaken, but turned topsy-turvy. My mother flew to my chamber; I was just rising, meaning on my part to awaken her, if she was asleep. We sat down in the forecourt of the house, which separated it by a short space from the sea. I know not whether I should call it courage or inexperience—I was not quite eighteen—but I called for a volume of Livy,[6] and began to read, and even went on with the extracts I was making from it, as if nothing were the matter. Lo and behold, a friend of my uncle's, who was just come to him from Spain, appears on the scene; observing my mother and me seated, and that I have actually a book in my hand, he sharply censures her patience and my indifference; nevertheless I still went on intently with my author.

It was now six o'clock in the morning, the light still ambiguous and faint. The buildings around us already tottered, and though we stood upon open ground, yet as the place was narrow and confined, there was certain and formidable danger from their collapsing. It was not till then we resolved to quit the town. The common people follow us in the utmost consternation, preferring the judgment of others to their own (wherein the extreme of fear resembles prudence), and impel us onwards by pressing in a crowd upon our rear. Being got outside the houses, we halt in the midst of a most strange and dreadful scene. The coaches which we had ordered out, though upon the most level ground, were sliding to and fro, and could not be kept steady even when stones were put against the wheels. Then we beheld the sea sucked back, and as it were repulsed by the convulsive motion of the earth; it is certain at least the shore was considerably enlarged, and now held many sea-animals captive on the dry sand. On the other side, a black and dreadful cloud bursting out in gusts

---

4. **"Though . . . tell":** a quotation from the second book of Virgil's *Aeneid*.

5. **Campania:** a district in southern Italy lying between the Apennine Mountains and the Tyrrhenian Sea.

6. **Livy:** a Roman historian (50 B.C.–A.D. 17).

of igneous serpentine vapor now and again yawned open to reveal long fantastic flames, resembling flashes of lightning but much larger.

Our Spanish friend already mentioned now spoke with more warmth and instancy: "If your brother—if your uncle," said he, "is yet alive, he wishes you both may be saved; if he has perished, it was his desire that you might survive him. Why therefore do you delay your escape?" We could never think of our own safety, we said, while we were uncertain of his. Without more ado our friend hurried off, and took himself out of danger at the top of his speed.

Soon afterwards, the cloud I have described began to descend upon the earth, and cover the sea. It had already begirt the hidden Capreae,[7] and blotted from sight the promontory of Misenum. My mother now began to beseech, exhort, and command me to escape as best I might; a young man could do it; she, burdened with age and corpulency, would die easy if only she had not caused my death. I replied, I would not be saved without her, and taking her by the hand, I hurried her on. She complies reluctantly and not without reproaching herself for retarding me. Ashes now fall upon us, though as yet in no great quantity. I looked behind me; gross darkness pressed upon our rear, and came rolling over the land after us like a torrent. I proposed while we yet could see, to turn aside, lest we should be knocked down in the road by the crowd that followed us and trampled to death in the dark. We had scarce sat down, when darkness overspread us, not like that of a moonless or cloudy night, but of a room when it is shut up, and the lamp put out. You could hear the shrieks of women, the crying of children, and the shouts of men; some were seeking their children, others their parents, others their wives or husbands, and only distinguishing them by their voices; one lamenting his own fate, another that of his family; some praying to die, from the very fear of dying; many lifting their hands to the gods; but the greater part imagining that there were no gods left anywhere, and that the last and eternal night was come upon the world.

There were even some who augmented the real perils by imaginary terrors. Newcomers reported that such or such a building at Misenum had collapsed or taken fire—falsely, but they were credited. By degrees it grew lighter; which we imagined to be rather the warning of approaching fire (as in truth it was) than the return of day: however, the fire stayed at a distance from us: then again came darkness, and a heavy shower of ashes; we were obliged every now and then to rise and shake them off, otherwise we should have been buried and even crushed under their weight. I might have boasted that amidst dangers so appalling, not a sigh or expression of fear escaped from me, had not my support been founded in that miserable, though strong consolation, that all mankind were involved in the same calamity, and that I was perishing with the world itself.

At last this dreadful darkness was attenuated by degrees to a kind of cloud or smoke, and passed away; presently the real day returned, and

---

7. **Capreae:** the island of Capri in the Bay of Naples.

even the sun appeared, though lurid as when an eclipse is in progress. Every object that presented itself to our yet affrighted gaze was changed, covered over with a drift of ashes, as with snow. We returned to Misenum, where we refreshed ourselves as well as we could, and passed an anxious night between hope and fear; though indeed with a much larger share of the latter, for the earthquake still continued, and several enthusiastic people were giving a grotesque turn to their own and their neighbors' calamities by terrible predictions. Even then, however, my mother and I, notwithstanding the danger we had passed, and that which still threatened us, had no thoughts of leaving the place, till we should receive some tidings of my uncle.

And now, you will read this narrative, so far beneath the dignity of a history, without any view of transferring it to your own; and indeed you must impute it to your own request, if it shall appear scarce worthy of a letter. Farewell.

BOOK 7, LETTER 27: TO SURA

Translated by William Melmoth

The present recess from business affords you leisure to give, and me to receive, instruction. I am extremely desirous therefore to know your sentiments concerning specters, whether you believe they actually exist and have their own proper shapes and a measure of divinity, or are only the false impressions of a terrified imagination?

What particularly inclines me to give credit to their existence, is a story which I heard of Curtius Rufus.[8] When he was in low circumstances and unknown in the world, he attended the newly-made governor of Africa into that province. One afternoon as he was walking in the public portico he was extremely daunted with the figure of a woman which appeared to him, of a size and beauty more than human. She told him she was the tutelar Genius that presided over Africa, and was come to inform him of the future events of his life:—that he should go back to Rome, where he should hold office, and return to that province invested with the proconsular dignity, and there should die. Every circumstance of this prophecy was actually accomplished. It is said farther, that upon his arrival at Carthage, as he was coming out of the ship, the same figure accosted him upon the shore. It is certain, at least, that being seized with a fit of illness, though there were no symptoms in his case that led his attendants to despair, he instantly gave up all hope of recovery; judging, it should seem, of the truth of the future part of the prediction, by that which had already been fulfilled; and of the misfortune which threatened him, by the success which he had experienced.

---

8. Curtius Rufus: a Roman historian (1st. century A.D.) and biographer of Alexander the Great.

To this story, let me add another as remarkable as the former, but attended with circumstances of greater horror; which I will give you exactly as it was related to me. There was at Athens a large and spacious, but ill-reputed and pestilential house. In the dead of the night a noise, resembling the clashing of iron, was frequently heard, which, if you listened more attentively, sounded like the rattling of fetters; at first it seemed at a distance, but approached nearer by degrees; immediately afterward a phantom appeared in the form of an old man, extremely meager and squalid, with a long beard and bristling hair, rattling the gyves[9] on his feet and hands. The poor inhabitants consequently passed sleepless nights under the most dismal terrors imaginable. This, as it broke their rest, threw them into distempers, which, as their horrors of mind increased, proved in the end fatal to their lives. For even in the day time, though the specter did not appear, yet the remembrance of it made such a strong impression upon their imaginations that it still seemed before their eyes, and their terror remained when the cause of it was gone. By this means the house was at last deserted, as being judged by everybody to be absolutely uninhabitable; so that it was now entirely abandoned to the ghost. However, in hopes that some tenant might be found who was ignorant of this great calamity which attended it, a bill was put up, giving notice that it was either to be let or sold.

It happened that Athenodorus[10] the philosopher came to Athens at this time, and reading the bill ascertained the price. The extraordinary cheapness raised his suspicion; nevertheless, when he heard the whole story, he was so far from being discouraged, that he was more strongly inclined to hire it, and, in short, actually did so. When it grew towards evening, he ordered a couch to be prepared for him in the fore-part of the house, and after calling for a light, together with his pen and tablets, he directed all his people to retire within. But that his mind might not, for want of employment, be open to the vain terrors of imaginary noises and apparitions, he applied himself to writing with all his faculties. The first part of the night passed with usual silence, then began the clanking of iron fetters; however, he neither lifted up his eyes, nor laid down his pen, but closed his ears by concentrating his attention. The noise increased and advanced nearer, till it seemed at the door, and at last in the chamber. He looked round and saw the apparition exactly as it had been described to him: it stood before him, beckoning with the finger. Athenodorus made a sign with his hand that it should wait a little, and bent again to his writing, but the ghost rattling its chains over his head as he wrote, he looked round and saw it beckoning as before. Upon this he immediately took up his lamp and followed it. The ghost slowly stalked along, as if encumbered with its chains; and having turned into the courtyard of the house, suddenly vanished. Athenodorus being thus deserted, marked the spot with

---

9. **gyves:** shackles.

10. **Athenodorus:** a Stoic philosopher, teacher of the young Augustus.

a handful of grass and leaves. The next day he went to the magistrates, and advised them to order that spot to be dug up. There they found bones commingled and intertwined with chains; for the body had moldered away by long lying in the ground, leaving them bare, and corroded by the fetters. The bones were collected, and buried at the public expense; and after the ghost was thus duly laid the house was haunted no more.

This story I believe upon the affirmation of others; I can myself affirm to others what I now relate. I have a freed-man named Marcus, who has some tincture of letters. One night, his younger brother, who was sleeping in the same bed with him, saw, as he thought, somebody sitting on the couch, who put a pair of shears to his head, and actually cut off the hair from the very crown of it. When morning came, they found the boy's crown was shorn, and the hair lay scattered about on the floor After a short interval, a similar occurrence gave credit to the former. A slave-boy of mine was sleeping amidst several others in their quarters, when two persons clad in white came in (as he tells the story) through the windows, cut off his hair as he lay, and withdrew the same way they entered. Daylight revealed that this boy too had been shorn, and that his hair was likewise spread about the room. Nothing remarkable followed, unless it were that I escaped prosecution; prosecuted I should have been, if Domitian[11] (in whose reign these things happened) had lived longer. For an information lodged by Carus against me was found in his scrutore.[12] Hence it may be conjectured, since it is customary for accused persons to let their hair grow, that this cutting of my servants' hair was a sign I should defeat the peril that hung over me.

I beg, then, you will apply learning to this question. It merits your prolonged and profound consideration; and I am not myself an unworthy recipient of your abounding knowledge. And though you should, after your manner, argue on both sides; yet I hope you will throw your weightiest reasons into one scale, lest you should dismiss me in suspense and uncertainty, whereas I consult you on purpose to determine my doubts. Farewell.

BOOK 9, LETTER 3: TO PAULINUS

Translated by William Melmoth

Mankind differ in their notions of supreme happiness; but in my opinion it consists in the foretaste of an honest and abiding fame, the assurance of being admired by posterity, the realization, while yet living, of future glory. I confess if I had not the reward of an immortal reputation in view, I should choose to live in the lap of Leisure, as people say. There

---

11. **Domitian:** Roman Emperor from A.D. 81 to 96.

12. **scrutore:** a desk.

seem to be but two points worthy our attention; either the endless duration of fame, or the short extent of life. Those who are governed by the former consideration, must pursue it with the full exertion of the most laborious efforts; while such as are influenced by the latter should quietly resign themselves to repose, nor wear out a short life in perishable pursuits: as some, we may observe, do, and then sink at last into self-contempt, in the midst of a wretched and fruitless course of false industry. These are my daily reflections, which I communicate to you, in order to renounce them if you do not join with me in the same sentiments: as undoubtedly you will, who are for ever meditating some glorious and immortal enterprise. Farewell.

DISCUSSION QUESTIONS

1. If you were making a movie about the eruption of Mt. Vesuvius, what details from Book 6, Letter 16 would you focus on? What aspects of crowd behavior would you emphasize?

2. What impression do you get of Pliny as a person from his description of his own behavior (Book 6, Letter 20) during the eruption of Mt. Vesuvius? What impression do you think he wants future readers to have of him?

3. Pliny describes three ghostly visitations in Book 7, Letter 27. What are the various motivations of these ghosts, that is, why do they decide to pay a visit?

4. According to Book 9, Letter 3, what was Pliny's primary goal in life?

SUGGESTION FOR WRITING

Imagine that you are a journalist who has decided to interview Pliny. You will either talk to him about his experiences during the eruption of Vesuvius or about his knowledge of ghosts. Your readers will be intensely interested in hearing what he says, and so you will want to ask probing questions. Write a script of this interview.

SUETONIUS

(C. A.D. 69–140)

A Roman historian and biographer, Suetonius is known primarily for *The Twelve Caesars*, from which the following selection is taken. His interest in history began when he was serving as secretary to the Emperor Hadrian and had access to documents containing information about past Roman emperors. Suetonius made use of these official documents to construct his biographies, but he also included a great deal of personal information gained from rumors and anecdotes. His writings are an interesting mixture of fact, speculation, and gossip.

The subject of the selection that follows is Nero (A.D. 37–68), the Roman emperor who eventually became one of the most despised rulers in world history. Nero neglected his duties and squandered money on circuses and spectacles. He executed any Roman senator who questioned his decisions and even ordered the murder of several family members, including his mother and two of his wives. In A.D. 64 most of Rome was destroyed by a huge fire, which Nero falsely blamed on the Christians. For years he persecuted and tortured them, but rumors persisted that Nero himself had started the fire so that he could lavishly rebuild the city.

In addition to his cruelty and wastefulness, Nero is also famous for his misguided artistic pursuits. Believing himself to be a gifted musician and poet, Nero constantly inflicted concerts, operas, and poetry readings on his helpless subjects. His last words are said to have been, "Alas, what an artist is dying in me." In the selection below, Suetonius humorously describes Nero's artistic and athletic endeavors. ■

from The Twelve Caesars

NERO THE IMPERIAL ARTIST

Translated by Robert Graves

Music formed part of Nero's childhood curriculum, and he early developed a taste for it. Soon after his accession, he summoned Terpnus, the greatest lyre-player of the day, to sing to him when dinner had ended, for several nights in succession, until very late. Then, little by little, he began to study and practice himself, and conscientiously undertook all the usual exercises for strengthening and developing the voice. He would lie on his back with a slab of lead on his chest, use enemas and emetics to keep down his weight, and refrain from eating apples and every other food considered deleterious to the vocal cords. Ultimately, though his voice was still feeble and husky, he was pleased enough with his progress to nurse theatrical ambitions, and would quote to his friends the Greek proverb: "Unheard melodies are never sweet." His first stage appearance was at Naples, where, disregarding an earthquake which shook the theater, he sang his piece through to the end. He often performed at Naples, for several consecutive days too; and even while giving his voice a brief rest, could not stay away from the theater, but went to dine in the orchestra—where he promised the crowd in Greek that, when he had downed a drink or two, he would give them something to make their ears ring. So captivated was he by the rhythmic applause of some Alexandrian sailors from a fleet which had just put in, that he sent to Egypt for more. He also chose a few young knights, and more than five thousand ordinary youths, whom he divided into claques to learn the Alexandrian method of applause—they were known, respectively, as "Bees," "Roof-tiles," and "Brick-bats"—and provide it liberally whenever he sang. It was easy to recognize them by their bushy hair, splendid dress, and the absence of rings on their left hands. The knights who led them earned five gold pieces a performance.

Appearances at Rome meant so much to Nero that he held the Neronia[1] again before the required five years elapsed. When the crowd clamored to hear his heavenly voice, he answered that he would perform in the Palace gardens later if anyone really wanted to hear him; but when the Guards on duty seconded the appeal, he delightedly agreed to oblige them. He wasted no time in getting his name entered on the list of competing lyre-players, and dropped his ticket into the urn with the others. The Guards colonels carried his lyre as he went up to play, and a group of military tribunes and close friends accompanied him. After taking his place and briefly begging the audience's kind attention, he made Cluvius Rufus, the ex-Consul, announce the title of the song. It was the whole of the opera *Niobe;* and he sang on until two hours before dusk. Since this allowed the remaining competitors no chance to perform, he postponed the award of a prize to the following year, which would give him another opportunity to sing. But since a year was a long time to wait, he continued to make frequent appearances. He toyed with the idea of playing opposite professional actors in public shows staged by magistrates: because one of the Praetors had offered him 12,500 gold pieces if he would consent. And he did actually appear in operatic tragedies, taking the parts of heroes and gods, sometimes even of heroines and goddesses, wearing masks either modeled on his own face, or on the face of whatever woman happened to be his current mistress. Among his performances were *Canace in Childbirth, Orestes the Matricide, Oedipus Blinded,* and *Distraught Hercules.* There is a story that a young recruit on guard in the wings recognized him in the rags and fetters demanded by the part of Hercules, and dashed boldly to his assistance.

Horses had been Nero's main interest since childhood; whatever his tutors might do, they could never stop his chatter about the chariot-races at the Circus. When scolded by one of them for telling his fellow-pupils about a Leek-Green charioteer who had the misfortune to get dragged by his team, Nero untruthfully explained that he had been discussing

---

1. the Neronia: games established by Nero to be held every five years. These games included dramatic contests as well as athletic events.

Hector's fate[2] in the *Iliad*. At the beginning of his reign he used every day to play with model ivory chariots on a board, and came up from the country to attend all the races, even minor ones, at first in secret and then without the least embarrassment; so that there was never any doubt at Rome when he would be in residence. He frankly admitted that he wished the number of prizes increased, which meant that the contest now lasted until a late hour and the faction-managers no longer thought it worth while to bring out their teams except for a full day's racing. Very soon Nero set his heart on driving a chariot himself, in a regular race, and, after a preliminary trial in the Palace Gardens before an audience of slaves and loungers, made a public appearance in the Circus Maximus; on this occasion one of his freedmen replaced the magistrate who dropped the napkin as the starting signal.

However, these amateur incursions into the arts at Rome did not satisfy him, and he headed for Greece, as I mentioned above. His main reason was that the cities which regularly sponsored musical contests had adopted the practice of sending him every available prize for lyre-playing; he always accepted these with great pleasure, giving the delegates the earliest audience of the day and invitations to private dinners. They would beg Nero to sing when the meal was over, and applaud his performance to the echo, which made him announce: "The Greeks alone are worthy of my genius; they really listen to music." So he sailed off hastily and, as soon as he arrived at Cassiope, gave his first song recital before the altar of Jupiter Cassius; after which he went the round of all the contests.

He ordered those contests which normally took place only at long intervals to be held during his visit, even if it meant repeating them; and broke tradition at Olympia by introducing a musical competition into the athletic games. When Helius, his freedman-secretary, reminded him that he was urgently needed at Rome, he would not be distracted by official business, but answered: "Yes, you have made yourself quite plain. I am aware that you want me to go home; you will do far better, however, if you encourage me to stay until I have proved myself worthy of my reputation."

No one was allowed to leave the theater during his recitals, however pressing the reason, and the gates were kept barred. We read of women in the audience giving birth, and of men being so bored with the music and the applause that they furtively dropped down from the wall at the rear, or shammed dead and were carried away for burial. Nero's stage fright and general nervousness, his jealousy of rivals, and his awe of the judges, were more easily seen than believed. Though usually gracious and charming to other competitors, whom he treated as equals, he abused them behind their backs, and often insulted them to their faces; and if any were particularly good singers, he would bribe them not to do themselves justice.

---

2. Hector's fate: In Homer's Iliad, the Greek hero Achilles kills the Trojan champion Hector. He then ties Hector's body to his chariot and drags him three times around the walls of Troy.

Before every performance he would address the judges with the utmost deference: saying that he had done what he could, and that the issue was now in Fortune's hands; but that since they were men of judgment and experience, they would know how to eliminate the factor of chance. When they told him not to worry, he felt a little better, but still anxious; and mistook the silence of some for severity, and the embarrassment of others for disfavor, admitting that he suspected every one of them.

He strictly observed the rules, never daring to clear his throat and even using his arm, rather than a handkerchief, to wipe the sweat from his brow. Once, while acting in a tragedy, he dropped his scepter and quickly recovered it, but was terrified of disqualification. The accompanist, however—who played a flute and made the necessary dumbshow to illustrate the words—swore that the slip had passed unnoticed, because the audience were listening with such rapt attention; so he took heart again. Nero insisted on announcing his own victories; which emboldened him to enter the competition for heralds. To destroy every trace of previous winners in these contests, he ordered all their statues and busts to be taken down, dragged away with hooks, and hurled into private privies. On several occasions he took part in the chariot-racing, and at Olympia drove a ten-horse team, a novelty for which he had censured King Mithridates[3] in one of his own poems. On this occasion he was thrown from the chariot, and had to be helped in again; but, though he failed to stay the course and retired before the finish, the judges nevertheless awarded him the prize. On the eve of his departure, he presented the whole province with its freedom and conferred Roman citizenship as well as large cash rewards on the judges. It was during the Isthmian Games at Corinth that he stood in the middle of the stadium and personally announced these benefits.

Physical characteristics of Nero:

> Height: average.
> Body: pustular and malodorous.
> Hair: light blond.
> Features: pretty, rather than handsome.
> Eyes: dullish blue.
> Neck: squat.
> Belly: protuberant.
> Legs: spindling.

His health was amazingly good: for all his extravagant indulgence he had only three illnesses in fourteen years, and none of them serious enough to stop him from drinking wine or breaking any other regular habit. He did not take the least trouble to dress as an Emperor should, but always had his hair set in rows of curls and, when he visited Greece, let it

---

3. King Mithridates: the name of several kings of Pontus, a region in northern Asia Minor. Presumably the reference here is to the last and most famous, Mithridates VI (c. 132–63 B.C.), who was involved in a series of wars with Rome.

grow long and hang down his back. He often gave audiences in an unbelted silk dressing-gown, slippers, and a scarf.

As a boy, Nero read most of the usual school subjects except philosophy which, Agrippina[4] warned him, was no proper study for a future ruler. His tutor Seneca[5] hid the works of the early rhetoricians from him, intending to be admired himself as long as possible. So Nero turned his hand to poetry, and would dash off verses without any effort. It is often claimed that he published other people's work as his own; but notebooks and loose pages have come into my possession, which contain some of Nero's best-known poems in his own handwriting, and have clearly been neither copied nor dictated. Many erasures and cancellations, as well as words substituted above the lines, prove that he was thinking things out for himself. Nero also took more than an amateur's interest in painting and sculpture.

His greatest weaknesses were his thirst for popularity and his jealousy of men who caught the public eye by any means whatsoever. Because he had swept the board of all public prizes offered for acting, and was also an enthusiastic wrestler—during his tour of Greece he had never missed a single athletic meeting—most people expected him to take part in the Classical events at the next Olympiad. He used to squat on the ground in the stadium, like the judges, and if any pair of competitors worked away from the center of the ring, would push them back himself. Because of his singing and chariot-driving he had been compared to Phoebus Apollo;[6] now, apparently, he planned to become a Hercules, for according to one story he had a lion so carefully trained that he could safely face it naked, before the entire amphitheater; and then either kill it with his club or else strangle it.

Just before the end, Nero took a public oath that if he managed to keep his throne, he would celebrate the victory with a music festival, performing successively on water-organ, flute, and bagpipes; and when the last day came, would dance the role of Turnus[7] in Virgil's *Aeneid*. He was supposed to have killed the actor Paris, because he considered him a serious professional rival.

---

4. **Agrippina:** Nero's mother.

5. **Seneca** (c. 5 B.C.–A.D. 64): Stoic philosopher and dramatist.

6. **Phoebus Apollo:** Greek god of music and poetry.

7. **Turnus:** in Virgil's *Aeneid*, champion of the Latins in their war with Aeneas and his Trojans. He is killed by Aeneas.

DISCUSSION QUESTIONS

1. Imagine that you are a talk show host and that Nero has agreed to appear on your show to discuss his recent awards. What questions would you ask Nero? How would you expect him to respond?

2. Relate the title to the contents of the biographical sketch. When did you first begin to suspect that Nero was not particularly talented?

3. Suetonius' attitude toward Nero is obvious, but how does he feel about the audiences that applauded the untalented emperor and the judges who awarded him prizes?

4. Suetonius was not born until after Nero's death, and yet his sketch of Nero strongly resembles a first-hand account. What features of Suetonius' account make it appear to be written by someone who actually knew Nero?

5. What are some of the tactics that Nero used to beat out his rivals?

SUGGESTIONS FOR WRITING

1. Sometimes a simple form of expression can communicate as much as a longer piece of writing. Try to capture something significant about Nero by creating one of the following:

- A humorous rhyming epitaph designed for Nero's tomb

- A political cartoon focusing on Nero

2. Few people have known a genuine tyrant, but almost everyone has had experience with someone who abused power. Write a description of a power abuser you have known, such as a teacher, coach, or boss. Aim for an entertaining sketch rather than a complaining one, and round out your description with plenty of specific details.

TACITUS

(C. A.D. 55–C. 120)

The son of a wealthy government official, Tacitus' training was in law and oratory. He became a successful lawyer and a persuasive orator, leading an active public life in a number of roles, including governor of several Roman provinces. In time he began withdrawing from public life to concentrate on his writing. His fame rests primarily on his *Histories* and his *Annals*, which describe Roman history from Augustus to Nero. Tacitus favored the republican form of government, and his works are extremely critical of the Roman emperors. In these works he examines how the diminishing role of the Senate permits the emperors to acquire overwhelming power, which they do not hesitate to abuse. Tacitus feared that Rome was in a serious decline and possibly headed toward ruin.

Tacitus, like most ancient historians, saw the purpose of history as moral evaluation rather than objective reporting. To a modern reader his works are more like literature than history, with their psychological analysis, powerful delineation of character, and brilliant conversations. In spite of his love for theatrical effects, Tacitus was extremely careful about checking facts and exercised good critical judgment when examining biased accounts. Unlike Suetonius, he did not spice up his accounts with gossip when there was no solid evidence to offer. His purpose, as he himself expressed it, was to write "without anger and partiality." ■

from THE ANNALS

Translated by Alfred John Church and William Jackson Brodribb

In the year[1] of the consulship of Marcus Asinius and Manius Acilius it was seen to be portended by a succession of prodigies that there were to be political changes for the worse. The soldiers' standards and tents were set in a blaze by lightning. A swarm of bees settled on the summit of the Capitol; births of monsters, half man, half beast, and of a pig with a hawk's talons, were reported. It was accounted a portent that every order of magistrates had had its number reduced, a quaestor, an aedile, a tribune, a praetor and consul having died within a few months. But Agrippina's terror was the most conspicuous. Alarmed by some words dropped by Claudius when half intoxicated, that it was his destiny to have to endure his wives' infamy[2] and at last punish it, she determined to act

---

1. **the year:** A.D. 54

2. **Agrippina . . . his wives' infamy:** Agrippina was the wife of the emperor Claudius. Messalina, his previous wife, was known for her shameless behavior. She was finally put to death by one of Claudius' freedmen for conspiring against him.

without a moment's delay. . . . Claudius had an attack of illness, and went to Sinuessa[3] to recruit his strength with its balmy climate and salubrious waters. Thereupon, Agrippina, who had long decided on the crime and eagerly grasped at the opportunity thus offered, and did not lack instruments, deliberated on the nature of the poison to be used. The deed would be betrayed by one that was sudden and instantaneous, while if she chose a slow and lingering poison, there was a fear that Claudius, when near his end, might, on detecting the treachery, return to his love for his son. She decided on some rare compound which might derange his mind and delay death. A person skilled in such matters was selected, Locusta by name, who had lately been condemned for poisoning, and had long been retained as one of the tools of despotism. By this woman's art the poison was prepared, and it was to be administered by a servant, Halotus, who was accustomed to bring in and taste the dishes.

All the circumstances were subsequently so well known, that writers of the time have declared that the poison was infused into some mushrooms, a favorite delicacy, and its effect, not at the instant perceived, from the emperor's lethargic, or intoxicated condition. His bowels too were relieved, and this seemed to have saved him. Agrippina was thoroughly dismayed. Fearing the worst, and defying the immediate obloquy of the deed, she availed herself of the complicity of Xenophon, the physician, which she had already secured. Under pretense of helping the emperor's efforts to vomit, this man, it is supposed, introduced into his throat a feather smeared with some rapid poison; for he knew that the greatest crimes are perilous in their inception, but well rewarded after their consummation.

Meanwhile the Senate was summoned, and prayers rehearsed by the consuls and priests for the emperor's recovery, though the lifeless body was being wrapped in blankets with warm applications, while all was being arranged to establish Nero on the throne.[4] At first Agrippina, seemingly overwhelmed by grief and seeking comfort, clasped Britannicus in her embraces, called him the very image of his father, and hindered him by every possible device from leaving the chamber. She also detained his sisters, Antonia and Octavia, closed every approach to the palace with a military guard, and repeatedly gave out that the emperor's health was better, so that the soldiers might be encouraged to hope, and that the fortunate moment foretold by the astrologers[5] might arrive.

At last, at noon on the 13th of October, the gates of the palace were suddenly thrown open, and Nero, accompanied by Burrus, went forth to

---

3. **Sinuessa:** a town on the Gulf of Gaeta north of Naples.

4. **on the throne:** Agrippina wished to see her own son Nero, Claudius' stepson, become emperor rather than Britannicus, Claudius' son and rightful heir.

5. **foretold by the astrologers:** Years earlier, Agrippina had consulted astrologers concerning her son's future. They had predicted that he would become emperor and also that he would kill her.

the cohort which was on guard after military custom. There, at the suggestion of the commanding officer, he was hailed with joyful shouts, and set on a litter. Some, it is said, hesitated, and looked round and asked where Britannicus was; then, when there was no one to lead a resistance, they yielded to what was offered them. Nero was conveyed into the camp, and having first spoken suitably to the occasion and promised a donative after the example of his father's bounty, he was unanimously greeted as emperor. The decrees of the Senate followed the voice of the soldiers, and there was no hesitation in the provinces. Divine honors were decreed to Claudius, and his funeral rites were solemnized on the same scale as those of Augustus; for Agrippina strove to emulate the magnificence of her great-grandmother, Livia. But his will was not publicly read, as the preference of the stepson to the son might provoke a sense of wrong and angry feeling in the popular mind. . . .

On the day of the funeral the prince pronounced Claudius's panegyric, and while he dwelt on the antiquity of his family and on the consulships and triumphs of his ancestors, there was enthusiasm both in himself and his audience. The praise of his graceful accomplishments, and the remark that during his reign no disaster had befallen Rome from the foreigner, were heard with favor. When the speaker passed on to his foresight and wisdom, no one could refrain from laughter, though the speech, which was composed by Seneca,[6] exhibited much elegance, as indeed that famous man had an attractive genius which suited the popular ear of the time. Elderly men who amuse their leisure with comparing the past and the present, observed that Nero was the first emperor who needed another man's eloquence. The dictator Caesar rivaled the greatest orators, and Augustus had an easy and fluent way of speaking, such as became a sovereign. Tiberius too thoroughly understood the art of balancing words, and was sometimes forcible in the expression of his thoughts, or else intentionally obscure. Even Caius Caesar's[7] disordered intellect did not wholly mar his faculty of speech. Nor did Claudius, when he spoke with preparation, lack elegance. Nero from early boyhood turned his lively genius in other directions; he carved, painted, sang, or practiced the management of horses, occasionally composing verses which showed that he had the rudiments of learning. . . .

Meanwhile the mother's influence was gradually weakened, as Nero fell in love with a freedwoman, Acte by name, and took into his confidence Otho and Claudius Senecio, two young men of fashion, the first of whom was descended from a family of consular rank, while Senecio's father was one of the emperor's freedmen. . . .

It happened at this time that the emperor after inspecting the apparel in which wives and mothers of the imperial house had been seen to glit-

---

6. Seneca: Stoic philosopher and dramatist (c. 5 B.C.–A.D. 64).

7. Caius Caesar: the emperor Caligula (A.D. 12–42), who became insane.

ter, selected a jeweled robe and sent it as a gift to his mother, with the unsparing liberality of one who was bestowing by preference on her a choice and much coveted present. Agrippina, however, publicly declared that so far from her wardrobe being furnished by these gifts, she was really kept out of the remainder, and that her son was merely dividing with her what he derived wholly from herself. . . . As she spoke, she raised her hand in menace and heaped insults on him, as she appealed to the deified Claudius, to the infernal shades of the Silani, and to those many fruitless crimes.[8]

Nero was confounded at this, and as the day was near on which Britannicus would complete his fourteenth year, he reflected, now on the domineering temper of his mother, and now again on the character of the young prince, which a trifling circumstance had lately tested, sufficient however to gain for him wide popularity. During the feast of Saturn, amid other pastimes of his playmates, at a game of lot drawing for king, the lot fell to Nero, upon which he gave all his other companions different orders, and such as would not put them to the blush; but when he told Britannicus to step forward and begin a song, hoping for a laugh at the expense of a boy who knew nothing of sober, much less of riotous society, the lad with perfect coolness commenced some verses which hinted at his expulsion from his father's house and from supreme power. This procured him pity, which was the more conspicuous, as night with its merriment had stripped off all disguise. Nero saw the reproach and redoubled his hate. Pressed by Agrippina's menaces, having no charge against his brother and not daring openly to order his murder, he meditated a secret device and directed poison to be prepared through the agency of Julius Pollio, tribune of one of the praetorian cohorts, who had in his custody a woman under sentence for poisoning, Locusta by name, with a vast reputation for crime. That every one about the person of Britannicus should care nothing for right or honor, had long ago been provided for. He actually received his first dose of poison from his tutors and passed it off his bowels, as it was rather weak or so qualified as not at once to prove deadly. But Nero, impatient at such slow progress in crime, threatened the tribune and ordered the poisoner to execution for prolonging his anxiety while they were thinking of the popular talk and planning their own defense. Then they promised that death should be as sudden as if it were the hurried work of the dagger, and a rapid poison of previously tested ingredients was prepared close to the emperor's chamber.

It was customary for the imperial princes to sit during their meals with other nobles of the same age, in the sight of their kinsfolk, at a table of their own, furnished somewhat frugally. There Britannicus was dining, and as what he ate and drank was always tested by the taste of a select attendant, the following device was contrived, that the usage might not be dropped or the crime betrayed by the death of both prince and atten-

---

8. crimes: such as her poisoning of her husband, the emperor Claudius.

dant. A cup as yet harmless, but extremely hot and already tasted, was handed to Britannicus; then, on his refusing it because of its warmth, poison was poured in with some cold water, and this so penetrated his entire frame that he lost alike voice and breath. There was a stir among the company; some, taken by surprise, ran hither and thither, while those whose discernment was keener, remained motionless, with their eyes fixed on Nero, who, as he still reclined in seeming unconsciousness, said that this was a common occurrence from a periodical epilepsy, with which Britannicus had been afflicted from his earliest infancy, and that his sight and senses would gradually return. As for Agrippina, her terror and confusion, though her countenance struggled to hide it, so visibly appeared, that she was clearly just as ignorant as was Octavia, Britannicus's own sister. She saw, in fact, that she was robbed of her only remaining refuge, and that here was a precedent for parricide. Even Octavia, notwithstanding her youthful inexperience, had learnt to hide her grief, her affection, and indeed every emotion.

And so after a brief pause the company resumed its mirth. One and the same night witnessed Britannicus's death and funeral, preparations having been already made for his obsequies, which were on a humble scale. He was however buried in the Campus Martius,[9] amid storms so violent, that in the popular belief they portended the wrath of heaven against a crime which many were even inclined to forgive when they remembered the immemorial feuds of brothers and the impossibility of a divided throne. The emperor apologized for the hasty funeral by reminding people that it was the practice of our ancestors to withdraw from view any grievously untimely death, and not to dwell on it with panegyrics or display. For himself, he said, that as he had now lost a brother's help, his remaining hopes centered in the State, and all the more tenderness ought to be shown by the Senate and people towards a prince who was the only survivor of a family born to the highest greatness.

He then enriched his most powerful friends with liberal presents. Some there were who reproached men of austere professions with having on such an occasion divided houses and estates among themselves, like so much spoil. It was the belief of others that a pressure had been put on them by the emperor, who, conscious as he was of guilt, hoped for merciful consideration if he could secure the most important men by wholesale bribery. But his mother's rage no lavish bounty could allay. She would clasp Octavia to her arms, and have many a secret interview with her friends; with more than her natural rapacity, she clutched at money everywhere, seemingly for a reserve, and courteously received tribunes and centurions. She honored the names and virtues of the nobles who still were left, seeking apparently a party and a leader. Of this Nero became aware, and he ordered the departure of the military guard now kept for the

---

9. the Campus Martius: a plain bounded by three of Rome's seven hills. It was the site of many temples and mausoleums, and at one time was used for army exercises.

emperor's mother, as it had formerly been for the imperial consort, along with some German troops, added as a further honor. He also gave her a separate establishment, that throngs of visitors might no longer wait on her, and removed her to what had been Antonia's[10] house; and whenever he went there himself, he was surrounded by a crowd of centurions, and used to leave her after a hurried kiss. . . .

In the year[11] of the consulship of Caius Vipstanus and Caius Fonteius, Nero deferred no more a long meditated crime. Length of power had matured his daring, and his passion for Poppaea[12] daily grew more ardent. As the woman had no hope of marriage for herself or of Octavia's divorce while Agrippina lived, she would reproach the emperor with incessant vituperation and sometimes call him in jest a mere ward who was under the rule of others, and was so far from having empire that he had not even his liberty. "Why," she asked, "was her marriage put off? Was it, forsooth, her beauty and her ancestors, with their triumphal honors, that failed to please, or her being a mother, and her sincere heart? No; the fear was that as a wife at least she would divulge the wrongs of the Senate, and the wrath of the people at the arrogance and rapacity of his mother. If the only daughter-in-law Agrippina could bear was one who wished evil to her son, let her be restored to her union with Otho. She would go anywhere in the world, where she might hear of the insults heaped on the emperor, rather than witness them, and be also involved in his perils."

These and the like complaints, rendered impressive by tears and by the cunning of an adulteress, no one checked, as all longed to see the mother's power broken, while not a person believed that the son's hatred would steel his heart to her murder. . . .

Nero accordingly avoided secret interviews with her,[13] and when she withdrew to her gardens or to her estates at Tusculum and Antium, he praised her for courting repose. At last, convinced that she would be too formidable, wherever she might dwell, he resolved to destroy her, merely deliberating whether it was to be accomplished by poison, or by the sword, or by any other violent means. Poison at first seemed best, but, were it to be administered at the imperial table, the result could not be referred to chance after the recent circumstances of the death of Britannicus. Again, to tamper with the servants of a woman who, from her familiarity with crime, was on her guard against treachery, appeared to be extremely difficult, and then, too, she had fortified her constitution by the use of antidotes. How again the dagger and its work were to be kept secret, no one could suggest, and it was feared too that whoever might be chosen to execute such a crime would spurn the order.

---

10. **Antonia:** daughter of Claudius, half-sister of Octavia and Britannicus.

11. **the year:** A.D. 59.

12. **Poppaea:** wife of Nero's friend Otho, whom Nero had appointed as a provincial governor in order that he might be free to pursue his affair with Poppaea at Rome. Nero married her in A.D. 62.

13. **her:** Agrippina.

An ingenious suggestion was offered by Anicetus, a freedman, commander of the fleet at Misenum,[14] who had been tutor to Nero in boyhood and had a hatred of Agrippina which she reciprocated. He explained that a vessel could be constructed, from which a part might by a contrivance be detached, when out at sea, so as to plunge her unawares into the water. "Nothing," he said, "allowed of accidents so much as the sea, and should she be overtaken by shipwreck, who would be so unfair as to impute to crime an offense committed by the winds and waves? The emperor would add the honor of a temple and of shrines to the deceased lady, with every other display of filial affection."

Nero liked the device, favored as it also was by the particular time, for he was celebrating Minerva's five days' festival at Baiae.[15] Thither he enticed his mother by repeated assurances that children ought to bear with the irritability of parents and to soothe their tempers, wishing thus to spread a rumor of reconciliation and to secure Agrippina's acceptance through the feminine credulity, which easily believes what gives joy. As she approached, he went to the shore to meet her (she was coming from Antium),[16] welcomed her with outstretched hand and embrace, and conducted her to Bauli. This was the name of a country house, washed by a bay of the sea, between the promontory of Misenum and the lake of Baiae. Here was a vessel distinguished from others by its equipment, seemingly meant, among other things, to do honor to his mother; for she had been accustomed to sail in a trireme, with a crew of marines. And now she was invited to a banquet, that night might serve to conceal the crime. It was well known that somebody had been found to betray it, that Agrippina had heard of the plot, and in doubt whether she was to believe it, was conveyed to Baiae in her litter. There some soothing words allayed her fear; she was graciously received, and seated at table above the emperor. Nero prolonged the banquet with various conversation, passing from a youth's playful familiarity to an air of constraint, which seemed to indicate serious thought, and then, after protracted festivity, escorted her on her departure, clinging with kisses to her eyes and bosom, either to crown his hypocrisy or because the last sight of a mother on the eve of destruction caused a lingering even in that brutal heart.

A night of brilliant starlight with the calm of a tranquil sea was granted by heaven, seemingly, to convict the crime. The vessel had not gone far, Agrippina having with her two of her intimate attendants, one of whom, Crepereius Gallus, stood near the helm, while Acerronia, reclining at Agrippina's feet as she reposed herself, spoke joyfully of her son's repentance and of the recovery of the mother's influence, when at a given signal the ceiling of the place, which was loaded with a quantity of lead, fell in, and Crepereius was crushed and instantly killed. Agrippina

---

14. **Misenum:** a cliff forming the north coast of the Bay of Naples, site of a Roman naval station.

15. **festival at Baiae:** Baiae was a town on the Bay of Naples; the festival of Minerva, the Roman goddess of wisdom, occurred during the latter half of March.

16. **Antium:** the town now called Anzio.

and Acerronia were protected by the projecting sides of the couch, which happened to be too strong to yield under the weight. But this was not followed by the breaking up of the vessel; for all were bewildered, and those too, who were in the plot, were hindered by the unconscious majority. The crew then thought it best to throw the vessel on one side and so sink it, but they could not themselves promptly unite to face the emergency, and others, by counteracting the attempt, gave an opportunity of a gentler fall into the sea. Acerronia, however, thoughtlessly exclaiming that she was Agrippina, and imploring help for the emperor's mother, was dispatched with poles and oars, and such naval implements as chance offered. Agrippina was silent and was thus the less recognized; still, she received a wound in her shoulder. She swam, then met with some small boats which conveyed her to the Lucrine lake,[17] and so entered her house.

There she reflected how for this very purpose she had been invited by a lying letter and treated with conspicuous honor, how also it was near the shore, not from being driven by winds or dashed on rocks, that the vessel had in its upper part collapsed, like a mechanism anything but nautical. She pondered too the death of Acerronia; she looked at her own wound, and saw that her only safeguard against treachery was to ignore it. Then she sent her freedman Agerinus to tell her son how by heaven's favor and his good fortune she had escaped a terrible disaster; that she begged him, alarmed, as he might be, by his mother's peril, to put off the duty of a visit, as for the present she needed repose. Meanwhile, pretending that she felt secure, she applied remedies to her wound, and fomentations to her person. She then ordered search to be made for the will of Acerronia, and her property to be sealed, in this alone throwing off disguise.

Nero, meantime, as he waited for tidings of the consummation of the deed, received information that she had escaped with the injury of a slight wound, after having so far encountered the peril that there could be no question as to its author. Then, paralyzed with terror and protesting that she would show herself the next moment eager for vengeance, either arming the slaves or stirring up the soldiery, or hastening to the Senate and the people, to charge him with the wreck, with her wound, and with the destruction of her friends, he asked what resource he had against all this, unless something could be at once devised by Burrus and Seneca. He had instantly summoned both of them, and possibly they were already in the secret. There was a long silence on their part; they feared they might remonstrate in vain, or believed the crisis to be such that Nero must perish, unless Agrippina were at once crushed. Thereupon Seneca was so far the more prompt as to glance back on Burrus, as if to ask him whether the bloody deed must be required of the soldiers. Burrus replied "that the praetorians were attached to the whole family of the Caesars, and remem-

---

17. **the Lucrine lake:** a small salt-water lake about nine miles northwest of Naples.

bering Germanicus[18] would not dare a savage deed on his offspring. It was for Anicetus to accomplish his promise."

Anicetus, without a pause, claimed for himself the consummation of the crime. At those words, Nero declared that that day gave him empire, and that a freedman was the author of this mighty boon. "Go," he said, "with all speed and take with you the men readiest to execute your orders." He himself, when he had heard of the arrival of Agrippina's messenger, Agerinus, contrived a theatrical mode of accusation, and, while the man was repeating his message, threw down a sword at his feet, then ordered him to be put in irons, as a detected criminal, so that he might invent a story how his mother had plotted the emperor's destruction and in the shame of discovered guilt had by her own choice sought death.

Meantime, Agrippina's peril being universally known and taken to be an accidental occurrence, everybody, the moment he heard of it, hurried down to the beach. Some climbed projecting piers; some the nearest vessels; others, as far as their stature allowed, went into the sea; some, again, stood with outstretched arms, while the whole shore rung with wailings, with prayers and cries, as different questions were asked and uncertain answers given. A vast multitude streamed to the spot with torches, and as soon as all knew that she was safe, they at once prepared to wish her joy, till the sight of an armed and threatening force scared them away. Anicetus then surrounded the house with a guard, and having burst open the gates, dragged off the slaves who met him, till he came to the door of her chamber, where a few still stood, after the rest had fled in terror at the attack. A small lamp was in the room, and one slave-girl with Agrippina, who grew more and more anxious, as no messenger came from her son, not even Agerinus, while the appearance of the shore was changed, a solitude one moment, then sudden bustle and tokens of the worst catastrophe. As the girl rose to depart, she exclaimed, "Do you too forsake me?" and looking round saw Anicetus, who had with him the captain of the trireme, Herculeius, and Obaritus, a centurion of marines. "If," said she, "you have come to see me, take back word that I have recovered, but if you are here to do a crime, I believe nothing about my son; he has not ordered his mother's murder."

The assassins closed in round her couch, and the captain of the trireme first struck her head violently with a club. Then, as the centurion bared his sword for the fatal deed, presenting her person, she exclaimed, "Smite my womb," and with many wounds she was slain.

So far our accounts agree. That Nero gazed on his mother after her death and praised her beauty, some have related, while others deny it. Her body was burnt that same night on a dining couch, with a mean funeral; nor, as long as Nero was in power, was the earth raised into a mound, or even decently closed. Subsequently, she received from the solicitude of her domestics, a humble sepulcher on the road to Misenum, near the coun-

---

18. Germanicus: brother of the emperor Claudius and father of Agrippina, a successful general who inspired devotion even after his death.

try house of Caesar the Dictator, which from a great height commands a view of the bay beneath. As soon as the funeral pile was lighted, one of her freedmen, surnamed Mnester, ran himself through with a sword, either from love of his mistress or from the fear of destruction.

Many years before Agrippina had anticipated this end for herself and had spurned the thought. For when she consulted the astrologers about Nero, they replied that he would be emperor and kill his mother. "Let him kill her," she said, "provided he is emperor."

But the emperor, when the crime was at last accomplished, realized its portentous guilt. The rest of the night, now silent and stupefied, now and still oftener starting up in terror, bereft of reason, he awaited the dawn as if it would bring with it his doom. He was first encouraged to hope by the flattery addressed to him, at the prompting of Burrus, by the centurions and tribunes, who again and again pressed his hand and congratulated him on his having escaped an unforeseen danger and his mother's daring crime. Then his friends went to the temples, and, an example having once been set, the neighboring towns of Campania[19] testified their joy with sacrifices and deputations. He himself, with an opposite phase of hypocrisy, seemed sad, and almost angry at his own deliverance, and shed tears over his mother's death. But as the aspects of places change not, as do the looks of men, and as he had ever before his eyes the dreadful sight of that sea with its shores (some too believed that the notes of a funereal trumpet were heard from the surrounding heights, and wailings from the mother's grave), he retired to Neapolis[20] and sent a letter to the Senate, the drift of which was that Agerinus, one of Agrippina's confidential freedmen, had been detected with the dagger of an assassin, and that in the consciousness of having planned the crime she had paid its penalty. . . .

A disaster followed, whether accidental or treacherously contrived by the emperor, is uncertain, as authors have given both accounts, worse, however, and more dreadful than any which have ever happened to this city by the violence of fire. It had its beginning in that part of the circus which adjoins the Palatine and Caelian hills, where, amid the shops containing inflammable wares, the conflagration both broke out and instantly became so fierce and so rapid from the wind that it seized in its grasp the entire length of the circus. For here there were no houses fenced in by solid masonry, or temples surrounded by walls, or any other obstacle to interpose delay. The blaze in its fury ran first through the level portions of the city, then rising to the hills, while it again devastated every place below them, it outstripped all preventive measures; so rapid was the mischief and so completely at its mercy the city, with those narrow winding passages and irregular streets, which characterized old Rome. Added to this were the wailings of terror-stricken women, the feebleness of age, the helpless inexperience of childhood, the crowds who sought to save

---

19. **Campania:** a district in southern Italy lying between the Apennine Mountains and the Tyrrhenian Sea.

20. **Neapolis:** the city now called Naples.

themselves or others, dragging out the infirm or waiting for them, and by their hurry in the one case, by their delay in the other, aggravating the confusion. Often, while they looked behind them, they were intercepted by flames on their side or in their face. Or if they reached a refuge close at hand, when this too was seized by the fire, they found that, even places, which they had imagined to be remote, were involved in the same calamity. At last, doubting what they should avoid or whither betake themselves, they crowded the streets or flung themselves down in the fields, while some who had lost their all, even their very daily bread, and others out of love for their kinsfolk, whom they had been unable to rescue, perished, though escape was open to them. And no one dared to stop the mischief, because of incessant menaces from a number of persons who forbade the extinguishing of the flames, because again others openly hurled brands, and kept shouting that there was one who gave them authority, either seeking to plunder more freely, or obeying orders.

Nero at this time was at Antium, and did not return to Rome until the fire approached his house, which he had built to connect the palace with the gardens of Maecenas. It could not, however, be stopped from devouring the palace, the house, and everything around it. However, to relieve the people, driven out homeless as they were, he threw open to them the Campus Martius and the public buildings of Agrippa, and even his own gardens, and raised temporary structures to receive the destitute multitude. Supplies of food were brought up from Ostia[21] and the neighboring towns, and the price of corn was reduced to three sesterces a peck. These acts, though popular, produced no effect, since a rumor had gone forth everywhere that, at the very time when the city was in flames, the emperor appeared on a private stage and sang of the destruction of Troy, comparing present misfortunes with the calamities of antiquity.

At last, after five days, an end was put to the conflagration at the foot of the Esquiline hill, by the destruction of all buildings on a vast space, so that the violence of the fire was met by clear ground and an open sky. But before people had laid aside their fears, the flames returned, with no less fury this second time, and especially in the spacious districts of the city. Consequently, though there was less loss of life, the temples of the gods, and the porticoes which were devoted to enjoyment, fell in a yet more widespread ruin. And to this conflagration there attached the greater infamy because it broke out on the Aemilian property of Tigellinus,[22] and it seemed that Nero was aiming at the glory of founding a new city and calling it by his name. Rome, indeed, is divided into fourteen districts, four of which remained uninjured, three were leveled to the ground, while in the other seven were left only a few shattered, half-burnt relics of houses.

It would not be easy to enter into a computation of the private mansions, the blocks of tenements, and of the temples, which were lost. Those

---

21. **Ostia:** the port of Rome, about sixteen miles distant at the mouth of the Tiber.

22. **Tigellinus:** one of Nero's close associates, who exerted a very evil influence on him.

with the oldest ceremonial, as that dedicated by Servius Tullius to Luna, the great altar and shrine raised by the Arcadian Evander to the visibly appearing Hercules, the temple of Jupiter the Stayer, which was vowed by Romulus, Numa's royal palace, and the sanctuary of Vesta, with the tutelary deities of the Roman people, were burnt. So too were the riches acquired by our many victories, various beauties of Greek art, then again the ancient and genuine historical monuments of men of genius, and, notwithstanding the striking splendor of the restored city, old men will remember many things which could not be replaced. Some persons observed that the beginning of this conflagration was on the 19th of July, the day on which the Senones captured and fired Rome.[23] Others have pushed a curious inquiry so far as to reduce the interval between these two conflagrations into equal numbers of years, months, and days.

Nero meanwhile availed himself of his country's desolation, and erected a mansion in which the jewels and gold, long familiar objects, quite vulgarized by our extravagance, were not so marvelous as the fields and lakes, with woods on one side to resemble a wilderness, and, on the other, open spaces and extensive views. The directors and contrivers of the work were Severus and Celer, who had the genius and the audacity to attempt by art even what nature had refused, and to fool away an emperor's resources. They had actually undertaken to sink a navigable canal from the lake Avernus[24] to the mouths of the Tiber along a barren shore or through the face of hills, where one meets with no moisture which could supply water, except the Pontine marshes.[25] The rest of the country is broken rock and perfectly dry. Even if it could be cut through, the labor would be intolerable, and there would be no adequate result. Nero, however, with his love of the impossible, endeavored to dig through the nearest hills to Avernus, and there still remain the traces of his disappointed hope.

Of Rome meanwhile, so much as was left unoccupied by his mansion, was not built up, as it had been after its burning by the Gauls, without any regularity or in any fashion, but with rows of streets according to measurement, with broad thoroughfares, with a restriction on the height of houses, with open spaces, and the further addition of colonnades, as a protection to the frontage of the blocks of tenements. These colonnades Nero promised to erect at his own expense, and to hand over the open spaces, when cleared of the debris, to the ground landlords. He also offered rewards proportioned to each person's position and property, and prescribed a period within which they were to obtain them on the completion of so many houses or blocks of building. He fixed on the marshes of Ostia for the reception of the rubbish, and arranged that the ships

---

23. **Senones . . . Rome:** The Senones were Gauls who captured and burned Rome in 390 B.C.

24. **the lake Avernus:** a deep lake about nine miles west of Naples.

25. **the Pontine marshes:** a swampy region southwest of Rome, between the Volscian Mountains and the Tyrrhenian Sea.

which had brought up corn by the Tiber, should sail down the river with cargoes of this rubbish. The buildings themselves, to a certain height, were to be solidly constructed, without wooden beams, of stone from Gabii or Alba, that material being impervious to fire. And to provide that the water which individual license had illegally appropriated, might flow in greater abundance in several places for the public use, officers were appointed, and everyone was to have in the open court the means of stopping a fire. Every building, too, was to be enclosed by its own proper wall, not by one common to others. These changes which were liked for their utility, also added beauty to the new city. Some, however, thought that its old arrangement had been more conducive to health, inasmuch as the narrow streets with the elevation of the roofs were not equally penetrated by the sun's heat, while now the open space, unsheltered by any shade, was scorched by a fiercer glow.

Such indeed were the precautions of human wisdom. The next thing was to seek means of propitiating the gods, and recourse was had to the Sibylline books,[26] by the direction of which prayers were offered to Vulcanus, Ceres, and Proserpina. Juno, too, was entreated by the matrons, first, in the Capitol, then on the nearest part of the coast, whence water was procured to sprinkle the fane[27] and image of the goddess. And there were sacred banquets and nightly vigils celebrated by married women. But all human efforts, all the lavish gifts of the emperor, and the propitiations of the gods, did not banish the sinister belief that the conflagration was the result of an order. Consequently, to get rid of the report, Nero fastened the guilt and inflicted the most exquisite tortures on a class hated for their abominations, called Christians by the populace. Christus, from whom the name had its origin, suffered the extreme penalty during the reign of Tiberius at the hands of one of our procurators, Pontius Pilatus, and a most mischievous superstition, thus checked for the moment, again broke out not only in Judaea, the first source of the evil, but even in Rome, where all things hideous and shameful from every part of the world find their center and become popular. Accordingly, an arrest was first made of all who pleaded guilty; then, upon their information, an immense multitude was convicted, not so much of the crime of firing the city, as of hatred against mankind. Mockery of every sort was added to their deaths. Covered with the skins of beasts, they were torn by dogs and perished, or were nailed to crosses, or were doomed to the flames and burnt, to serve as a nightly illumination, when daylight had expired.

Nero offered his gardens for the spectacle, and was exhibiting a show in the circus, while he mingled with the people in the dress of a charioteer or stood aloft on a car. Hence, even for criminals who deserved extreme and exemplary punishment, there arose a feeling of compassion;

---

26. **Sibylline books:** books or oracles kept at Rome and consulted during times of crisis.

27. **fane:** temple.

for it was not, as it seemed, for the public good, but to glut one man's cruelty, that they were being destroyed.

Meanwhile Italy was thoroughly exhausted by contributions of money, the provinces were ruined, as also the allied nations and the free states, as they were called. Even the gods fell victims to the plunder; for the temples in Rome were despoiled and the gold carried off, which, for a triumph or a vow, the Roman people in every age had consecrated in their prosperity or their alarm.

DISCUSSION QUESTIONS

1. If given a choice between Tacitus and Suetonius, which man would you choose to write your biography? Why?

2. What was the most common method for overcoming political rivals in Nero's time? If Agrippina and Nero were alive today, what strategies might they use for gaining victory over their rivals?

3. What strategies were executed by Nero to appear innocent of Britannicus' murder, his mother's murder, and the great Roman fire?

4. Describe the character of Agrippina as it emerges in the first part of this account. How does she react to the almost certain knowledge that her son is trying to kill her? What does the murder scene reveal about her character?

5. Nero has long been rumored to be the person who started the great fire of Rome. What is Tacitus' view of this rumor? Does he try to prove it or disprove it?

6. Many readers have commented that Tacitus' historical accounts read like novels. What particular techniques make this account of Nero seem like a novel?

7. What is Tacitus' view of the moral climate of Rome at this time?

SUGGESTION FOR WRITING

Select a current public figure and write a paragraph about him or her as Suetonius might have written it. Then write a paragraph about the same figure as Tacitus might have written it.

Acknowledgments

127 "A Gravestone at Corinth" (anonymous) translated by Kenneth Rexroth, from *Poems from the Greek Anthology*. Ann Arbor: The University of Michigan Press, 1962. Reprinted by permission.

xii Excerpt from *The Odyssey of Homer* translated by Robert Fitzgerald. Translation copyright © 1961 and translation copyright renewed © 1989 by Benedict R. C. Fitzgerald on behalf of the Fitzgerald children. This edition copyright © 1998 by Farrar, Straus & Giroux, Inc. Reprinted by permission of Farrar, Straus & Giroux, Inc.

xii From *The Odyssey* by Homer, translated by Robert Fagles, Translation copyright © 1996 by Robert Fagles. Used by permission of Viking Penguin, a division of Penguin Putnam Inc.

ix Quotation from "Translation and Transposition" by D. S. Carne-Ross in *The Craft and Context of Translation*, ed. William Arrowsmith and Roger Shattuck. New York: Doubleday Anchor Books, 1964.

xi "Liber Duo, Carmen Decem" by Horace, Latin text from the Oxford University Press edition. Reprinted by permission.

4 *The House of Atreus by Aeschylus*, adapted from the *Oresteia* by John Lewin. Copyright © 1966 by the University of Minnesota. Reprinted by permission of the University of Minnesota Press.

74 "The Cranes and the Farmer" by Aesop, translated by Denison B. Hull, from *Aesop's Fables* told by Valerius Babrius. © 1960 by the University of Chicago. All rights reserved. Reprinted by permission.

74 "The Field Mouse and the House Mouse" by Aesop, translated by Denison B. Hull, from *Aesop's Fables* told by Valerius Babrius. © 1959 by the University of Chicago. All rights reserved. Reprinted by permission.

76 "The North Wind and the Sun" by Aesop, translated by Denison B. Hull, from *Aesop's Fables* told by Valerius Babrius. © 1959 by the University of Chicago. All rights reserved. Reprinted by permission.

76 "The Old Man and His Children" by Aesop, translated by Denison B. Hull, *from Aesop's Fables* told by Valerius Babrius. © 1959 by the University of Chicago. All rights reserved. Reprinted by permission.

77 "The Two Packs" by Aesop, translated by Denison B. Hull, from *Aesop's Fables* told by Valerius Babrius. © 1959 by the University of Chicago. All rights reserved.

Reprinted by permission.

79 From *On the Art of Poetry* by Aristotle, translated by Ingram Bywater. Reprinted by permission of Oxford University Press.

89 *Iphigenia in Aulis* by Euripedes translated by F. M. Stawell. New York: Oxford University Press, 1929.

127 "Never Again, Orpheus" by Antipatros, translated by Kenneth Rexroth, from *Poems from the Greek Anthology*. Ann Arbor: The University of Michigan Press, 1962. Reprinted by permission.

128 "Where Is Your Famous Beauty?" by Antipatros, translated by Kenneth Rexroth, from *Poems from the Greek Anthology*. Ann Arbor: The University of Michigan Press, 1962. Reprinted by permission.

128 "A Physician's Touch" from *Greek Lyric Poetry*, trans. Willis Barnstone. New York: Bantam, 1962. Reprinted by permission of Willis Barnstone.

129 "Of the Sensual World" from *Greek Lyric Poetry*, trans. Willis Barnstone. New York: Bantam, 1962. Reprinted by permission of Willis Barnstone.

129 "Ten Ages in the Life of Man" from *Greek Lyric Poetry*, trans. Willis Barnstone. New York: Bantam, 1962. Reprinted by permission of Willis Barnstone.

129 "The Darkness of Human Life" from *Greek Lyric Poetry*, trans. Willis Barnstone. New York: Bantam, 1962. Reprinted by permission of Willis Barnstone.

130 "The Last Utterance of the Delphic Oracle" (anonymous) translated by Kenneth Rexroth, from *Poems from the Greek Anthology*. Ann Arbor: The University of Michigan Press, 1962. Reprinted by permission.

132 From *The History* by Herodotus, translated by George Rawlinson. New York: Tudor Publishing Company, 1928.

150 From *The Dialogues of Plato*, translated by Benjamin Jowett, 1953. Reprinted by permission of the Oxford University Press.

175 "Ceremony" from *Greek Lyric Poetry*, trans. Willis Barnstone. New York: Bantam, 1962. Reprinted by permission of Willis Barnstone.

175 "Full Moon" from *Greek Lyric Poetry*, trans. Willis Barnstone. New York: Bantam, 1962. Reprinted by permission of Willis Barnstone.

175 "World" from *Greek Lyric Poetry*, trans. Willis Barnstone. New York: Bantam, 1962. Reprinted by permission of Willis Barnstone.

176 "Aphrodite and the Nereids" from *Greek Lyric Poetry*, trans. Willis Barnstone. New York: Bantam, 1962. Reprinted by permission of Willis Barnstone.

176 "Kleïs" from *Greek Lyric Poetry*, trans. Willis Barnstone. New York: Bantam, 1962. Reprinted by permission of Willis Barnstone.

176 "Andromeda, What Now?" from *Greek Lyric Poetry*, trans. Willis Barnstone. New York: Bantam, 1962. Reprinted by permission of Willis Barnstone.

176 "A Lanky Groom" from *Greek Lyric Poetry*, trans. Willis Barnstone. New York: Bantam, 1962. Reprinted by permission of Willis Barnstone.

177 "Wedding Song" from *Greek Lyric Poetry*, trans. Willis Barnstone. New York: Bantam, 1962. Reprinted by permission of Willis Barnstone.

177 "Wedding of Andromache" from *Greek Lyric Poetry*, trans. Willis Barnstone. New York: Bantam, 1962. Reprinted by permission of Willis Barnstone.

178 "To Dika, Not to Go Bareheaded" from *Greek Lyric Poetry*, trans. Willis Barnstone. New York: Bantam, 1962. Reprinted by permission of Willis Barnstone.

178 "To an Uneducated Woman" from *Greek Lyric Poetry*, trans. Willis Barnstone. New York: Bantam, 1962. Reprinted by permission of Willis Barnstone.

178 "Her Wealth" from *Greek Lyric Poetry*, trans. Willis Barnstone. New York: Bantam, 1962. Reprinted by permission of Willis Barnstone.

179 "Money and Virtue" from *Greek Lyric Poetry*, trans. Willis Barnstone. New York: Bantam, 1962. Reprinted by permission of Willis Barnstone.

179 "Someone, I Tell You" from *Greek Lyric Poetry*, trans. Willis Barnstone. New York: Bantam, 1962. Reprinted by permission of Willis Barnstone.

179 "Then" from *Greek Lyric Poetry*, trans. Willis Barnstone. New York: Bantam, 1962. Reprinted by permission of Willis Barnstone.

181 © Oxford University Press 1962. Reprinted from *Sophocles: Three Tragedies*, translated by H. D. F. Kitto (1962) by permission of Oxford University Press.

225 "Happiness" by Catullus, from *The Lyrical Genius of Catullus*, translated by E. A. Havelock. Copyright © 1966 by E. A. Havelock. Reprinted courtesy of Christine M. Havelock.

228 Book I, Ode 15 from *The Odes* by Horace, trans. James Michie. Copyright © James Michie. Reprinted with permission.

229 Book I, Ode 37 from *The Odes of Horace*, translated by Helen Rowe Henze. Copyright © 1961 by University of Oklahoma Press. Reprinted by permission.

230 Book II, Ode 15 from *The Odes* by Horace, trans. James Michie. Copyright © James Michie. Reprinted with permission.

231 Book III, Ode 30 from *The Odes of Horace*, translated by Helen Rowe Henze. Copyright © 1961 by University of Oklahoma Press. Reprinted by permission.

236 "The Town Mouse and the Country Mouse" by Horace from *The Satires and Epistles of Horace*, translated by Smith Palmer Bovie. © 1959 by The University of Chicago. All rights reserved. Reprinted by permission.

241 "The Fifth Satire: Against Mean Patrons and Despicable Clients" from *The Satires of Juvenal* translated by Rolfe Humphries. Copyright © 1958 by Indiana University Press. Reprinted by permission.

247 "The Thirteenth Satire: For a Defrauded Friend" from *The Satires of Juvenal* translated by Rolfe Humphries. Copyright © 1958 by Indiana University Press. Reprinted by permission.

256 "The Cook" by Martial, translated by J. A. Pott, from *The Epigrams of Martial* by J. A. Pott and F. A. Wright. London: Routledge, 1924.

257 "A Promising Youth" by Martial, translated by J. A. Pott, from *The Epigrams of Martial* by J. A. Pott and F. A. Wright. London: Routledge, 1924.

258 "To Ligurinus" by Martial, translated by F. A. Wright, from *The Epigrams of Martial* by J. A. Pott and F. A. Wright. London: Routledge, 1924.

261 "The Creation" from *The Metamorphoses* by Ovid, translated by Rolfe Humphries. Copyright © 1955 by Indiana University Press. Reprinted by permission.

263 "The Story of Baucis and Philemon" from *The Metamorphoses* by Ovid, translated by Rolfe Humphries. Copyright © 1955 by Indiana University Press. Reprinted by permission.

266 "The Story of Daedalus and Icarus" from *The Metamorphoses* by Ovid, translated by Rolfe Humphries. Copyright © 1955 by Indiana University Press. Reprinted by permission.

279 "Nero the Imperial Artist" from *The Twelve Caesars* by Suetonius, translated by Robert Graves. Copyright © 1957 by Robert Graves. Reprinted by permission of Carcanet Press, Ltd.

285 From *The Complete Works of Tacitus* by Tacitus, translated by Alfred John Church and Wm. Jackson Brodribb. Edited by Moses Hadas. Reprinted by permission of Random House, Inc.

Pronunciation Key

a	bat	ē	me	ô	ornate	ch	change		a	in along
ā	cage	ėr	her	oi	soil	ng	song		e	in shaken
ä	star	i	hit	ou	scout	sh	shell	ə	i	in stencil
â	dare	ī	nice	u	up	th	think		o	in lemon
au	law	o	cot	u̇	put	TH	there		u	in circus
e	bet	ō	old	ü	tube	zh	pleasure			

Index of Authors, Titles and Translators